MOSES

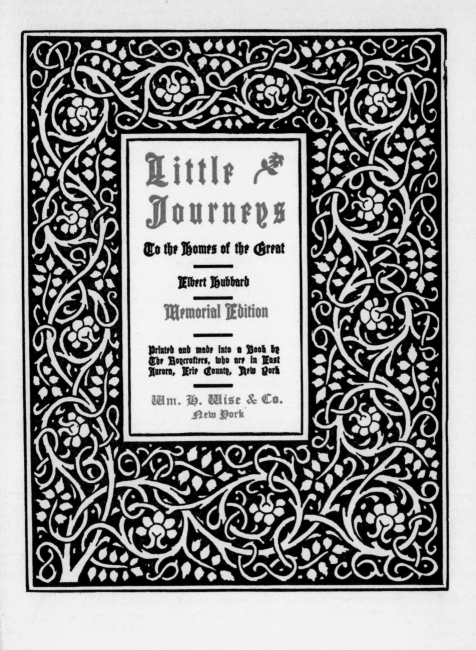

Little Journeys

To the Homes of the Great

Elbert Hubbard

Memorial Edition

Printed and made into a Book by
The Roycrofters, who are in East
Aurora, Erie County, New York

Wm. H. Wise & Co.
New York

CONTENTS

Little Journeys
To the Homes
of
Great Teachers

MOSES

And God said unto Moses, I AM THAT I AM: and he said, Thus shalt thou say unto the children of Israel, I AM hath sent me unto you. And God said, moreover, unto Moses: Thus shalt thou say unto the children of Israel, The Lord God of your Fathers, the God of Abraham, the God of Isaac, and the God of Jacob, hath sent me unto you: this is my name forever, and this is my memorial unto all generations.

—*Exodus iii: 14, 15*

MOSES

OSES was the world's first great teacher. He is still one of the world's great teachers. Seven million people yet look to his laws for special daily guidance, and more than two hundred millions read his books and regard them as Holy Writ. And these people as a class are of the best and most enlightened who live now or who have ever lived ✳ ✳

Moses did not teach of a life after this—he gives no hint of immortality—all of his rewards and punishments refer to the present. If there is a heaven for the good and a hell for the bad, he did not know of them. ¶ The laws of Moses were designed for the Now and the Here. Many of them ring true and correct even today, after all this interval of more than three thousand years. Moses had a good knowledge of physiology, hygiene, sanitation. He knew the advantages of cleanliness, order, harmony, industry and good habits. He also knew psychology, or the science of the mind: he knew the things that influence humanity, the limits of the average intellect, the plans and methods of government that will work and those which will not.

He was practical. He did what was expedient. He considered the material with which he had to deal, and he did what he could and taught that which his people would and could believe. The Book of Genesis was plainly written for the child-mind.

The problem that confronted Moses was one of practical politics, not a question of philosophy or of absolute or final truth. The laws he put forth were for the guidance of the people to whom he gave them, and his precepts were such as they could assimilate.

It were easy to take the writings of Moses as they have come down to us, translated, re-translated, colored and tinted with the innocence, ignorance and superstition of the nations who have kept them alive for thirty-three centuries, and then compile a list of the mistakes of the original writer. The writer of these records of dreams and hopes and guesses, all cemented with stern commonsense, has our profound reverence and regard. The "mistakes" lie in the minds of the people who, in the face of the accumulated knowledge of the centuries, have persisted that things once written were eternally sufficient ✄ ✄

In point of time there is no teacher within many hundred years following him who can be compared with him in originality and insight.

Moses lived fourteen hundred years before Christ.

The next man after him to devise a complete code of conduct was Solon, who lived seven hundred years after. A little later came Zoroaster, then Confucius, Buddha, Lao-tsze, Pericles, Socrates, Plato, Aristotle

—contemporaries, or closely following each other, their philosophy woven and interwoven by all and each and each by all.

Moses, however, stands out alone. That he did not know natural history as did Aristotle, who lived a thousand years later, is not to his discredit, and to emphasize the fact were irrelevant.

Back of it all lies the undisputed fact that Moses led a barbaric people out of captivity and so impressed his ideals and personality upon them that they endure as a distinct and peculiar people, even unto this day. He founded a nation. And chronologically he is the civilized world's first author.

Moses was a soldier, a diplomat, an executive, a writer, a teacher, a leader, a prophet, a stonecutter. Beside all these he was a farmer—a workingman, one who when forty years of age tended flocks and herds for a livelihood. Every phase of the outdoor life of the range was familiar to him. And the greatness of the man is revealed in the fact that his plans and aspirations were so far beyond his achievements that at last he thought he had failed. Exultant success seems to go with that which is cheap and transient. All great teachers have, in their own minds, been failures—they saw so much further than they were able to travel.

MOSES

ALL ancient chronology falls easily into three general divisions: the fabulous, the legendary, and the probable or natural.

In the understanding of history, psychology is quite as necessary as philology.

To reject anything that has a flaw in it is quite as bad as to have that excess of credulity which swallows everything presented.

It is not necessary to throw away the fabulous nor deny the legendary. But it is certainly not wise to construe the fabulous as the actual and maintain the legendary as literally true. Things may be true allegorically and false literally, and to be able to distinguish the one from the other, and prize each in its proper place, is the mark of wisdom.

If, however, we were asked to describe the man Moses to a jury of sane, sensible, intelligent and unprejudiced men and women, and show why he is worthy of the remembrance of mankind, we would have to eliminate the fabulous, carefully weigh the traditional, and rest our argument upon records that are fair, sensible and reasonably free from dispute.

The conclusions of professional retainers, committed before they begin their so-called investigations to a literal belief in the fabulous, should be accepted with great caution. For them to come to conclusions outside of that which they have been taught, is not only to forfeit their social position, but to lose their actual means of livelihood. Perhaps the truth in the final summing up can best be gotten from those who have made no vows that they will not change their opinions, and have nothing to lose if they fail occasionally to gibe with the popular.

On a certain occasion after Colonel Ingersoll had delivered his famous lecture entitled, "Some Mistakes of Moses," he was entertained by a local club. At the meeting, which was of the usual informal kind known as "A Dutch Feed," a young lawyer made bold to address the great orator thus: " Colonel Ingersoll, you are a lover of freedom—with you the word liberty looms large. All great men love liberty, and no man lives in history, respected and revered, save as he has sought to make men free. Moses was a lover of liberty. Now, would n't it be gracious and generous in you to give Moses, who in some ways was in the same business as yourself, due credit as a liberator and law-giver and not emphasize his mistakes to the total exclusion of his virtues? "

Colonel Ingersoll listened—he was impressed by the fairness of the question. He listened, paused and replied: " Young man, you have asked a reasonable question, and all you suggest about the greatness of Moses, in spite of his mistakes, is well taken. The trouble in your logic lies in the fact that you do not understand my status in this case. You seem to forget that I am not the attorney for Moses. He has more

15

than two million men looking after his interests. I am
retained on the other side!"

Like unto Colonel Ingersoll, I am not an attorney for
Moses. I desire, however, to give a fair, clear and
judicial account of the man. I will attempt to present
a brief for the people, and neither prosecute nor defend.
I will simply try to picture the man as he once existed,
nothing extenuating, nor setting down aught in malice.
As the original office of the State's Attorney was
rather to protect the person at the bar than to indict
him, so will I try to bring out the best in Moses,
rather than hold up his mistakes and raise a laugh by
revealing his ignorance. Modesty, which is often egotism turned wrong side out, might here say, "Oh,
Moses requires no defense at this late day!" But
Moses, like all great men, has suffered at the hands of
his friends. To this man has been attributed powers
which no human being ever possessed.

Moses lived thirty-three hundred years ago. In one
sense thirty-three centuries is a very long time. All is
comparative—children regard a man of fifty as "awful
old." I have seen several persons who have lived a
hundred years, and they did n't consider a century
long, "and thirty-five is n't anything," said one of
them to me.

Geologically, thirty-three centuries is only an hour ago.
It does not nearly take us back to the time when men
of the Stone Age hunted the hairy mammoth in what is

now Nebraska, nor does thirty-three centuries give us any glimpse of the time when tropical animals, plants and probably men lived and flourished at the North Pole ᔍ ᔍ

Egyptian civilization, at the time of Moses, was more than three thousand years old. Egypt was then in the first stage of senility, entering upon her decline, for her best people had settled in the cities, and this completes the cycle and spells deterioration. She had passed through the savage, barbaric, nomadic and agricultural stages and was living on her unearned increment, a part of which was Israelitish labor. Moses looked at the Pyramids, which were built more than a thousand years before his birth, and asked in wonder about who built them, very much as we do today. He listened for the Sphinx to answer, but she was silent, then as now. The date of the exodus has been fixed as having probably occurred during the reign of the Great Pharaoh, Mineptah, or the nineteenth Egyptian Dynasty. The date is, say, fourteen hundred years before Christ. An inscription has recently been found which seems to show that Joseph settled in Egypt during the reign of Mineptah, but the best scholars now have gone back to the conclusions I have stated.

At the time of the Pharaohs, Egypt was the highest civilized country on earth. It had a vast system of canals, an organized army, a goodly degree of art, and there were engineers and builders of much ability.

17

MOSES

Philosophy, poetry and ethics were recognized, prized and discussed.

The storage of grain by the government to bank against famine had been practised for several hundred years. There were also treasure-cities built to guard against fire, thieves or destruction by the elements. It will thus be seen that foresight, thrift, caution, wisdom, played their parts. The Egyptians were not savages.

MOSES

BOUT five hundred years before the birth of Moses there lived in Arabia a powerful Sheik or Chief, known as Abraham. This man had a familiar spirit, or guide, or guardian-angel known as Yaveh or Jehovah. All of the desert tribes had such tutelary gods; and all of these gods were once men of power who lived on earth. The belief in special gods has often been held by very great men: Socrates looked to his " demon " for guidance; Themistocles consulted his oracle; a President of the United States visited a clairvoyant, who consented to act as a medium and interpret the supernatural. This idea, which is a variant of ancestor worship, still survives, and very many good people do not take journeys or make investments until they believe they are being dictated to by Shakespeare, Emerson, Beecher or Phillips Brooks. These people also believe that there are bad spirits to which we must not harken.

Abraham was led by Jehovah; what Jehovah told him to do he did; when Jehovah told him to desist or change his plans, he obeyed. Jehovah promised him many things, and some of these promises were fulfilled.

Whether these tutelary gods or controlling spirits had any actual existence outside of the imagination of the people who believed in them—whether they were merely pictures thrown upon the screen by a subconscious spiritual stereopticon—is not the question now under discussion. Something must be left for a

19

later time: the fact remains that special providences are yet relied upon by sincere and intelligent people. ¶ Abraham had a son named Isaac. And Isaac was the father of Jacob, or Israel, " the Soldier of God," so called on account of his successful wrestling with the angel. And Jacob was the father of twelve sons. All of these people believed in Jehovah, the god of their tribe; and while they did not disbelieve in the gods of the neighboring tribes, they yet doubted their power and had grave misgivings as to their honesty. Therefore, they had nothing to do with them, praying to their own god only and looking to him for support. They were the chosen people of Jehovah, just as the Babylonians were the chosen people of Baal; the Canaanites the chosen people of Ishitar; the Moabites the chosen people of Chemos; the Ammonites the chosen people of Rimmon.

Now Joseph was the favorite son of Jacob, and his brethren were naturally jealous of him. So one day out on the range they sold him into slavery to a passing caravan, and went home and told their father the boy was dead, having been killed by a wild beast. To make the matter plausible they took the coat of Joseph and smeared it with the blood of a goat which they had killed. Nowadays, the coat would have been sent to a chemist's laboratory and the blood-spots tested to see whether it was the blood of beast or human. But Jacob believed the story and mourned his son as dead.

MOSES

Now Joseph was taken to Egypt and there arose to a position of influence and power through his intelligence and diligence. How eventually his brethren, starving, came to him for food, there being a famine in their own land, is one of the most natural and beautiful stories in all literature. It is a folklore legend, free from the fabulous, and has all the corroborating marks of the actual.

For us it is history undisputed, unrefuted, because it is so natural. It could all easily happen in various parts of the world even now. It shows the identical traits of human nature that are alive and pulsing today. ¶ Joseph having made himself known to his brethren induced some of them and their neighbors to come down into Egypt, where the pasturage was better and the water more sure, and settle there. The Bible tells us that there were seventy of these settlers and gives us their names.

These emigrants, called Israelites, or Children of Israel, account for the presence of the enslaved people whom Moses led out of captivity three hundred years later. ¶ One thing seems quite sure, and that is that they were a peculiar people then, with the pride of the desert in their veins, for they stood socially aloof and did not mix with the Egyptians. They still had their own god and clung to their own ways and customs.

That very naive account in the first chapter of Exodus of how they had two midwives, " and the name of one

21

was Shiphrah and the other Puah," is as fine in its
elusive exactitude as an Uncle Remus story. Children
always want to know the names of people. These two
Hebrew midwives were bribed by the King of Egypt
—ruler over twenty million people—in person, to kill
all the Hebrew boy babies. Then the account states
that Jehovah was pleased with these Hebrew women
who proved false to their master, and Jehovah rewarded
them by giving them houses.

This order to kill the Hebrew children must have
gone into execution, if at all, about the time of the
birth of Moses, because Aaron, the brother of Moses,
and three years older, certainly was not killed.

Whether Moses was the son of Pharaoh's daughter,
his father an Israelite, or both of his parents were
Israelites, is problematic. Royal families are not apt
to adopt an unknown waif into the royal household
and bring him up as their royal own, especially if this
waif belongs to what is regarded as an inferior race.
The tie of motherhood is the only one that could over-
rule caste and override prejudice. If the daughter of
Pharaoh, or more properly " the Pharaoh," were the
mother of Moses, she had a better reason for hiding
him in the bulrushes than did the daughter of a Levite,
for the order to kill these profitable workers is extremely
doubtful. The strength, skill and ability of the Israelites
formed a valuable acquisition to the Egyptians, and
what they wanted was more Israelites, not fewer.

Judging from the statement that there were only two midwives, there were only a few hundred Israelites— perhaps between one and two thousand, at most ⚜ So leaving the legend of the childhood of Moses with just enough mystery mixed in it to give it a perpetual piquancy, we learn that he was brought up an Egyptian, as the son of Pharaoh's daughter, and that it was she who gave him his name.

Philo and Josephus give various sidelights on the life and character of Moses. The Midrash or Commentaries on the History of the Jews, composed, added to or modified by many men, extending over a period of twenty centuries, also add their weight, even though the value of these Commentaries is conjectural.

Egyptian accounts of Moses and the Israelites come to us through Hellenic sources, and very naturally are not complimentary. These picture Moses, or Osarsiph, as they call him, as an agitator, an undesirable citizen, who sought to overturn the government, and failing in this, fled to the desert with a few hundred outlaws. They managed to hold out against the forces sent to capture them, were gradually added to by other refugees, and through the organizing genius of Moses were rounded into a strong tribe.

That Moses was their supreme ruler, and that to better hold his people in check he devised a religious ritual for them, and impressed his god, Jehovah, upon them, almost to the exclusion of all other gods, and thus formed them into a religious whole, is beyond question. No matter what the cause of the uprising, or who was to blame for it, the fact is undisputed that Moses led a revolt in Egypt, and the people he carried with him in this exodus formed the nucleus of the Hebrew Nation. And further, the fact is beyond dispute that the personality of Moses was the prime cementing factor in the making of the nation. The power, poise, patience and unwavering self-reliance of the man, through his faith in the god Jehovah, are all beyond dispute. Things happen because the man makes them happen.

MOSES

HE position of the Israelites in Egypt was one of voluntary vassalage. The government was a feudal monarchy. The Israelites had come into Egypt of their own accord, but had never been admitted into the full rights of citizenship. This exclusion by the Egyptians had no doubt tended to fix the Children of Israel in their religious beliefs, and on the other hand, their proud and exclusive nature had tended to keep them from a full fellowship with the actual owners of the land.

The Egyptians never attempted to traffic in them as they did in slaves of war, being quite content to use them as clerks, laborers and servants, paying them a certain wage, and also demanding an excess of labor in lieu of taxation. In other words, they worked out their " road-tax," which no doubt was excessive. Many years later, Athens and also Rome had similar "slaves," some of whom were men of great intellect and worth. If one reads the works of modern economic prophets, it will be seen that wage-workers in America are often referred to as " slaves " or " bondmen," terms which will probably give rise to confusion among historians to come ✤ ✤

Moses was brought up in the court of the king, and became versed in all the lore of the Egyptians. We are led to suppose that he also looked like an Egyptian, as we are told that people seeing him for the first time, he being a stranger to them, went away and referred to him as " that Egyptian." He was handsome, commanding, silent by habit and slow of speech, strong as a counselor, a safe man. That he was a most valuable man in the conduct of Egyptian official affairs, there is no doubt. And although he was nominally an Egyptian, living with the Egyptians, adopting their manners and customs, yet his heart was with " his brethren," the Israelites, who he saw were sore oppressed through governmental exploitation.

Moses knew that a government which does not exist for the purpose of adding to human happiness has no excuse for being. And once when he was down among his own people he saw an Egyptian taskmaster or foreman striking an Israelitish workman, and in wrath he arose and killed the oppressor. The only persons who were witnesses to this affair were two Hebrews. The second day after the fight, when Moses was attempting to separate two Hebrews who had gotten into an altercation with each other, they taunted him by saying, " Who gavest thee to be a ruler over us?—wilt thou also kill us as thou didst the Egyptian? "
¶ This gives us a little light upon the quality and character of the people with whom Moses had to deal. It also shows that the ways of the reformer and peacemaker are not flower-strewn. The worst enemies of a reformer are not the Egyptians—he has also to deal with the Israelites.

I once heard Terence V. Powderly, who organized the

Knights of Labor—the most successful labor organization ever formed—say, "Any man who devotes his life to helping laboring men will be destroyed by them." And then he added, " But this should not deter us from the effort to benefit."

As the Hebrew account plainly states that the killing of all the male Hebrew children was carried out with the connivance of Hebrew women who pretended to be ministering to the Hebrew mothers, so was the flight of Moses from Egypt caused by the Hebrews, who turned informants and brought him into disgrace with Pharaoh, who sought his life.

Very naturally, the Egyptians deny and have always denied that the order to kill children was ever issued by a Pharaoh. They also point to the fact that the Israelites were a source of profit—a valuable asset to the Egyptians. And moreover, the proposition that the Egyptians killed the children to avoid trouble is preposterous, since no possible act that man can commit would so arouse sudden rebellion and fan into flame the embers of hate as the murder of the young. If the Egyptians had attempted to carry out any such savage cruelty, they would not only have had to fight the Israelitish men, but the outraged mothers as well. The Egyptians were far too wise to invite the fury of frenzied motherhood. To have done this would have destroyed the efficiency of the entire Hebrew population. An outraged and heartbroken people do not work.

MOSES

¶ When one person becomes angry with another, his mental processes work overtime making up a list of the other's faults and failings.

When a people arise in revolt they straightway prepare an indictment against the government against which they revolted, giving a schedule of outrages, insults, plunderings and oppressions. This is what is politely called partisan history. " Uncle Tom's Cabin " was a literary indictment of the South by featuring its supposed brutalities. And the attitude of the South is mirrored in a pretty parable concerning a Southern girl who came North on a visit, and seeing in print the words " damned Yankee," innocently remarked that she always thought they were one word. A description of the enemy, made by a person or a people, must be taken cum grano Syracuse ⚹ ⚹

MOSES

HEN Moses fled, after killing the Egyptian, he went northward and east into the land of the Midianites, who were also descendants of Abraham. At this time he was forty years of age, and still unmarried, his work in the Egyptian Court having evidently fully absorbed his time.

It is a pretty little romance, all too brief in its details, of how the tired man stopped at a well, and the seven daughters of Jethro came to draw water for their flocks. Certain shepherds came also and drove the girls away, when Moses, true to his nature, took the part of the young ladies, to the chagrin and embarrassment of the male rustics who had left their manners at home. The story forms a melodramatic stage-setting which the mummers have not been slow to use, representing the seven daughters as a ballet, the shepherds as a male chorus, and Moses as basso-profundo and hero. We are told that the girls went home and told their father of the chivalrous stranger they had met, and he, with all the deference of the desert, sent for him " that he might eat bread."

Very naturally Moses married one of the girls.

And Moses tended the flocks of Jethro, his father-in-law, taking the herds a long distance, living with them and sleeping out under the stars.

Now Jethro was the chief of his tribe. Moses calls him a " priest," but he was a priest only incidentally, as all the Arab chiefs were.

29

MOSES

The clergy originated in Egypt. Before the Israelites were in Goshen, the "sacra," or sacred utensils, belonged to the family; and the head of the tribe performed the religious rites, propitiating the family deity, or else delegated some one else to do so. This head of the tribe, or chief, was called a " Cohen "; and the man who assisted him, or whom he delegated, was called a " Levi." The plan of making a business of being a " Levi " was borrowed from the Egyptians, who had men set apart, exclusively, to deal in the mysterious. Moses calls himself a Levi, or Levite.

After the busy life he had led, Moses could not settle down to the monotonous existence of a shepherd. It is probable that then he wrote the Book of Job, the world's first drama and the oldest book of the Bible. Moses was full of plans. Very naturally he prayed to the Israelitish god, and the god harkened unto his prayer and talked to him.

The silence, the loneliness, the majesty of the mountains, the great stretches of shining sand, the long peaceful nights, all tend to hallucinations. Sheepmen are in constant danger of mental aberration. Society is needed quite as much as solitude.

From talking with God, Moses desired to see Him. One day, from the burning red of an acacia-tree, the Lord called to him, " Moses, Moses! "

And Moses answered, " Here am I ! "

Moses was a man born to rule—he was a leader of men

30

—and here at middle life the habits of twenty-five years were suddenly snapped and his occupation gone. He yearned for his people, and knowing their unhappy lot, his desire was to lead them out of captivity. He knew the wrongs the Egyptian government was visiting upon the Israelites. Rameses the Second was a ruler with the builder's eczema: always and forever he made gardens, dug canals, paved roadways, constructed model tenements, planned palaces, erected colossi. He was a worker, and he made everybody else work. It was in this management of infinite detail that Moses had been engaged; and while he entered into it with zest, he knew that the hustling habit can be overdone and its votaries may become its victims—not only that, but this strenuous life may turn freemen into serfs, and serfs into slaves.

And now Rameses was dead, and the proud, vain, fretful and selfish Mineptah ruled in his place. It was worse with the Israelites than ever!

The more Moses thought of it the more he was convinced that it was his duty to go back to Egypt and lead his people out of bondage. He himself, having been driven out, made the matter a burning one with him: he had lost his place in the Egyptian Court, but he would get it back and hold it under better conditions than ever before!

He heard the "Voice"! All strong people hear the Voice calling them. And harkening to the Inner Voice

is simply doing what you want to do. ¶ " Moses,
Moses! "
And Moses answered, " Lord, here am I."
The laws of Moses still influence the world, but not
even the orthodox Jews follow them literally. We bring
our reason to bear upon the precepts of Moses, and
those which are not for us we gently pass over. In fact,
the civil laws of most countries prohibit many of the
things which Moses commanded. For instance, the
eighteenth verse of the twenty-second chapter of
Exodus says, " Thou shalt not suffer a witch to live."
Certainly no Jewish lawyer nor Rabbi, in any part of
the world, advocates the killing of persons supposed to
be witches. We explain that in this instance the inspired
writer lapsed and merely mirrored the ignorance of his
time. Or else we fall back upon the undoubted fact that
various writers and translators have tampered with the
original text—this must be so, since the book written
by Moses makes record of his death.
But when we find passages in Moses requiring us to
benefit our enemies, we say with truth that this was
the first literature to express for us the brotherhood of
man ⚶ ⚶
" Thou shalt take no gift: for the gift blindeth the wise
and perverteth the words of the righteous." Here we
get Twentieth-Century Wisdom. And very many passages as fine and true can be found, which prove
for us beyond cavil that Moses was right a part of the

time, and to say this of any man, living or dead, is a very great compliment.

In times of doubt the Jewish people turn to the Torah, or Book of the Law. This book has been interpreted by the Rabbis, or the learned men, and to meet the exigencies of living under many conditions, it has been changed, enlarged and augmented. In these changes the people were not consulted. Very naturally it was done secretly, for inspired men must be well dead before the many accept their edict. To be alive is always more or less of an offense, especially if you be a person and not a personage.

The murmurings against Moses during his lifetime often broke into a rumble and a roar. The mob accused him of taking them out into the wilderness to perish. To get away from the constant bickering and criticisms of the little minds, Moses used to go up into the mountains alone to find rest, and there he communicated with his god. It was surely a great step in advance when all the Elohims were combined into one Supreme Elohim that was everywhere present and ruled the world. Instead of dozens of little gods, jealous, jangling, fearful, fretful, fussy, boastful, changing walking-sticks to serpents, or doing other things quite as useless, it was a great advance to have one Supreme Being, dispassionate, a God of Love and Justice, " with whom can be no variation, neither shadow that is cast by turning." This gradual ennobling of the conception of Divinity reveals

33

the extent to which man is ennobling his own nature. ¶ Up to within a very few years God had a rival in the Devil, but now the Devil lives only as a pleasantry. Until the time of Moses, the God of Sinai was only the God of the Hebrew people, and this accounts for His violence, wrath, jealousy, and all of those qualities which went to make up a barbaric chief, including the tendency of His sons and servants to make love to the daughters of earth.

It is probable that the idea of God—in opposition to a god, one of many gods—was a thought that grew up very gradually in the mind of Moses. The ideal grew, and Moses grew with the ideal.

Then from God being a Spirit, to being Spirit, is a natural, easy and beautiful evolution.

The thought of angels, devils, heavenly messengers, like Gabriel and the Holy Ghost, constantly surrounding the Throne, is a suggestion that comes from the court of the absolute monarch. The Trinity is the oligarchy refined, and the one son who gives himself as a sacrifice for all the people who have offended the monarch is the retreating vision of that night of ignorance when all nations sought to appease the wrath of their god by the death of human beings.

God to us is Spirit, realized everywhere in unfolding Nature. We are a part of Nature—we, too, are Spirit. When Moses commands his people that they must return the stray animal of their enemy to its rightful owner, we behold a great man struggling to benefit humanity by making them recognize the laws of Spirit. We are all one family—we can not afford to wrong or harm even an enemy.

Instead of thousands of warring, jarring families or tribes, we have now a few strong federations of States, or countries, which, if they would make war on one another, would today quickly face a larger foe. Already the idea of one government for all the world is taking form—there must be one Supreme Arbiter, and all this monstrous expense of money and flesh and blood and throbbing hearts for purposes of war, must go, just as we have sent to limbo the jangling, jarring, jealous gods. Also, the better sentiment of the world will send the czars, emperors, kings, grand dukes, and the greedy grafters of so-called democracy, into the dust-heap of oblivion, with all the priestly phantoms that have obscured the sun and blackened the sky. The gods have gone, but MAN IS HERE.

MOSES

HE plagues that befell the Egyptians were the natural ones to which Egypt was liable: drought, flood, flies, lice, frogs, disease. The Israelites very naturally declared that these things were sent as a punishment by the Israelitish god. I remember a farmer, in my childhood days, who was accounted by his neighbors as an infidel. He was struck by lightning and instantly killed, while standing in his doorway. The Sunday before, this man had worked in the fields, and just before he was killed he had said, " dammit," or something quite as bad. Our preacher explained at length that this man's death was a " judgment." Afterward, when our church was struck by lightning, it was regarded as an accident.

Ignorant and superstitious people always attribute special things to special causes. When the grasshoppers overran Kansas in Eighteen Hundred Eighty-five, I heard a good man from the South say it was a punishment on the Kansans for encouraging Old John Brown. The next year the boll-weevil ruined the cotton crop, and certain preachers in the North, who thought they knew, declared it was the lingering wrath of God on account of slavery. ¶ Three nations unite to form our present civilization. These are the Greek, the Roman and the Judaic. The lives of Perseus, Romulus and Moses all teem with the miraculous, but if we accept the supernatural in one we must in all. Which of these three great nations has contributed most to our well-being is a question largely decided by temperament; but just now the star of Greece seems to be in the ascendant. We look to art for solace. Greece stands for art; Rome for conquest; Judea for religion.

And yet Moses was a lover of beauty, and the hold he had upon his people was quite as much through training them to work as through his moral teaching. Indeed, his morality was expediency—which is reason enough according to modern science. When he wants them to work, he says, "Thus saith the Lord," just the same as when he wishes to impress upon them a thought. ¶ No one can read the twenty-sixth, twenty-seventh and twenty-eighth chapters of Exodus without being impressed with the fact that the man who wrote them had in him the spirit of the Master Workman—a King's Craftsman. His carving the ten commandments on tablets of stone also shows his skill with mallet and chisel, a talent he had acquired in Egypt, where Rameses the Second had thousands of men engaged in sculpture and in making inscriptions in stone.

Several chapters in Exodus might have been penned by Albrecht Durer or William Morris. The commandment, "Thou shalt not make unto thyself any graven image," was unmistakably made merely to correct a local evil: the tendency to worship the image instead of the thing it symbolized. People who do not contribute to the creation of an object fall easy victims to this error. With all the stern good sense that Moses

37

revealed, it is but fair to assume that he did not mean the command to be perpetual. It was only through so much moving about that the Jews seemed to lose their art spirit.

And certainly the flame of art in the Jewish heart has never died out, even though at times it has smoldered, for wherever there has been peace and security for the Jews, they have not been slow to evolve the talent which creates. History teems with the names of Jews who, in music, painting, poetry and sculpture, have devoted their days to beauty. And the germ of genius is seen in many of the Jewish children who attend the manual-training and art schools of America.

Art has its rise in the sense of sublimity. It seems at times to be a fulfilment of the religious impulse. The religion which balks at work, stopping at prayer and contemplation, is a form of arrested development.

¶ The number of people in the exodus was probably two or three thousand. Renan says that one century only elapsed between the advent of Joseph into Egypt and the revolt. Very certain it was not a great number that went forth into the desert. A half-million women could not have borrowed jewelry of their neighbors—the secret could not have been kept. And in the negotiations between Moses and the King, it will be remembered that Moses asked only for the privilege of going three days' journey into the wilderness to make sacrifices. It was a kind of picnic or religious campmeeting. A vast multitude

38

could not have taken part in any such exercise. We also hear of their singing their gratitude on account of reaching Elim, where there were " twelve springs and seventy palm-trees." Had there been several million people, as we have been told, the insignificant shade of seventy trees would have meant nothing to them. ¶ The distance from Goshen in Egypt to Canaan in Palestine was about one hundred seventy-five miles. But by the circuitous route they traveled it was nearly a thousand miles. It took forty years to make the passage, for the way had to be fought through the country of foes who very naturally sought to block the way. Quick transportation was out of the question. The rate of speed was about twenty-five miles a year. ¶ Here was a people without homes, or fixed habitation, beset on every side with the natural dangers of the desert, and compelled to face the fury of the inhabitants whose lands they overran, fearful, superstitious, haunted by hunger, danger and doubt. By night a man sent ahead with a lantern on a pole led the way; by day a cavalcade that raised a cloud of dust. One was later sung by the poets as a pillar of fire, and the other a cloud. Chance flocks of quail blown by a storm into their midst were regarded as a miracle; the white exuding wax of the manna-plant was told of as " bread " —or more literally food.

Those who had taken part in the original exodus were nearly all dead—their children and grandchildren survived, desert born and savage bred. Canaan was not the land flowing with milk and honey that had been described. Milk and honey are the results of labor applied to land. Moses knew this and tried to teach this great truth. He was true to his divine trust. Through doubt, hardship, poverty, misunderstanding, he held high the ideal—they were going to a better place. ¶ At last, worn by his constant struggle, aged one hundred twenty, " his eye not dim nor his natural force abated "—for only those live long who live well —Moses went up into the mountain to find solace in solitude as was his custom. His people waited for him in vain—he did not return. Alone there with his God he slept and forgot to awaken. His pilgrimage was done. "And no man knoweth his grave even unto this day." ¶ History is very seldom recorded on the spot—certainly it was not then. Centuries followed before fact, tradition, song, legend and folklore were fused into the form we call Scripture. But out of the fog and mist of that far-off past there looms in heroic outline the form and features of a man—a man of will, untiring activity, great hope, deep love, a faith which at times faltered, but which never died. Moses was the first man in history who fought for human rights and sought to make men free, even from their own limitations. "And there arose not a prophet since Israel like unto Moses, whom the Lord knew face to face."

CONFUCIUS

The highest study of all is that which teaches us to develop those principles of purity and perfect virtue which Heaven bestowed upon us at our birth, in order that we may acquire the power of influencing for good those amongst whom we are placed, by our precepts and example; a study without an end—for our labors cease only when we have become perfect—an unattainable goal, but one that we must not the less set before us from the very first. It is true that we shall not be able to reach it, but in our struggle toward it we shall strengthen our characters and give stability to our ideas, so that, whilst ever advancing calmly in the same direction, we shall be rendered capable of applying the faculties with which we have been gifted to the best possible account.

—*" The Annals " of Confucius*

CONFUCIUS

CONFUCIUS

THE Chinese comprise one-fourth of the inhabitants of the earth. There are four hundred millions of them ✂ They can do many things which we can not do, and we can do a few things which they have not yet been able to do; but they are learning from us, and possibly we would do well to learn from them. In China there are now trolley-cars, telephone-lines, typewriters, cash-registers and American plumbing. China is a giant awaking from sleep. He who thinks that China is a country crumbling into ruins has failed to leave a call at the office and has overslept.

The West can not longer afford to ignore China. And not being able to waive her, perhaps the next best thing is to try to understand her.

The one name that looms large above any other name in China is Confucius. He of all men has influenced China most. One-third of the human race love and cherish his memory, and repeat his words as sacred writ. ¶ Confucius was born at a time when one of those tidal waves of reason swept the world—when the nations were full of unrest, and the mountains of thought were shaken with discontent.

It was just previous to the blossoming of Greece.

CONFUCIUS

Pericles was seventeen years old when Confucius died. Themistocles was preparing the way for Pericles; for then was being collected the treasure of Delos, which made Phidias and the Parthenon possible. During the life of Confucius lived Leonidas, Miltiades, Cyrus the Great, Cambyses, Darius, Xerxes. And then quite naturally occurred the battles of Marathon, Salamis and Thermopylæ. Then lived Buddha-Gautama, Laotsze, Ezekiel, Daniel, Haggai, Zechariah, Pythagoras, Pindar, Æschylus and Anacreon.

The Chinese are linked to the past by ties of language and custom beyond all other nations. They are a peculiar people, a chosen people, a people set apart. Just when they withdrew from the rest of mankind and abandoned their nomadic habits, making themselves secure against invasion by building a wall one hundred feet high, and settled down to lay the foundations of a vast empire, we do not know. Some historians have fixed the date about ten thousand years before Christ—let it go at that. There is a reasonably well-authenticated history of China that runs back twenty-five hundred years before Christ, while our history merges into mist seven hundred fifty years before the Christian era.

The Israelites wandered; the Chinese remained at home. Walls have this disadvantage: they keep people in as well as shut the barbarians out. But now there are vast breaches in the wall, through which the inhabitants

44

ooze, causing men from thousands of miles away to cry in alarm, " the Yellow Peril! " And also through these breaches, Israelites, Englishmen and Yankees enter fearlessly, settle down in heathen China, and do business. ¶ It surely is an epoch, and what the end will be few there are who dare forecast.

CONFUCIUS

THIS then is from the pen of Edward Carpenter, the Church of England curate who was so great a friend and admirer of our own Walt Whitman that he made a trip across the sea to join hands with him in preaching the doctrine of democracy and the religion of humanity.

In the interior of China, along low-lying plains and great river-valleys, and by lake-sides, and far away up into hilly and even mountainous regions,
Behold! an immense population, rooted in the land, rooted in the clan and the family,
The most productive and stable on the whole Earth.
A garden one might say—a land of rich and recherche crops, of rice and tea and silk and sugar and cotton and oranges;
Do you see it?—stretching away endlessly over river-lines and lakes, and the gentle undulations of the lowlands, and up the escarpments of the higher hills;
The innumerable patchwork of civilization—the poignant verdure of the young rice; the somber green of orange-groves; the lines of tea-shrubs, well hoed, and showing the bare earth beneath; the pollard mulberries; the plots of cotton and maize and wheat and yam and clover; the little brown and green tiled cottages with spreading recurbed eaves, the clumps of feathery bamboo, or of sugar-canes;
The endless silver threads of irrigation canals and ditches, skirting the hills for scores and hundreds of miles, tier above tier, and serpentining down to the lower slopes and plains—

46

CONFUCIUS

The accumulated result, these, of centuries upon centuries of ingenious industry, and innumerable public and private benefactions, continued from age to age;
¶ The grand canal of the Delta plain extending, a thronged waterway, for seven hundred miles, with sails of junks and bankside villages innumerable;

The chain-pumps, worked by buffaloes or men, for throwing the water up slopes and hillsides, from tier to tier, from channel to channel;

The endless rills and cascades flowing down again into pockets and hollows of verdure, and on fields of steep and plain;

The bits of rock and wildwood left here and there, with the angles of Buddhist or Jain temples projecting from among the trees;

The azalea and rhododendron bushes, and the wild deer and pheasants unharmed;

The sounds of music and the gong—the Sin-fa sung at eventide—and the air of contentment and peace pervading;

A garden you might call the land, for its wealth of crops and flowers,

A town almost for its population.

A population denser, on a large scale, than anywhere else on earth—

Five or six acre holdings, elbowing each other, with lesser and larger, continuously over immense tracts, and running to plentiful market centers;

A country of few roads, but of innumerable footpaths and waterways.

Here, rooted in the land, and rooted in the family, each family clinging to its portion of ancestral earth, each

47

offshoot of the family desiring nothing so much as to secure its own patrimonial field,

Each member of the family answerable primarily to the family assembly for his misdeeds or defalcations,
¶ All bound together in the common worship of ancestors, and in reverence for the past and its sanctioned beliefs and accumulated prejudices and superstitions;
¶ With many ancient, wise, simple customs and ordinances, coming down from remote centuries, and the time of Confucius,

This vast population abides—the most stable and the most productive in the world.

And Government touches it but lightly—can touch it but lightly.

With its few officials (only some twenty-five thousand for the whole of its four hundred millions), and its scanty taxation (about one dollar per head), and with the extensive administration of justice and affairs by the clan and the family—little scope is left for government ❧ ❧

The great equalized mass population pursues its even and accustomed way, nor pays attention to edicts and foreign treaties, unless these commend themselves independently;

Pays readier respect, in such matters, to the edicts and utterances of its literary men, and the deliberations of the Academy.

And religious theorizing touches it but lightly—can touch it but lightly.

Established on the bedrock of actual life, and on the living unity and community of present, past and future

CONFUCIUS

generations. ¶ Each man stands bound already, and by the most powerful ties, to the social body—nor needs the dreams and promises of Heaven to reassure him ✄ And all are bound to the Earth.

Rendering back to it as a sacred duty every atom that the Earth supplies to them (not insensately sending it in sewers to the sea),

By the way of abject commonsense they have sought the gates of Paradise—and to found on human soil their City Celestial!

CONFUCIUS

THE first general knowledge of Confucius came to the Western world in the latter part of the Sixteenth Century from Jesuit missionaries. Indeed, it was they who gave him the Latinized name of "Confucius," the Chinese name being Kung-Fu-tsze.

So impressed were these missionaries by the greatness of Confucius that they urged upon the Vatican the expediency of placing his name upon the calendar of Saints. They began by combating his teachings, but this they soon ceased to do, and the modicum of success which they obtained was through beginning each Christian service by the hymn which may properly be called the National Anthem of China. Its opening stanza is as follows:

> Confucius! Confucius!
> Great was our Confucius!
> Before him there was no Confucius,
> Since him there was no other,
> Confucius! Confucius!
> Great was our Confucius!

The praise given by these early Jesuits to Confucius was at first regarded at Rome as apology for the meager success of their ministrations. But later scientific study of Chinese literature corroborated all that the Jesuit Fathers proclaimed for Confucius, and he stands today in a class with Socrates and the scant half-dozen whom we call the saviors of the world.

50

CONFUCIUS

¶ Yet Confucius claimed no " divine revelation," nor did he seek to found a religion. He was simply a teacher, and what he taught was the science of living— living in the present, with the plain and simple men and women who make up the world, and bettering our condition by bettering theirs. Of a future life he said he knew nothing, and concerning the supernatural he was silent, even rebuking his disciples for trying to pry into the secrets of Heaven. The word " God " he does not use, but his recognition of a Supreme Intelligence is limited to the use of a word which can best be translated " Heaven," since it tokens a place more than it does a person. Constantly he speaks of " doing the will of Heaven." And then he goes on to say that " Heaven is speaking through you," " Duty lies in mirroring Heaven in our acts," and many other such New-Thought aphorisms or epigrams.

That the man was a consummate literary stylist is beyond doubt. He spoke in parables and maxims, short, brief and musical. He wrote for his ear, and always his desire, it seems, was to convey the greatest truth in the fewest words. The Chinese, even the lowly and uneducated, know hundreds of Confucian epigrams, and still repeat them in their daily conversation or in writing, just as educated Englishmen use the Bible and Shakespeare for symbol.

Minister Wu, in a lecture delivered in various American cities, compared Confucius with Emerson, showing how in many ways these two great prophets paralleled each other. Emerson, of all Americans, seems the only man worthy of being so compared.

The writer who lives is the man who supplies the world with portable wisdom—short, sharp, pithy maxims which it can remember, or, better still, which it can not forget.

Confucius said, "Every truth has four corners: as a teacher I give you one corner, and it is for you to find the other three."

The true artist in words or things is always more or less impressionistic—he talks in parables, and it is for the hearer to discover the meaning for himself.

An epigram is truth in a capsule. The disadvantage of the epigram is the temptation it affords to good people to explain it to the others who are assumed to be too obtuse to comprehend it alone. And since explanations seldom explain, the result is a mixture or compound that has to be spewed utterly or taken on faith. Confucius is simple enough until he is explained. Then we evolve sects, denominations and men who make it their profession to render moral calculi opaque. China, being peopled by human beings, has suffered from this tendency to make truth concrete, just as all the rest of the world has suffered. Truth is fluid and should be allowed to flow. Ankylosis of a fact is superstition. Confucius was a free-trader.

CONFUCIUS

HINA has always been essentially feudal in her form of government. China is made up of a large number of States, each presided over by a prince or governor, and these States are held together by a rather loose federal government, the Emperor being the supreme ruler. State rights prevail. State may fight with State, or States may secede—it is n't of much moment. They are glad enough, after a few years, to get back, like boys who run away from home, or farmhands who quit work in a tantrum. The Chinese are very patient—they know that time cures all things, a truth the West has not yet learned. States that rebel, like individuals who place themselves beyond the protection of all, assume grave responsibilities.

The local prince usually realizes the bearing of the Social Contract—that he holds his office only during good behavior, and that his welfare and the welfare of his people are one.

Heih, the father of Confucius, was governor of one of these little States, and had impoverished himself in an effort to help his people. Heih was a man of seventy, wedded to a girl of seventeen, when their gifted son was born. When the boy was three years old the father died, and the lad's care and education depended entirely on the mother. This mother seems to have been a woman of rare mental and spiritual worth. She deliberately chose a life of poverty and honest toil

53

for herself and child, rather than allow herself to be
cared for by rich kinsmen. The boy was brought up
in a village, and he was not allowed to think himself
any better than the other village children, save as he
proved himself so. He worked in the garden, tended
the cattle and goats, mended the pathways, brought
wood and water, and waited on his elders. Every
evening his mother used to tell him of the feats of
strength of his father, of his heroic qualities in friendship, of deeds of valor, of fidelity to trusts, of his
absolute truthfulness, and his desire for knowledge in
order that he might better serve his people.

The coarse, plain fare, the long walks across the fields,
the climbing of trees, the stooping to pull the weeds in
the garden, the daily bath in the brook, all combined to
develop the boy's body to a splendid degree. He went
to bed at sundown, and at the first flush of dawn was up
that he might see the sunrise. There were devotional
rites performed by the mother and son, morning and
evening, which consisted in the playing upon a lute and
singing or chanting the beauty and beneficence of
creation ✤ ✤

Confucius, at fifteen, was regarded as a phenomenal
musician, and the neighbors used to gather to hear him
perform. At nineteen he was larger, stronger, comelier,
more skilled, than any other youth of his age in all the
country round.

The simple quality of his duties as a prince can be

guessed when we are told that his work as keeper of the herds required him to ride long distances on horseback to settle difficulties between rival herders. The range belonged to the State, and the owners of goats, sheep and cattle were in continual controversies. Montana and Colorado will understand this matter. Confucius summoned the disputants and talked to them long about the absurdity of quarreling and the necessity of getting together in complete understanding. Then it was that he first put forth his best-known maxim: " You should not do to others that which you would not have others do to you."

This negative statement of the Golden Rule is found expressed in various ways in the writings of Confucius. A literal interpretation of the Chinese language is quite impossible, as the Chinese have single signs or symbols that express a complete idea. To state the same matter, we often use a whole page.

Confucius had a single word which expressed the Golden Rule in such a poetic way that it is almost useless to try to convey it to people of the West. This word, which has been written into English as " Shu," means: My heart responds to yours, or my heart's desire is to meet your heart's desire, or I wish to do to you even as I would be done by. This sign, symbol or word Confucius used to carve in the bark of trees by the roadside. The French were filled with a like impulse when they cut the words Liberty, Fraternity,

CONFUCIUS

Equality, over the entrances to all public buildings.
¶ Confucius had his symbol of love and friendship
painted on a board, which he stuck into the ground
before the tent where he lodged; and finally it was
worked upon a flag by some friends and presented to
him, and became his flag of peace.

His success in keeping down strife among the herders,
and making peace among his people, soon gave him a
fame beyond the borders of his own State. As a judge
he had the power to show both parties where they were
wrong, and arranged for them a common meeting-
ground ⚅ ⚅

His qualifications as an arbiter were not, however,
limited to his powers of persuasion—he could shoot an
arrow farther and hurl a spear with more accuracy than
any man he ever met. Very naturally there are a great
number of folklore stories concerning his prowess, some
of which make him out a sort of combination Saint
George and William Tell, with the added kingly graces
of Alfred the Great. Omitting the incredible, we are
willing to believe that this man had a giant's strength,
but was great enough not to use it like a giant.

We are willing to believe that when attacked by
robbers, he engaged them in conversation and that,
seated on the grass, he convinced them they were in
a bad business. Also, he did not later hang them, as did
our old friend Julius Cæsar under like conditions.

When twenty-seven he ceased going abroad to hold

court and settle quarrels, but sending for the disputants, they came, and he gave them a course of lectures
in ethics. In a week, by a daily lesson of an hour's
length, they were usually convinced that to quarrel is
very foolish, since it reduces bodily vigor, scatters the
mind, and disturbs the secretions, so the man is the
loser in many ways.

This seems to us like a very queer way to hold court,
but Confucius maintained that men should learn to
govern their tempers, do equity, and thus be able to
settle their own disputes, and this without violence.
" To fight decides who is the stronger, the younger
and the more skilful in the use of arms, but it does not
decide who is right. That is to be settled by the Heaven
in your own heart."

To let the Heaven into your heart, to cultivate a conscience so sensitive that it can conceive the rights of
the other man, is to know wisdom.

To decide specific cases for others he thought was to
cause them to lose the power of deciding for themselves. When asked what a just man should do when he
was dealing with one absolutely unjust, he said, " He
who wrongs himself sows in his own heart nettles."
And when some of his disciples, after the Socratic
method, asked him how this helped the injured man,
he replied, " To be robbed or wronged is nothing unless
you continue to remember it." When pushed still
further, he said, "A man should fight, only when he does

57

---

so to protect himself or his family from bodily harm."
¶ Here a questioner asked, " If we are to protect our
persons, must we not learn to fight? "

And the answer comes, " The just man, he who partakes moderately of all good things, is the only man to
fear in a quarrel, for he is without fear."

Over and over is the injunction in varying phrase,
"Abolish fear—abolish fear!" When pressed to give in
one word the secret of a happy life, he gives a word
which we translate, " Equanimity."

58

CONFUCIUS

THE mother of Confucius died during his early manhood. For her he ever retained the most devout memories.

Before going on a journey he always visited her grave, and on returning, before he spoke to any one, he did the same. On each anniversary of her death he ate no food and was not to be seen by his pupils. This filial piety, which is sometimes crudely and coarsely called " ancestor worship," is something which for the Western world is rather difficult to appreciate. But in it there is a subtle, spiritual significance, suggesting that it is only through our parents that we are able to realize consciousness or personal contact with Heaven. These parents loved us into being, cared for us with infinite patience in infancy, taught us in youth, watched with high hope our budding manhood; and as reward and recognition for the service rendered us, the least we can do is to remember them in all our prayers and devotions. The will of Heaven used these parents for us, therefore parenthood is divine.

That this ancestor worship is beautiful and beneficial is quite apparent, and rightly understood no one could think of it as " heathendom." Confucius used to chant the praises of his mother, who brought him up in poverty, thus giving a close and intimate knowledge of a thousand things from which princes, used to ease and luxury, are barred.

So close was he to nature and the plain people that

59

he ordered that all skilful charioteers in his employ should belong to the nobility. This giving a title or degree to men of skill—men who can do things—we regard as essentially a modern idea.

China, I believe, is the first country in the world to use the threads of a moth or worm for fabrics. The patience and care and inventive skill required in first making silk were very great. But it gives us an index to invention when we hear that Confucius regarded the making of linen, using the fiber of a plant, as a greater feat than utilizing the strands made by the silkworm. Confucius had a sort of tender sentiment toward the moth, similar to the sentiments which our vegetarian friends have toward killing animals for food. Confucius wore linen in preference to silk, for sentimental reasons. The silkworm dies at his task of making himself a cocoon, so to evolve in a winged joy, but falls a victim of man's cupidity. Likewise, Confucius would not drink milk from a cow until her calf was weaned, because to do so were taking an unfair advantage of the maternal instincts of the cow. It will thus be seen that Confucius had a very fair hold on the modern idea which we call " Monism," or " The One." He, too, said, "All is one." In his attitude toward all living things he was ever gentle and considerate ✄ ✄

No other prophet so much resembles Confucius in doctrine as Socrates. But Confucius does not suffer from the comparison. He had a beauty, dignity and grace of person which the great Athenian did not possess. Socrates was more or less of a buffoon, and to many in Athens he was a huge joke—a town fool. Confucius combined the learning and graces of Plato with the sturdy, practical commonsense of Socrates. No one ever affronted or insulted him; many did not understand him, but he met prince or pauper on terms of equality 🌿 🌿

In his travels Confucius used often to meet recluses or monks—men who had fled the world in order to become saints. For these men Confucius had more pity than respect. "The world's work is difficult, and to live in a world of living, striving and dying men and women requires great courage and great love. Now we can not all run away, and for some to flee from humanity and to find solace in solitude is only another name for weakness." 🌿 🌿

This sounds singularly like our Ralph Waldo who says, " It is easy in the world to live after the world's opinions; it is easy in solitude to live after our own; but the Great Man is he who in the midst of the crowd keeps with perfect sweetness the independence of solitude." 🌿 🌿

Confucius is the first man in point of time to proclaim the divinity of service, the brotherhood of man, and the truth that in useful work there is no high nor low degree. In talking to a group of young men he says:

61

"When I was keeper of the herds I always saw to it that all of my cattle were strong, healthy and growing, that there was water in abundance and plenty of feed. When I had charge of the public granaries I never slept until I knew that all was secure and cared for against the weather, and my accounts as true and correct as if I were going on my long journey to return no more. My advice is to slight nothing, forget nothing, never leave things to chance, nor say, 'Nobody will know—this is good enough.'"

In all of his injunctions Confucius never has anything in mind beyond the present life. Of a future existence he knows nothing, and he seems to regard it as a waste of energy and a sign of weakness to live in two worlds at a time. "Heaven provides us means of knowing all about what is best here, and supplies us in abundance every material thing for present happiness, and it is our business to realize, to know, to enjoy."

He taught rhetoric, mathematics, economics, the science of government and natural history. And always and forever running through the fabric of his teaching was the silken thread of ethics—man's duty to man, man's duty to Heaven. Music was to him a necessity, since "it brings the mind in right accord with the will of Heaven." Before he began to speak he played softly on a stringed instrument which perhaps would compare best with our guitar, but it was much smaller, and this instrument he always carried with him, suspended from his shoulder by a silken sash. Yet with all of his passion for music, he cautioned his disciples against using it as an end. It was merely valuable as an introduction to be used in attuning the mind and heart to an understanding of great truth.

Confucius was seventy-two years old at his death. During his life his popularity was not great. When he passed away his followers numbered only about three thousand persons, and his " disciples," or the teachers who taught his philosophy, were seventy in number ॐ ॐ

There is no reason to suppose that Confucius assumed that a vast number of people would ever ponder his words or regard him as a prophet.

At the time that Confucius lived, also lived Lao-tsze. As a youth Confucius visited Lao-tsze, who was then an old man. Confucius often quotes his great contemporary and calls himself a follower of Lao-tsze. The difference, however, between the men is marked. Laotsze's teachings are full of metaphysics and strange and mystical curiosities, while Confucius is always simple, lucid and practical.

CONFUCIUS

CONFUCIUS has been revered for twenty centuries, revered simply as a man, not as a god or as a divinely appointed savior. He offered no reward of heaven, nor did he threaten non-believers with hell. He claimed no special influence nor relationship to the Unseen. In all his teachings he was singularly open, frank and free from all mystery or concealment. In reference to the supernatural he was an agnostic. He often said, " I do not know." He was always an inquirer, always a student, always open to conviction. History affords no instance of another individual who has been so well and so long loved, who still holds his place, and who, so far as his reasoning went, is unassailed and unassailable. Even the two other great religions in China that rival Confucianism—Buddhism and Taoism (the religion of Lao-tsze) —do not renounce Confucius: they merely seek to amend and augment him.

During his lifetime Confucius made many enemies by his habit of frankly pointing out the foibles of society and the wrongs visited upon the people by officials who pretended to serve them. Of hypocrisy, selfishness, vanity, pretense, he was severe in his denunciation. ¶ Politicians at that time had the very modern habit of securing the office and then leaving all the details of the work to menials, they themselves pocketing the perquisites. As Minister of State, Confucius made himself both feared and detested on account of

his habit of summoning the head of the office before
him and questioning him concerning his duties. In fact,
this insistence that those paid by the State should work
for the State caused a combination to be formed against
him, which finally brought about his deposition and
exile, two things which troubled him but little, since one
gave him leisure and the other opportunity for travel.
¶ The personal followers of Confucius did not belong
to the best society; but immediately after his death,
many who during his life had scorned the man made
haste to profess his philosophy and decorate their
houses with his maxims. Humanity is about the same,
whether white or yellow, the round world over, and
time modifies it but little. It will be recalled how John
P. Altgeld was feared and hated by both press and pul-
pit, especially in the State and city he served. But rigor
mortis had scarcely seized upon that slight and tired
body before the newspapers that had disparaged the
man worst were vying with one another in glowing
eulogies and warm testimonials to his honesty, sincerity, purity of motive and deep insight. A personality
which can neither be bribed, bought, coerced, flattered
nor cajoled is always regarded by the many—especially
by the party in power—as " dangerous." Vice, masked
as virtue, breathes easier when the honest man is
safely under the sod.
The plain and simple style of Confucius' teaching can be
gathered by the following sayings, selected at random

CONFUCIUS

from the canonical books of Confucianism, consisting of the teachings of the great master which were gathered together and grouped by his disciples and followers after his death:

The men of old spoke little. It would be well to imitate them, for those who talk much are sure to say something it would be better to have left unsaid.

Let a man's labor be proportioned to his needs. For he who works beyond his strength does but add to his cares and disappointments. A man should be moderate even in his efforts.

Be not over-anxious to obtain relaxation or repose. For he who is so, will get neither.

Beware of ever doing that which you are likely, sooner or later, to repent of having done.

Do not neglect to rectify an evil because it may seem small, for, though small at first, it may continue to grow until it overwhelms you.

As riches adorn a house, so does an expanded mind adorn and tranquillize the body. Hence it is that the superior man will seek to establish his motives on correct principles.

The cultivator of the soil may have his fill of good things, but the cultivator of the mind will enjoy a continual feast.

CONFUCIUS

It is because men are prone to be partial toward those they love, unjust toward those they hate, servile toward those above them, arrogant to those below them, and either harsh or over-indulgent to those in poverty and distress, that it is so difficult to find any one capable of exercising a sound judgment with respect to the qualities of others.

He who is incapable of regulating his own family can not be capable of ruling a nation. The superior man will find within the limits of his own home, a sufficient sphere for the exercise of all those principles upon which good government depends. How, indeed, can it be otherwise, when filial piety is that which should regulate the conduct of a people toward their prince; fraternal affection, that which should regulate the relations which should exist between equals, and the conduct of inferiors toward those above them; and paternal kindness, that which should regulate the bearing of those in authority toward those over whom they are placed?

Be slow in speech, but prompt in action.

He whose principles are thoroughly established will not be easily led from the right path.

The cautious are generally to be found on the right side.

By speaking when we ought to keep silence, we waste our words.

If you would escape vexation, reprove yourself liberally and others sparingly.

There is no use attempting to help those who can not help themselves.

Make friends with the upright, intelligent and wise; avoid the licentious, talkative and vain.

Disputation often breeds hatred.

Nourish good principles with the same care that a mother would bestow on her newborn babe. You may not be able to bring them to maturity, but you will nevertheless be not far from doing so.

The decrees of Heaven are not immutable, for though a throne may be gained by virtue, it may be lost by vice.

There are five good principles of action to be adopted: To benefit others without being lavish; to encourage labor without being harsh; to add to your resources without being covetous; to be dignified without being supercilious; and to inspire awe without being austere. Also, we should not search for love or demand it, but so live that it will flow to us.

Personal character can only be established on fixed principles, for if the mind be allowed to be agitated by violent emotions, to be excited by fear, or unduly moved by the love of pleasure, it will be impossible for it to be made perfect. A man must reason calmly, for without reason he would look and not see, listen and not hear.

When a man has been helped around one corner of a square, and can not manage by himself to get around the other three, he is unworthy of further assistance.

PYTHAGORAS

Consult and deliberate before you act, that thou mayest not commit foolish actions. For 't is the part of a miserable man to speak and to act without reflection. But do that which will not afflict thee afterwards, nor oblige thee to repentance.

—*Pythagoras*

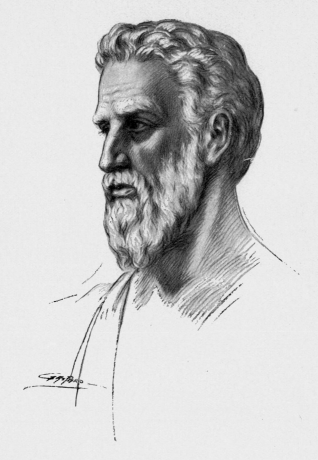

PYTHAGORAS

PYTHAGORAS

ITH no desire to deprive Mr. Bok of his bread, I wish to call attention to Pythagoras, who lived a little more than five hundred years before Christ ᔥ ᔥ

Even at that time the world was old. Memphis, which was built four thousand years ago, had begun to crumble into ruins. Troy was buried deep in the dust which an American citizen of German birth was to remove. Nineveh and Babylon were dying the death that success always brings, and the star of empire was preparing to westward wend its way.

Pythagoras ushered in the Golden Age of Greece. All the great writers whom he immediately preceded, quote him and refer to him. Some admire him; others are loftily critical; most of them are a little jealous; and a few use him as a horrible example, calling him a poseur, a pedant, a learned sleight-of-hand man, a bag of books.

Trial by newspaper was not invented in the time of Pythagoras; but personal vilification has been popular since Balaam talked gossip with his vis-a-vis.

Anaxagoras, who gave up his wealth to the State that he might be free, and who was the teacher of Pericles, was a pupil of Pythagoras, and used often to mention

71

PYTHAGORAS

him ❧ In this way Pericles was impressed by the Pythagorean philosophy, and very often quotes it in his speeches. Socrates gave Pythagoras as an authority on the simple life, and stated that he was willing to follow him in anything save his injunction to keep silence. Socrates wanted silence optional; whereas Pythagoras required each of his pupils to live for a year without once asking a question or making an explanation. In aggravated cases he made the limit five years. ¶ In many ways Pythagoras reminds us of our friend Muldoon, both being beneficent autocrats, and both proving their sincerity by taking their own medicine. Pythagoras said, " I will never ask another to do what I have not done, and am not willing to do myself."

To this end he was once challenged by his three hundred pupils to remain silent for a year. He accepted the defi, not once defending himself from the criticisms and accusations that were rained upon him, not once complaining, nor issuing an order. Tradition has it, however, that he made averages good later on, when the year of expiation was ended.

There are two reasonably complete lives of Pythagoras, one by Diogenes Laertius, and another by Iamblichus. Personally, I prefer the latter, as Iamblichus, as might be inferred from his name, makes Pythagoras a descendant of Æneas, who was a son of Neptune. This is surely better than the abrupt and somewhat sensational statement to the effect that his father was Apollo.

72

PYTHAGORAS

HE birthplace of Pythagoras was Samos, an isle of Greece. He was born of wealthy but honest parents, who were much in love with each other—a requisite, says Pythagoras, for parentage on its highest plane. It is probable that Pythagoras was absolutely correct in his hypothesis ‸ That he was a very noble specimen of manhood— physically and mentally—there is no doubt. He was tall, lithe, dignified, commanding and silent by nature, realizing fully that a handsome man can never talk as well as he looks.

He was quite aware of his physical graces, and in following up the facts of his early life, he makes the statement that his father was a sea-captain and trader. He then incidentally adds that the best results are obtained for posterity where a man is absent from his family eleven months in the year. This is an axiom agreed upon by many modern philosophers, few of whom, however, live up to their ideals. Aristophanes, who was on friendly terms with some of the disciples of Pythagoras, suggested in one of his plays that the Pythagorean domestic time-limit should be increased at least a month for the good of all concerned.

Plato, Xenophon and Aristotle make frequent references to Pythagoras. In order to impress men like these, the man must have taught a very exalted philosophy. In truth, Pythagoras was a teacher of teachers. And like all men who make a business of wisdom he sometimes came tardy off, and indulged in a welter of words that wrecked the original idea—if there were one.

There are these three: Knowledge, Learning, Wisdom. And the world has until very recent times assumed that they were practically one and the same thing. ¶ Knowledge consists of the things we know, not the things we believe or the things we assume. Knowledge is a personal matter of intuition, confirmed by experience. Learning consists largely of the things we memorize and are told by persons or books. Tomlinson of Berkeley Square was a learned man. When we think of a learned man, we picture him as one seated in a library surrounded by tomes that top the shelves.

Wisdom is the distilled essence of what we have learned from experience. It is that which helps us to live, work, love and make life worth living for all we meet. Men may be very learned, and still be far from wise.

Pythagoras was one of those strange beings who are born with a desire to know, and who finally comprehending the secret of the Sphinx, that there is really nothing to say, insist on saying it. That is, vast learning is augmented by a structure of words, and on this is built a theogony. Practically he was a priest.

Worked into all priestly philosophies are nuggets of wisdom that shine like stars in the darkness and lead men on and on.

All great religions have these periods of sanity, otherwise

they would have no followers at all. The followers, understanding little bits of this and that, hope finally to understand it all. Inwardly the initiates at the shrine of their own conscience know that they know nothing. When they teach others they are obliged to pretend that they, themselves, fully comprehend the import of what they are saying. The novitiate attributes his lack of perception to his own stupidity, and many great teachers encourage this view.

" Be patient, and you shall some day know," they say, and smile frigidly.

And when credulity threatens to balk and go no further, magic comes to the rescue and the domain of Hermann and Kellar is poached upon.

Mystery and miracle were born in Egypt. It was there that a system was evolved, backed up by the ruler, of religious fraud so colossal that modern deception looks like the bungling efforts of an amateur. The government, the army, the taxing power of the State, were sworn to protect gigantic safes in which was hoarded —nothing. That is to say, nothing but the pretense upon which cupidity and self-hypnotized credulity battened and fattened.

All institutions which through mummery, strange acts, dress and ritual, affect to know and impart the inmost secrets of creation and ultimate destiny, had their rise in Egypt. In Egypt now are only graves, tombs, necropolises and silence. The priests there need no

---

soldiery to keep their secrets safe. Ammon-Ra, who once ruled the universe, being finally exorcised by Yaveh, is now as dead as the mummies who once were men and upheld his undisputed sway.

PYTHAGORAS

HE Egyptians guarded their mysteries with jealous dread.

We know their secret now. It is this—there are no mysteries.

That is the only secret upon which any secret society holds a caveat. Wisdom can not be corraled with gibberish and fettered in jargon. Knowledge is one thing—palaver another. The Greek-letter societies of our callow days still survive in bird's-eye, and next to these come the Elks, who take theirs with seltzer and a smile, as a rare good joke, save that brotherhood and good-fellowship are actually a saving salt which excuses much that would otherwise be simply silly.

All this mystery and mysticism was once official, and later, on being discarded by the authorities, was continued by the students as a kind of prank.

Greek-letter societies are the rudimentary survivals of what was once an integral part of every college. Making dead languages optional was the last convulsive kick of the cadaver.

And now a good many colleges are placing the seal of their disapproval on secret societies among the students; and the day is near when the secret society will not be tolerated, either directly or indirectly, as a part of the education of youth. All this because the sophomoric mind is prone to take its Greek-letter mysteries seriously, and regard the college curriculum as a joke of the faculty.

PYTHAGORAS

If knowledge were to be gained by riding a goat, any petty crossroads, with its lodge-room over the grocery, would contain a Herbert Spencer; and the agrarian mossbacks would have wisdom by the scruff and detain knowledge with a tail-hold.

There can be no secrets in life and morals, because Nature has so provided that every beautiful thought you know and every precious sentiment you feel, shall shine out of your face so that all who are great enough may see, know, understand, appreciate and appropriate. You can keep things only by giving them away.

PYTHAGORAS

HEN Pythagoras was only four or five years old, his mother taught him to take his morning bath in the cold stream, and dry his baby skin by running in the wind. As he ran, she ran with him, and together they sang a hymn to the rising sun, that for them represented the god Apollo. ¶ This mother taught him to be indifferent to cold, heat, hunger, to exult in endurance, and to take a joy in the glow of the body.

So the boy grew strong and handsome, and proud; and perhaps it was in those early years, from the mother herself, that he gathered the idea, afterward developed, that Apollo had appeared to his mother, and so great was the beauty of the god that the woman was actually overcome, it being the first god at which she had ever had a good look.

The ambition of a great mother centers on her son. Pythagoras was filled with the thought that he was different, peculiar, set apart to teach the human race. ¶ Having compassed all there was to learn in his native place, and, as he thought, being ill appreciated, he started for Egypt, the land of learning. The fallacy that knowledge was a secret to be gained by word of mouth and to be gotten from books existed then as now. The mother of Pythagoras wanted her son to comprehend the innermost secrets of the Egyptian mysteries. He would then know all. To this end she sold her jewels, in order that her son might have the advantages of an

79

Egyptian education. ¶ Women were not allowed to know the divine secrets—only just a few little ones. This woman wanted to know, and she said her son would learn, and tell her.

The family had become fairly rich by this time, and influential. Letters were gotten from the great ones of Samos to the Secretary of State in Egypt. And so Pythagoras, aged twenty, " the youth with the beautiful hair," went on his journey to Egypt and knocked boldly at the doors of the temples at Memphis, where knowledge was supposed to be in stock. Religion then monopolized all schools and continued to do so for quite some time after Pythagoras was dead.

He was turned away with the explanation that no foreigner could enter the sacred portals—that the initiates must be those born in the shadows of the temples and nurtured in the faith from infancy by holy virgins.

Pythagoras still insisted, and it was probably then that he found a sponsor who made for him the claim that he was a son of Apollo. And the holy men peeped out of their peep-holes in holy admiration for any one who could concoct as big a lie as they themselves had ever invented ❧ ❧

The boy surely looked the part. Perhaps, at last, here was one who was what they pretended to be! Frauds believe in frauds, and rogues are more easily captured by roguery than are honest men.

PYTHAGORAS

His admittance to the university became a matter of international diplomacy. At last, being too hard-pressed, the wise ones who ran the mystery monopoly gave in, and Pythagoras was informed that at midnight of a certain night, he should present himself, naked, at the door of a certain temple and he would be admitted. ¶ On the stroke of the hour, at the appointed time, Pythagoras, the youth with the beautiful hair, was there, clothed only in his beautiful hair. He knocked on the great, bronze doors, but the only answer was a faint, hollow echo.

Then he got a stone and pounded, but still no answer. ¶ The wind sprang up fresh and cold. The young man was chilled to the bone, but still he pounded and then called aloud demanding admittance. His answer now was the growling and barking of dogs, within. Still he pounded! After an interval a hoarse voice called out through a little slide, ordering him to be gone or the dogs would be turned loose upon him.

He demanded admittance.

" Fool, do you not know that the law says these doors shall admit no one except at sunrise? "

" I only know that I was told to be here at midnight and I would be admitted."

"All that may be true, but you were not told when you would be admitted—wait, it is the will of the gods."

So Pythagoras waited, numbed and nearly dead ⚡ The dogs which he had heard had, in some way, gotten out, and came tearing around the corner of the great stone building. He fought them with desperate strength. The effort seemed to warm his blood, and whereas before he was about to retreat to his lodgings he now remained.

The day broke in the east, and gangs of slaves went by to work. They jeered at him and pelted him with pebbles ✄ ✄

Suddenly across the desert sands he saw the faint pink rim of the rising sun. On the instant the big bronze doors against which he was leaning swung suddenly in. He fell with them, and coarse, rough hands seized his hair and pulled him into the hall.

The doors swung to and closed with a clang. Pythagoras was in dense darkness, lying on the stone floor.

A voice, seemingly coming from afar, demanded, "Do you still wish to go on?"

And his answer was, "I desire to go on."

A black-robed figure, wearing a mask, then appeared with a flickering light, and Pythagoras was led into a stone cell.

His head was shaved, and he was given a coarse robe and then left alone. Toward the end of the day he was given a piece of black bread and a bowl of water. This he was told was to fortify him for the ordeal to come.

¶ What that ordeal was we can only guess, save that it consisted partially in running over hot sands where he sank to his waist. At a point where he seemed about to perish a voice called loudly, " Do you yet desire to go on? "

And his answer was, " I desire to go on."

Returning to the inmost temple he was told to enter a certain door and wait therein. He was then blindfolded and when he opened the door to enter, he walked off into space and fell into a pool of ice-cold water ✄ While floundering there the voice again called, " Do you yet desire to go on? "

And his answer was, " I desire to go on."

At another time he was tied upon the back of a donkey and the donkey was led along a rocky precipice, where lights danced and flickered a thousand feet below.

" Do you yet want to go on? " called the voice.

And Pythagoras answered, " I desire to go on."

The priests here pushed the donkey off the precipice, which proved to be only about two feet high, the gulf below being an illusion arranged with the aid of lights that shone through apertures in the wall.

These pleasing little diversions Pythagoras afterward introduced into the college which he founded, so to teach the merry freshmen that nothing, at the last, was as bad as it seemed, and that most dangers are simply illusions.

The Egyptians grew to have such regard for Pythagoras that he was given every opportunity to know the inmost secrets of the mysteries. He said he encompassed them all, save those alone which were incomprehensible.

PYTHAGORAS

This was probably true. ¶ The years spent in Egypt were not wasted—he learned astronomy, mathematics, and psychology, a thing then not named, but pretty well understood—the management of men.

It was twenty years before Pythagoras returned to Samos. His mother was dead, so she passed away in ignorance of the secrets of the gods—which perhaps was just as well.

Samos now treated Pythagoras with great honor ✄ Crowds flocked to his lectures, presents were given him, royalty paid him profound obeisance.

But Samos soon tired of Pythagoras. He was too austere, too severe; and when he began to rebuke the officials for their sloth and indifference, he was invited to go elsewhere and teach his science of life. And so he journeyed into Southern Italy, and at Crotona built his Temple to the Muses and founded the Pythagorean School. He was the wisest as well as the most learned man of his time.

PYTHAGORAS

OME unkind person has said that Pythagoras was the original charter member of the Jesuits Society. The maxim that the end justifies the means was the cornerstone of Egyptian theology. When Pythagoras left Egypt he took with him this cornerstone as a souvenir. That the priests could hold their power over the masses only through magic and miracle was fully believed, and as a good police system the value of organized religion was highly appreciated. In fact, no ruler could hold his place, unsupported by the priest. Both were divine propositions. One searches in vain for simple truth among the sages, solons, philosophers, poets and prophets that existed down to the time of Socrates. Truth for truth's sake was absolutely unimagined; freethought was unguessed.

Expediency was always placed before truth.

Truth was furnished with frills—the people otherwise would not be impressed. Chants, robes, ritual, processions, banging of bells, burning of incense, strange sounds, sights and smells: these were considered necessary factors in teaching divine truth.

To worship with a noise seems to us a little like making love with a brass band.

Pythagoras was a very great man, but for him to eliminate theological chaff entirely was impossible. So we find that when he was about to speak, red fire filled the building as soon as he arose. It was all a little like the alleged plan of the late Reverend T. DeWitt Talmage, who used to have an Irishman let loose a white pigeon from the organ-loft at an opportune time. ¶ When Pythagoras burned the red fire, of course the audience thought a miracle was taking place, unable to understand a simple stage-trick which all the boys in the gallery who delight in " Faust " now understand. ¶ However, the Pythagorean School had much virtue on its side, and made a sincere and earnest effort to solve certain problems that yet are vexing us.

The Temple of the Muses, built by Pythagoras at Crotona, is described by Iamblichus as a stone structure with walls twenty feet thick, the light being admitted only from the top. It was evidently constructed after the Egyptian pattern, and the intent was to teach there the esoteric doctrine. But Pythagoras improved upon the Egyptian methods and opened his temple on certain days to all and any who desired to come. Then at times he gave lectures to women only, and then to men only, and also to children, thus showing that modern revival methods are not wholly modern. ¶ These lectures contain the very essence of Pythagorean philosophy, and include so much practical commonsense that they are still quoted. These are some of the sayings that impressed Socrates, Pericles, Aristotle and Pliny. What the Egyptians actually taught we really do not know—it was too gaseous to last. Only the good endures. Says Pythagoras:

PYTHAGORAS

Cut not into the grape. Exaltation coming from wine is not good. You hope too much in this condition, so are afterwards depressed. Wise men are neither cast down in defeat nor exalted by success. Eat moderately, bathe plentifully, exercise much in the open air, walk far, and climb the hills alone.

Above all things, learn to keep silence—hear all and speak little. If you are defamed, answer not back. Talk convinces no one. Your life and character proclaim you more than any argument you can put forth. Lies return to plague those who repeat them.

The secret of power is to keep an even temper, and remember that no one thing that can happen is of much moment. The course of justice, industry, courage, moderation, silence, means that you shall receive your due of every good thing. The gods may be slow, but they never forget.

It is not for us to punish men nor avenge ourselves for slights, wrongs and insults—wait, and you will see that Nemesis unhorses the man intent on calumny.

A woman's ornaments should be modesty, simplicity, truth, obedience. If a woman would hold a man captive she can only do it by obeying him. Violent women are even more displeasing to the gods than violent men— both are destroying themselves. Strife is always defeat. ¶ Debauchery, riot, splendor, luxury, are attempts to get a pleasure out of life that is not our due, and so Nemesis provides her penalty for the idle and gluttonous ⚬ Fear and honor the gods. They guide our ways and watch over us in our sleep. After the gods, a man's first thought should be of his father and mother. Next to these his wife, then his children.

87

PYTHAGORAS

So great was this power of Pythagoras over the people that many of the women who came, hearing his discourse on the folly of pride and splendor, threw off their cloaks, and left them with their rings, anklets and necklaces on the altar.

With these and other offerings Pythagoras built another temple, this time to Apollo, and the Temple to the Muses was left open all the time for the people.

His power over the multitude alarmed the magistrates, so they sent for him to examine him as to his influence and intents. He explained to them that as the Muses were never at variance among themselves, always living in subjection to Apollo, so should magistrates agree among themselves and think only of being loyal to the king. All royal edicts and laws are reflections of divine law, and therefore must be obeyed without question. And as the Muses never interrupt the harmony of Heaven, but in fact add to it, so should men ever keep harmony among themselves.

All officers of the government should consider themselves as runners in the Olympian games, and never seek to trip, jostle, harass or annoy a rival, but run the race squarely and fairly, satisfied to be beaten if the other is the stronger and better man. An unfair victory gains only the anger of the gods.

All disorders in the State come from ill education of the young. Children not brought up to be patient, to endure, to work, to be considerate of their elders and respectful to all, grow diseased minds that find relief at last in anarchy and rebellion. So to take great care of children in their infancy, and then leave them at puberty to follow their own inclinations, is to sow disorder. Children well loved and kept close to their parents grow up into men and women who are an ornament to the State and a joy to the gods. Lawless, complaining, restless, idle children grieve the gods and bring trouble upon their parents and society.

The magistrates were here so pleased, and satisfied in their own minds that Pythagoras meant the State no harm, that they issued an order that all citizens should attend upon his lectures at least once a week, and take their wives and children with them.

They also offered to pay Pythagoras—that is, put him on the payroll as a public teacher—but he declined to accept money for his services. In this, Iamblichus says, he was very wise, since by declining a fixed fee, ten times as much was laid upon the altar of the Temple of the Muses, and not knowing to whom to return it, Pythagoras was obliged to keep it for himself and the poor.

PYTHAGORAS

HURCHMEN of the Middle Ages worked the memory of Pythagoras great injustice by quoting him literally in order to prove how much they were beyond him. Symbols and epigrams require a sympathetic hearer, otherwise they are as naught ✄ ✄

For instance, Pythagoras remarks, " Sit thou not down upon a bushel measure." What he probably meant was, get busy and fill the measure with grain rather than use it for a seat.

" Eat not the heart "—do not act so as to harrow the feelings of your friends, and do not be morbid.

" Never stir the fire with a sword "—do not inflame people who are wrathful.

" Wear not the image of God upon your jewelry "— do not make religion a proud or boastful thing.

" Help men to a burden, but never unburden them." This saying was used by Saint Francis to prove that the pagan philosophers had no tenderness, and that the humanities came at a later date. We can now easily understand that to relieve men of responsibilities is no help; rather do we grow strong by carrying burdens.

¶ "Leave not the mark of the pot upon the ashes" —wipe out the past, forget it, look to the future.

" Feed no animal that has crooked claws "—do not encourage rogues by supplying them a living.

" Eat no fish whose fins are black "—have nothing to do with men whose deeds are dark.

90

PYTHAGORAS

"Always have salt upon your table"—this seems the original of "cum grano salis" of the Romans.

" Leave the vinegar at a distance "—keep sweet.

" Speak not in the face of the sun "—even Erasmus thought this referred to magic. To us it is quite reasonable to suppose that it meant, " do not talk too much in public places."

" Pick not up what falls from the table "—Plutarch calls this superstition, but we can just as easily suppose it was out of consideration for cats, dogs or hungry men. The Bible has a command against gleaning too closely, and leaving nothing for the traveler.

" When making sacrifice, never pare your nails "—that is to say, do one thing at a time: wind not the clock at an inopportune time.

" Eat not in the chariot "—when you travel, travel.

¶ " Feed not yourself with your left hand "—get your living openly and avoid all left-handed dealings.

And so there are hundreds of these Pythagorean sayings that have vexed our classic friends for over two thousand years. All Greek scholars who really pride themselves on their scholarship have taken a hand at them, and agitated the ether just as the members of the Kokomo Woman's Club discuss obscure passages in Bliss Carman or Ella Wheeler Wilcox. Learned people are apt to comprehend anything but the obvious.

PYTHAGORAS

HE School of Pythagoras grew until it became the chief attraction of Crotona. The size of the town was doubled through the pilgrims who came to study music, mathematics, medicine, ethics and the science of government.

The Pythagorean plan of treating the sick by music was long considered as mere incantation, but there is a suspicion now that it was actual science. Once there was a man who rode a hobby all his life; and long after he was dead, folks discovered it was a real live horse and had carried the man long miles.

Pythagoras reduced the musical scale to a mathematical science. In astronomy he anticipated Copernicus, and indeed, it was cited as the chief offense of Copernicus that he had borrowed from a pagan. Copernicus, it seems, set the merry churchmen digging into Greek literature to find out just how bad Pythagoras was. This did the churchmen good, but did not help the cause of Copernicus.

Pythagoras for a time sought to popularize his work, but he soon found to his dismay that he was attracting cheap and unworthy people, who came not so much out of a love of learning as to satisfy a morbid curiosity and gain a short cut to wisdom. They wanted secrets, and knowing that Pythagoras had spent twenty years in Egypt, they came to him, hoping to get them.

Said Pythagoras, " He who digs, always finds." At another time, he put the same idea reversely, thus,

92

PYTHAGORAS

" He who digs not, never finds." ¶ Pythagoras was well past forty when he married a daughter of one of the chief citizens of Crotona. It seems that, inspired by his wife, who was first one of his pupils and then a disciple, he conceived a new mode of life, which he thought would soon overthrow the old manner of living.

Pythagoras himself wrote nothing, but all his pupils kept tablets, and Athens in the century following Pythagoras was full of these Pythagorean notebooks, and these supply us the scattered data from which his life was written.

Pythagoras, like so many other great men, had his dream of Utopia: it was a college or, literally, "a collection of people," where all were on an equality. Everybody worked, everybody studied, everybody helped everybody, and all refrained from disturbing or distressing any one. It was the Oneida Community taken over by Brook Farm and fused into a religious and scientific New Harmony by the Shakers.

One smiles to see the minute rules that were made for the guidance of the members. They look like a transcript from a sermon by John Alexander Dowie, revised by the shade of Robert Owen.

This Pythagorean Community was organized out of a necessity in order to escape the blow-ins who sailed across from Greece intent on some new thing, but principally to get knowledge and a living without work.
¶ And so Pythagoras and his wife formed a close

corporation. For each member there was an initiation, strict and severe, the intent of which was absolutely to bar the transient triflers. Each member was to turn over to the Common Treasury all the money and goods he had of every kind and quality. They started naked, just as did Pythagoras when he stood at the door of the temple in Egypt.

Simplicity, truth, honesty and mutual service were to govern. It was an outcrop of the monastic impulse, save that women were admitted, also. Unlike the Egyptians, Pythagoras believed now in the equality of the sexes, and his wife daily led the women's chorus, and she also gave lectures. The children were especially cared for by women set apart as nurses and teachers. By rearing perfect children, it was hoped and expected to produce in turn a perfect race.

The whole idea was a phase of totemism and tabu. ¶ That it flourished for about thirty years is very certain. Two sons and a daughter of Pythagoras grew to maturity in the college, and this daughter was tried by the Order on the criminal charge of selling the secret doctrines of her father to outsiders.

One of the sons it seems made trouble, also, in an attempt to usurp his father's place and take charge of affairs, as " next friend." One generation is about the limit of a Utopian Community. When those who have organized the community weaken and one by one pass away, and the young assume authority, the old ideas of austerity are forgotten and dissipation and disintegration enter. So do we move in circles.

The final blow to the Pythagorean College came through jealousy and misunderstanding of the citizens outside. It was the old question of Town versus Gown. The Pythagoreans numbered nearly three hundred people. They held themselves aloof, and no doubt had an exasperating pride. No strangers were ever allowed inside the walls—they were a law unto themselves.

Internal strife and tales told by dissenters excited the curiosity, and then the prejudice, of the townspeople. ¶ Then the report got abroad that the Pythagoreans were collecting arms and were about to overthrow the local government and enslave the officials.

On a certain night, led by a band of drunken soldiers, a mob made an assault upon the college. The buildings were fired, and the members were either destroyed in the flames or killed as they rushed forth to escape. Tradition has it that Pythagoras was later seen by a shepherd on the mountains, but the probabilities are that he perished with his people. But you can not dispose of a great man by killing him. Here we are reading, writing and talking yet of Pythagoras.

PLATO

How well I remember the aged poet Sophocles, when in answer to the question, " How does love suit with age, Sophocles—are you still the man you were? "

" Peace," he replied; " most gladly have I escaped that, and I feel as if I had escaped from a mad and furious master."

That saying of his has often come into my mind since, and seems to me still as good as at the time when I heard him. For certainly old age has a great sense of calm and freedom; when the passions relax their hold, then, as Sophocles says, you have escaped from the control not of one master only, but of many. And of these regrets, as well as of the complaint about relations, Socrates, the cause is to be sought, not in men's ages, but in their characters and tempers; for he who is of a calm and happy nature will hardly feel the pressure of age, but he who is of an opposite disposition will find youth and age equally a burden.

— *The Republic*

PLATO

PLATO

THINKING man is one of the most recent productions evolved from Nature's laboratory. The first man of brains to express himself about the world in an honest, simple and natural way, just as if nothing had been said about it before, was Socrates ❧ ❧

Twenty-four centuries have passed since Socrates was put to death on the charge of speaking disrespectfully of the gods and polluting the minds of the youths of Athens. During ten of these centuries that have passed since then, the race lost the capacity to think, through the successful combination of the priest and the soldier. These men blocked human evolution. The penalty for making slaves is that you become one.

To suppress humanity is to suppress yourself.

The race is one. So the priests and the soldiers who in the Third Century had a modicum of worth themselves, sank and were submerged in the general slough of superstition and ignorance. It was a panic that continued for a thousand years, all through the endeavor of faulty men to make people good by force. At all times, up to within our own decade, frank expression on religious, economic and social topics has been fraught with great peril. Even yet any man who hopes for popularity as a writer, orator, merchant or politician, would do well to conceal studiously his inmost beliefs. On such simple themes as the taxation of real estate, regardless of the business of the owner, and a payment of a like wage for a like service without consideration of sex, the statesman who has the temerity to speak out will be quickly relegated to private life. Successful merchants depending on a local constituency find it expedient to cater to popular superstitions by heading subscription-lists for the support of things in which they do not believe. No avowed independent thinker would be tolerated as chief ruler of any of the so-called civilized countries.

The fact, however, that the penalty for frank expression is limited now to social and commercial ostracism is very hopeful—a few years ago it meant the scaffold.

¶ We have been heirs to a leaden legacy of fear that has well-nigh banished joy and made of life a long nightmare ⚜ ⚜

In very truth, the race has been insane.

Hallucinations, fallacies, fears, have gnawed at our hearts, and men have fought men with deadly frenzy. The people who interfered, trying to save us, we have killed. Truly did we say, " There is no health in us," which repetition did not tend to mend the malady ⚜ We are now getting convalescent. We are hobbling out into the sunshine on crutches. We have discharged most of our old advisers, heaved the dulling and deadly bottles out of the windows, and are intent on studying and understanding our own case. Our motto is twenty-four centuries old—it is simply this: KNOW THYSELF.

PLATO

OCRATES was a street preacher, with a beautiful indifference as to whether people liked him or not. To most Athenians he was the town fool. Athens was a little city (only about one hundred fifty thousand), and everybody knew Socrates. The popular plays caricatured him; the topical songs misquoted him; the funny artists on the street-corners who modeled things in clay, while you waited, made figures of him.

Everybody knew Socrates—I guess so!

Plato, the handsome youth of nineteen, wearing a purple robe, which marked him as one of the nobility, paused to listen to this uncouth man who gave everything and wanted nothing.

Ye gods! But it is no wonder they caricatured him— he was a temptation too great to resist.

Plato smiled—he never laughed, being too well-bred for that. Then he sighed, and moved a little nearer in. ¶ " Individuals are nothing. The State is all. To offend the State is to die. The State is an organization and we are members of it. The State is only as rich as its poorest citizen. We are all given a little sample of divinity to study, model and marvel at. To understand the State you must KNOW THYSELF."

Plato lingered until the little crowd had dispersed, and when the old man with the goggle-eyes and full-moon face went shuffling slowly down the street, he approached and asked him a question.

102

PLATO

This man Socrates was no fool—the populace was wrong—he was a man so natural and free from cant that he appeared to the triflers and pretenders like a pretender, and they asked, " Is he sincere? "

What Plato was by birth, breeding and inheritance, Socrates was by nature—a noble man.

Up to this time the ambition of Plato had been for place and power—to make the right impression on the people in order to gain political preferment. He had been educated in the school of the Sophists, and his principal studies were poetry, rhetoric and deportment. ¶ And now straightway he destroyed the manuscript of his poems, for in their writing he had suddenly discovered that he had not written what he inwardly believed was true, but simply that which he thought was proper and nice to say. In other words, his literature had been a form of pretense.

Daily thereafter, where went Socrates there went Plato. Side by side they sat on the curb—Socrates talking, questioning the bystanders, accosting the passers-by; Plato talking little, but listening much.

Socrates was short, stout and miles around. Plato was tall, athletic and broad-shouldered. In fact, the word, " plato," or " platon," means broad, and it was given him as a nickname by his comrades. His correct name was Aristocles, but " Plato " suited him better, since it symbols that he was not only broad of shoulder, but likewise in mind. He was not only noble by birth,

PLATO

but noble in appearance. ¶ Emerson calls him the universal man. He absorbed all the science, all the art, all the philosophy of his day. He was handsome, kindly, graceful, gracious, generous, and lived and died a bachelor. He never collided with either poverty or matrimony.

PLATO

LATO was twenty-eight years old when Socrates died. For eight years they had been together daily. After the death of Socrates, Plato lived for forty-six years, just to keep alive the name and fame of the great philosopher ✣ Socrates comes to us through Plato. Various other contemporaries mention Socrates and quote him, some to his disadvantage, but it was left for Plato to give us the heart of his philosophy, and limn his character for all time in unforgetable outline.

Plato is called the "Pride of Greece." His contribution to the wealth of the world consists in the fact that he taught the joys of the intellect—the supreme satisfaction that comes through thinking. This is the pure Platonic philosophy: to find our gratifications in exalted thought and not in bodily indulgence. Plato's theory that five years should be given in early manhood to abstract thought, abstaining from all practical affairs, so as to acquire a love for learning, has been grafted upon a theological stalk and comes down to our present time. It has, however, now been discarded by the world's best thinkers as a fallacy. The unit of man's life is the day, not the month or year, much less a period of five years. Each day we must exercise the mind, just as each day we must exercise the body. We can not store up health and draw upon it at will over long-deferred periods. The account must be kept active. To keep physical energy we must expend

physical energy every day. The opinion of Herbert
Spencer that thought is a physical function—a vibra-
tion set up in a certain area of brain-cells—is an idea
never preached by Plato. The brain, being an organ,
must be used, not merely in one part for five years to
the exclusion of all other parts, but all parts should
be used daily. To this end the practical things of life
should daily engage our attention, no less than the
contemplation of beauty as manifest in music, poetry,
art or dialectics. The thought that every day we should
look upon a beautiful picture, read a beautiful poem, or
listen for a little while to beautiful music, is highly
scientific, for this contemplation and appreciation of
harmony is a physical exercise as well as a spiritual one,
and through it we grow, develop, evolve.

That we could not devote five years of our time to
purely esthetic exercises, to the exclusion of practical
things, without very great risk, is now well known.
And when I refer to practical affairs, I mean the effort
which Nature demands we should put forth to get a
living. Every man should live like a poor man, regardless of the fact that he may have money. Nature knows
nothing of bank-balances. In order to have an appetite
for dinner, you must first earn your dinner. If you
would sleep at night, you must first pay for sweet sleep
by physical labor.

PLATO

LATO was born on the Island of Ægina, where his father owned an estate. His mother was a direct descendant of Solon, and his father, not to be outdone, traced to Codrus. ¶ The father of Socrates was a stonecutter and his mother a midwife, so very naturally the son had a beautiful contempt for pedigree. Socrates once said to Plato, "Anybody can trace to Codrus—by paying enough to the man who makes the family-tree." This seems to show that genealogy was a matter of business then as now, and that nothing is new under the sun. Yet with all his contempt for heredity, we find Socrates often expressing pride in the fact that he was a " native son," whereas Plato, Aspasia, the mother of Themistocles, and various other fairly good people, were Athenian importations ✂ ✂

Socrates belonged to the leisure class and had plenty of time for extended conversazione, so just how much seriousness we should mix in his dialogues is still a problem. Each palate has to season to suit. Also, we can never know how much is Socrates and how much essence of Plato. Socrates wrote nothing, and Plato ascribes all of his wisdom to his master. Whether this was simple prudence or magnanimity is still a question. ¶ The death of Socrates must have been a severe blow to Plato. He at once left Athens. It was his first intention never to return. He traveled through the cities of Greece, Southern Italy and down to Egypt, and everywhere was treated with royal courtesies. ¶ After many solicitations from Dionysius, Tyrant of Syracuse, he went to visit that worthy, who had a case of philosophic and literary scabies. Dionysius prided himself on being a Beneficent Autocrat, with a literary and artistic attachment. He ruled his people, educated them, cared for them, disciplined them.

Some people call this slavery; others term it applied socialism. Dionysius wanted Syracuse to be the philosophic center of the world, and to this end Plato was importuned to make Syracuse his home and dispense his specialty—truth.

This he consented to do.

It was all very much like the arrangement between Mæcenas and Horace, or Voltaire and Frederick the Great. The patron is a man who patronizes—he wants something, and the particular thing that Dionysius wanted was to have Plato hold a colored light upon the performances of His Altruistic, Beneficent, Royal Jackanapes. But Plato was a simple, honest and direct man: he had caught the habit from Socrates.

Charles Ferguson says that the simple life does not consist in living in the woods and wearing overalls and sandals, but in getting the cant out of one's cosmos and eliminating the hypocrisy from one's soul.

Plato lived the simple life. When he spoke he stated what he thought. He discussed exploitation, war, taxation, and the Divine Right of Kings. Kings are very

108

PLATO

unfortunate—they are shut off and shielded from truth on every side. They get their facts at second hand and are lied to all day long. Consequently they become in time incapable of digesting truth. A court, being an artificial fabric, requires constant bracing. Next to capital, nothing is so timid as a king. Heine says that kings have to draw their nightcaps on over their crowns when they go to bed, in order to keep them from being stolen, and that they are subject to insomnia. ¶ Walt Whitman, with nothing to lose—not even a reputation or a hat—was much more kingly walking bareheaded past the White House than Nicholas of Russia or Alfonso of Spain can ever possibly be.

Dionysius thought that he wanted a philosophic court, but all he wanted was to make folks think he had a philosophic court. Plato supplied him the genuine article, and very naturally Plato was soon invited to vacate ✄ ✄

After he had gone, Dionysius, fearful that Plato would give him a bad reputation in Athens—somewhat after the manner and habit of the " escaped nun "—sent a fast-rowing galley after him. Plato was arrested and sold into slavery on his own isle of Ægina.

This all sounds very tragic, but the real fact is it was a sort of comedy of errors—as a king's doings are when viewed from a safe and convenient distance. De Wolf Hopper's kings are the real thing. Dionysius claimed that Plato owed him money, and so he got out a body-attachment, and sold the philosopher to the highest bidder ⚹ ⚹

This was a perfectly legal proceeding, being simply peonage, a thing which exists in some parts of the United States today. I state the fact without prejudice, merely to show how hard custom dies.

Plato was too big a man conveniently either to secrete or kill. Certain people in Athens plagiarized Doctor Johnson who, on hearing that Goldsmith had debts of several thousand pounds, in admiration exclaimed, " Was ever poet so trusted before! " Other good friends ascertained the amount of the claim and paid it, just as Colonel H. H. Rogers graciously cleared up the liabilities of Mark Twain, after the author of " Huckleberry Finn " had landed his business craft on a sandbar. ¶ And so Plato went free, arriving back in Athens, aged forty, a wiser and a better man than when he left ⚹

PLATO

OTHING absolves a reputation like silence and absence, or what the village editors call " the grim reaper." To live is always more or less of an offense, especially if you have thoughts and express them. Athens exists, in degree, because she killed Socrates, just as Jerusalem is unforgetable for a similar reason. The South did not realize that Lincoln was her best friend until the assassin's bullet had found his brain. Many good men in Chicago did not cease to revile their chiefest citizen, until the ears of Altgeld were stopped and his hands stiffened by death. The lips of the dead are eloquent.

Plato's ten years of absence had given him prestige. He was honored because he had been the near and dear friend of Socrates, a great and good man who was killed through mistake.

Most murders and killings of men, judicial and otherwise, are matters of misunderstandings.

Plato had been driven out of Syracuse for the very reasons that Socrates had been killed at Athens. And now behold, when Dionysius saw how Athens was honoring Plato, he discovered that it was all a mistake of his bookkeeper, so he wrote to Plato to come back and all would be forgiven.

THOSE who set out to live the Ideal Life have a hard trail to travel. The road to Jericho is a rocky one—especially if we are a little in doubt as to whether it really is the road to Jericho or not. Perhaps if we ever find the man who lives the Ideal Life he will be quite unaware of it, so occupied will he be in his work—so forgetful of self ⌥ Time had taught Plato diplomacy. He now saw that to teach people who did not want to be taught was an error in judgment for which one might forfeit his head. ¶ Socrates was the first Democrat: he stood for the demos—the people. Plato would have done the same, but he saw that the business was extra hazardous, to use the phrase of our insurance friends. He who works for the people will be destroyed by the people. Hemlock is such a rare and precious commodity that few can afford it; the cross is a privilege so costly that few care to pay the price.

The genius is a man who first states truths; and all truths are unpleasant on their first presentation. That which is uncommon is offensive. " Who ever heard anything like that before? " ask the literary and philosophic hill tribes in fierce indignation. Says James Russell Lowell, " I blab unpleasant truths, you see, that none may need to state them after me."

Plato was a teacher by nature: this was his business, his pastime, and the only thing in life that gave him joy. But he dropped back to the good old ways of making truth esoteric as did the priests of Egypt, instead of exoteric as did Socrates. He founded his college in the grove of his old friend Academus, a mile out of Athens on the road to Eleusis. In honor of Academus the school was called " The Academy." It was secluded, safe, beautiful for situation. In time Plato bought a tract of land adjoining that of Academus, and this was set apart as the permanent school. All the teaching was done out of doors, master and pupils seated on the marble benches, by the fountain-side, or strolling through the grounds, rich with shrubs and flowers and enlivened by the song of birds. The climate of Athens was about like that of Southern California, where the sun shines three hundred days in the year ✄ Plato emphasized the value of the spoken word over the written, a thing he could well afford to do, since he was a remarkably good writer. This for the same reason that the only man who can afford to go ragged is the man with a goodly bank-balance. The shibboleth of the modern schools of oratory is, " We grow through expression." And Plato was the man who first said it. Plato's teaching was all in the form of the " quiz," because he believed that truth was not a thing to be acquired from another—it is self-discovery.

Indeed, we can imagine it was very delightful—this walking, strolling, lying on the grass, or seated in semicircles, indulging in endless talk, easy banter, with now and then a formal essay read to start the vibrations. ¶ Here it was that Aristotle came from his wild home in the mountains of Macedonia, to remain for twenty years and to evolve into a rival of the master ✠ We can well imagine how Aristotle, the mountain-climber and horseman, at times grew heartily tired of the faultily faultless garden with its high wall and graveled walks and delicate shrubbery, and shouted aloud in protest, "The whole world of mountain, valley and plain should be our Academy, not this pent-up Utica that contracts our powers."

Then followed an argument as to the relative value of talking about things or doing them, or Poetry versus Science ✠ ✠

Poetry, philosophy and religion are very old themes, and they were old even in Plato's day; but natural science came in with Aristotle. And science is only the classification of the common knowledge of the common people. It was Aristotle who named things, not Adam. He contended that the classification and naming of plants, rocks and animals was quite as important as to classify ideas about human happiness and make guesses at the state of the soul after death.

Of course he got himself beautifully misunderstood, because he was advocating something which had never been advocated before. In this lay his virtue, that he outran human sympathy, even the sympathy of the great Plato.

Yet for a while the unfolding genius of this young

114

PLATO

barbarian was a great joy to Plato, as the earnest,
eager intellect of an ambitious pupil always is to his
teacher. Plato was great in speculation; Aristotle was
great in observation. Well has it been said that it was
Aristotle who discovered the world. And Aristotle in
his old age said, " My attempts to classify the objects
of Nature all came through Plato's teaching me first how
to classify ideas." And forty years before this Plato had
said, " It was Socrates who taught me this game of the
correlation and classification of thoughts."

PLATO

HE writings of Plato consist of thirty-five dialogues, and one essay which is not cast in the dramatic form—"The Apology." These dialogues vary in length from twenty pages, of, say, four hundred words each, to three hundred pages. In addition to these books are many quotations from Plato and references to him by contemporary writers. Plato's work is as impersonal as that of Shakespeare. All human ideas, shades of belief, emotions and desires pass through the colander of his mind. He allows everybody to have his say.

What Plato himself thought can only be inferred, and this each reader does for himself. We construct our man Plato in our own image. A critic's highest conception of Plato's philosophy is the highest conception of the critic's own. We, however, are reasonably safe in assuming that Plato's own ideas were put into the mouth of Socrates, for the one intent of Plato's life was to redeem Socrates from the charges that had been made against him. The characters Shakespeare loved are the ones that represent the master, not the hated and handmade rogues.

Plato's position in life was that of a spectator rather than that of an actor. He stood and saw the procession pass by, and as it passed, commented on it. He charged his pupils no tuition and accepted no fees, claiming that to sell one's influence or ideas was immoral.

It will be remembered that Byron held a similar

position at the beginning of his literary career, and declared i' faith, he " would not prostitute his genius for hire." He gave his poems to the world. Later, when his income was pinched, he began to make bargains with Barabbas and became an artist in per centum, collecting close, refusing to rhyme without collateral. ¶ Byron's humanity is not seriously disputed. Plato also was human. He had a fixed income and so knew the worthlessness of riches. He issued no tariff, but the goodly honorarium left mysteriously on a marble bench by a rich pupil he accepted, and for it gave thanks to the gods. He said many great things, but he never said this: " I would have every man poor that he might know the value of money."

" The Republic " is the best known and best read of any of Plato's dialogues. It outlines an ideal form of government where everybody would be healthy, happy and prosperous. It has served as inspiration to Sir Thomas More, Erasmus, Jean Jacques Rousseau, William Morris, Edward Bellamy, Brigham Young, John Humphrey Noyes and Eugene Debs. The subdivision of labor, by setting apart certain persons to do certain things—for instance, to care for the children —has made its appeal to Upton Sinclair, who jumped from his Utopian woodshed into a rubber-plant and bounced off into oblivion.

Plato's plan was intended to relieve marriage from the danger of becoming a form of slavery. The rulers,

117

teachers and artists especially were to be free, and the
State was to assume all responsibilities. The reason is
plain: he wanted them to reproduce themselves. But
whether genius is an acquirement or a natural endow-
ment he touches on but lightly. Also, he seemingly did
not realize " that no hovel is safe from it."

If all marriage-laws were done away with, Plato thought
that the men and women who were mated would still
be true to each other, and that the less the police interfered in love-relations, the better.

In one respect at least, Plato was certainly right: he
advocated the equality of the sexes, and declared that
no woman should be owned by a man nor forced into a
mode of life, either by economic exigency or marriage,
that was repulsive to her. Also, that her right to bear
children or not should be strictly her own affair, and
to dictate to a mother as to who should father her
children tended to the production of a slavish race.
¶ The eugenics of " The Republic " were tried for
thirty years by the Oneida Community with really
good results, but one generation of communal marriages was proved to be the limit, a thing Plato now
knows from his heights in Elysium, but which he in
his bachelor dreams on earth did not realize.

In his division of labor each was to do the thing he was
best fitted to do, and which he liked to do. It was
assumed that each person had a gift, and that to use
this gift all that was necessary was to give him an

118

opportunity. That very modern cry of "equality of opportunity" harks back to Plato.

The monastic impulse was a very old thing, even in the time of Plato. The monastic impulse is simply cutting for sanctuary when the pressure of society gets intense—a getting rid of the world by running away from it. This usually occurs when the novitiate has exhausted his capacity for sin, and so tries saintship in the hope of getting a new thrill.

Plato had been much impressed by the experiments of Pythagoras, who had actually done the thing of which Plato only talked. Plato now picked the weak points in the Pythagorean philosophy and sought, in imagination, to construct a fabric that would stand the test of time.

However, all Utopias, like all monasteries and penitentiaries, are made up of picked people. The Oneida Community was not composed of average individuals, but of people who were selected with great care, and only admitted after severe tests. And great as was Plato, he could not outline an ideal plan of life except for an ideal people.

To remain in the world of work and share the burdens of all—to ask for nothing which other people can not have on like terms—not to consider yourself peculiar, unique and therefore immune and exempt—is now the ideal of the best minds. We have small faith in monasticism or monotheism, but we do have great faith

in monism. We believe in the Solidarity of the Race.
We must all progress together. Whether Pythagoras,
John Humphrey Noyes and Brigham Young were
ahead of the world or behind it is really not to the
point—the many would not tolerate them. So their
idealism was diluted with danger until it became as
somber, sober and slaty-gray as the average existence,
and fades as well as shrinks in the wash.

A private good is no more possible for a community
than it is for an individual. We help ourselves only as
we advance the race—we are happy only as we minister
to the whole. The race is one, and this is monism ✄
And here Socrates and Plato seemingly separate, for
Socrates in his life wanted nothing, not even joy, and
Plato's desire was for peace and happiness. Yet the
ideal of justice in Plato's philosophy is very exalted.
¶ No writer in that flowering time of beauty and reason
which we call " The Age of Pericles " exerted so profound an influence as Plato. All the philosophers
that follow him were largely inspired by him. Those
who berated him most were, very naturally, the ones
he had most benefited. Teach a boy to write, and the
probabilities are that his first essay, when he has cut
loose from his teacher's apron-strings and starts a
brownie bibliomag, will be in denunciation of the man
who taught him to push the pen and wield the Faber.
¶ Xenophon was more indebted, intellectually, to Plato
than to any other living man, yet he speaks scathingly

of his master. Plutarch, Cicero, Iamblichus, Pliny, Horace and all the other Roman writers read Plato religiously. The Christian Fathers kept his work alive, and passed it on to Dante, Petrarch and the early writers of the Renaissance, so all of their thought is well flavored with essence of Plato. Well does Addison put into the mouth of Cato those well-known words:

> It must be so—Plato, thou reasonest well!—
> Else whence this pleasing hope, this fond desire,
> This longing after immortality?
> Or whence this secret dread, and inward horror,
> Of falling into nought? Why shrinks the soul
> Back on herself, and startles at destruction?
> 'T is the divinity that stirs within us;
> 'T is heaven itself, that points out an hereafter,
> And intimates eternity to man.

All of that English group of writers in Addison's day knew their Plato, exactly as did Cato and the other great Romans of near two thousand years before. From Plato you can prove that there is a life after this for each individual soul, as Francis of Assisi proved, or you can take your Plato, as did Hume, and show that man lives only in his influence, his individual life returning to the mass and becoming a part of all the great pulsing existence that ebbs and flows through plant and tree and flower and flying bird. And today we turn to Plato and find the corroboration of our thought that to live now and here, up to our highest and best,

is the acme of wisdom. We prepare to live by living.
If there is another world we better be getting ready
for it. If heaven is an Ideal Republic it is founded on
unselfishness, truth, reciprocity, equanimity and co-
operation, and only those will be at home there who
have practised these virtues here. Man was made for
mutual service. This way lies Elysium.

Plato was a teacher of teachers, and like every other
great teacher who has ever lived, his soul goes marching
on, for to teach is to influence, and influence never dies.
Hail, Plato!

KING ALFRED

A saint without superstition, a scholar without ostentation, a warrior who fought only in defense of his country, a conqueror whose laurels were never stained with cruelty, a prince never cast down by adversity, nor lifted up to insolence in the hour of triumph—there is no other name in English history to compare with his.

—*Freeman*

KING ALFRED.

KING ALFRED

JULIUS CÆSAR, the greatest man of initiative the world has ever seen, had a nephew known as Cæsar Augustus ✳ ✳

The grandeur that was Rome occurred in the reign of Augustus. It was Augustus who said, " I found your city mud and I left it marble!"

The impetus given to the times by Julius Cæsar was conserved by Augustus. He continued the work his uncle had planned, but before he had completed it, he grew very weary, and the weariness he expressed was also the old age of the nation. There was lime in the bones of the boss.

When Cæsar Augustus said, " Rome is great enough— here we rest," he merely meant that he had reached his limit, and had had enough of road-building. At the boundaries of the Empire and the end of each Roman road he set up a statue of the god Terminus. This god gave his blessing to those going beyond, and a welcome to those returning, just as the Stars and Stripes welcome the traveler coming to America from across the sea. This god Terminus also supplied the world, especially the railroad world, a word.

Julius Cæsar reached his terminus and died, aged fifty-six, from compulsory vaccination.

Augustus, aged seventy-seven, died peacefully in bed. ¶ The reign of Augustus marks the crest of the power of Rome, and a crest is a place where no man nor nation stays—when you reach it, you go over and down on the other side.

When Augustus set up his Termini, announcing to all mankind that this was the limit, the enemies of Rome took courage and became active. The Goths and Vandals, hanging on the skirts of Rome, had learned many things, and one of the things was that, for getting rich quick, conquest is better than production. The barbarians, some of whom evidently had a sense of humor, had a way of picking up the Termini and carrying them inward, and finally they smashed them entirely, somewhat as country boys, out hunting, shoot railroad-signs full of holes ⌘

N the Middle Ages the soldier was supreme, and in the name of protecting the people he robbed the people, a tradition much respected, but not in the breach.

To escape the scourge of war, certain families and tribes moved northward. It was fight and turmoil in Southern Europe that settled Norway, Sweden and Denmark, and produced the Norsemen. And in making for themselves a home in the wilderness, battling with the climate and unkind conditions, there was evolved a very strong and sturdy type of man.

On the north shore of the Baltic dwelt the Norsemen. Along the southern shore were scattered several small tribes or families who were not strong enough in numbers to fight the Goths, and so sought peace with them, and were taxed—or pillaged—often to the point of starvation. They were so poor and insignificant that the Romans really never heard of them, and they never heard of the Romans, save in myth and legend. They lived in caves and rude stone huts. They fished, hunted, raised goats and farmed, and finally, about the year Three Hundred, they secured horses, which they bought from the Goths, who stole them from the Romans. ¶ Their Government was the Folkmoot, the germ of the New England Town Meeting. All the laws were passed by all the people, and in the making of these laws, the women had an equal voice with the men. ¶ When important steps were to be taken where the interests of the whole tribe were at stake, great deference was paid to the opinions of the mothers. For the mother spoke not only for herself, but for her children. The mother was the home-maker. The word " wife " means weaver; and this deference to the one member of the family who invented, created, preparing both the food and the clothing, is a marked Teutonic instinct. Its survival is seen yet in the sturdy German of the middle class, who takes his wife and children with him when he goes to the concert or to the beer-garden. So has he always taken his family with him on his migrations; whereas the Greeks and the Romans left their women behind.

South America was colonized by Spanish men. And the Indians and the Negroes absorbed the haughty grandee, yet preserved the faults and failings of both. ¶ The German who moves to America comes to stay— his family is a part of himself. The Italian comes alone, and his intent is to make what he can and return. This is a modified form of conquest.

The Romans who came to Brittany in Cæsar's time were men. Those who remained " took to themselves wives among the daughters of Philistia," as strong men ever are wont to do when they seek to govern savage tribes. And note this—instead of raising the savages or barbarians to their level, they sink to theirs. The child takes the status of the mother. The white man who marries an Indian woman becomes an Indian and their

128

children are Indians. With the Negro race the same law holds.

The Teutonic races have conquered the world because they took their women with them on their migrations, mental and physical. And the moral seems to be this, that the men who progress financially, morally and spiritually are those who do not leave their women-folk behind ⚘ ⚘

KING ALFRED

HEN we think of the English, we usually have in mind the British Isles. But the original England was situated along the southern shore of the Baltic Sea. This was the true Eng-Land, the land of the Engles or Angles. To one side lay Jute-Land, the home of the Jutes. On the other was Saxony, where dwelt the Saxons.

Jute-Land still lives in Jutland; the land of the Saxons is yet so indicated on the map; but Eng-Land was transported bodily a thousand miles, and her original territory became an abandoned farm where barbarians battled ✠ ✠

And now behold how England has diffused herself all over the world, with the British Isles as a base of supplies, or a radiating center. Behind this twenty miles of water that separates Calais and Dover she found safety and security, and there her brain and brawn evolved and expanded. So there are now Anglo-Americans, Anglo-Africans, Anglo-Indians, Anglo-Australians, and Anglo-New-Zealanders. As the native Indians of America and the Maoris of New Zealand have given way before the onward push and persistence of the English, so likewise did the ancient Britons give way and were absorbed by the Anglo-Saxons; and then the Saxons, being a little too fine for the stern competitor, allowed the Engles to take charge. And as Dutch, Germans, Slavs and Swedes are transformed with the second generation into English-Americans when they come to America, so did the people from Eng-Land fuse Saxons, Norsemen, Jutes, Celts and Britons into one people and fix upon them the indelible stamp of Eng-Land ✥ ✥

Yet it is obvious that the characters of the people of England have been strengthened, modified and refined by contact with the various races she has met, mixed with and absorbed. To influence others is to grow. Had England been satisfied to people and hold the British Isles, she would ere this have been outrun and absorbed by Spain or France. To stand still is to retreat. It is the same with men as it is with races. England's Colonies have been her strength. They have given her poise, reserve, ballast—and enough trouble to prevent either revolution, stagnation or introspection.

Nations have their periods of youth, manhood and old age. Whether England is now passing into decline, living her life in her children, the Colonies, might be indelicate to ask. Perhaps as Briton, Celt, Jute and Saxon were fused to make that hardy, courageous, restless and sinewy man known as the Englishman, so are the English, the Dutch, the Swede, the German, the Slav, transplanted into America, being fused into a composite man who shall surpass any type that the world has ever seen. In the British Isles, just as in the great cities, mankind gets pot-bound. In the newer lands, the roots strike deep into the soil, and find the sustenance the human plant requires

Walls keep folks in as well as shut other folks out. The British Isles, rock-faced and sea-girted, shut out the enemies of England without shutting the English in. A country surrounded by the sea produces sailors, and England's position bred a type of man that made her mistress of the seas. As her drum-taps, greeting the rising sun, girdle the world, so do her lighthouses flash protection to the mariner wherever the hungry sea lies in wait along rocky coasts, the round world over. England has sounded the shallows, marked the rocks and reefs, and mapped the coasts.

The first settlement of Saxons in Britain occurred in the year Four Hundred Forty-nine. They did not come as invaders, as did the Romans five hundred years before; their numbers were too few, and their arms too crude to mean menace to the swarthy, black-haired Britons. These fair stranger-folk were welcomed as curiosities and were allowed to settle and make themselves homes. Word was sent back to Saxony and Jute-Land and more settlers came. In a few years came a shipload of Engles, with their women and children, red-haired, freckled, tawny. They tilled the soil with a faith and an intelligence such as the Britons never brought to bear: very much as the German settlers follow the pioneers and grow rich where the Mudsock fails. Naturally the fair-haired girls found favor in the sight of the swarthy Britons. Marriages occurred, and a new type of man-child appeared as the months went by.

132

More Engles came. A century passed, and the coast, from Kent to the Firth of Forth, was dotted with the farms and homes of the people from the Baltic. There were now occasional protests from the original holders, and fights followed, when the Britons retreated before the strangers, or else were very glad to make terms. Victory is a matter of staying-power. The Engles had come to stay.

But a new enemy had appeared—the Norsemen or Danes. These were sea-nomads who acknowledged no man as master. Rough, bold, laughing at disaster, with no patience to build or dig or plow, they landed but to ravish, steal and lay waste, and then boarded their craft, sailing away, joying in the ruin they had wrought. ¶ The next year they came back. The industry and the thrift of the Engles made Britain a land of promise, a storehouse where the good things of life could be secured much more easily than by creating or producing them. And so now, before this common foe, the Britons, Jutes, Celts, Saxons and Engles united to punish and expel the invaders.

The calamity was a blessing—as most calamities are. From being a dozen little kingdoms, Britain now became one. A " Cyng," or captain, was chosen—an Engle, strong of arm, clear of brain, blue of eye, with long yellow hair. He was a man who commanded respect by his person and by his deeds. His name was Egbert. ¶ King Alfred, or Elfred, was born at Wantage, Berk-

133

shire, in the year Eight Hundred Forty-nine. He was the grandson of Egbert, a great man, and the son of Ethelwulf, a man of mediocre qualities. Alfred was shrewd enough to inherit the courage and persistence of his grandfather. Our D. A. R. friends are right and Mark Twain is wrong—it is really more necessary to have a grandfather than a father.

English civilization begins with Alfred. If you will refer to the dictionary you will find that the word "civilization" simply means to be civil. That is, if you are civilized you are gentle instead of violent—gaining your ends by kindly and persuasive means, instead of through coercion, intimidation and force.

Alfred was the first English gentleman, and let no joker add "and the last." Yet it is needless and quite irrelevant to say that civilized people are not always civil; nor are gentlemen always gentle—so little do words count. Many gentlemen are only gents.

Alfred was civil and gentle. He had been sent to Rome in his boyhood, and this transplantation had done him a world of good. Superior men are always transplanted men: people who do not travel have no perspective. To stay at home means getting pot-bound. You neither search down in the soil for color and perfume nor reach out strong toward the sunshine.

It was only a few years before the time of Alfred that a Christian monk appeared at Edin-Borough, and told the astonished Engles and Saxons of the gentle Jesus,

134

who had been sent to earth by the All-Father to tell
men they should love their enemies and be gentle and
civil and not violent, and should do unto others as they
would be done by. The natural religion of the Great
Spirit which the ancient Teutonic people held had much
in it that was good, but now they were prepared for
something better—they had the hope of a heaven of
rest and happiness after death.

Christianity flourishes best among a downtrodden, poor,
subdued and persecuted people. Renan says it is a
religion of sorrow. And primitive Christianity—the
religion of conduct—is a beautiful and pure doctrine
that no sane person ever flouted or scoffed.

The parents of Alfred, filled with holy zeal, allowed
one of the missionary monks to take the boy to Rome,
The idea was that he should become a bishop in the
Church ❧ ❧

Ethelred, the elder brother of Alfred, had succeeded
Ethelwulf, his father, as King. The Danes had overrun
and ravished the country. For many years these
marauding usurpers had fed their armies on the products
of the land. And now they had more than two-thirds of
the country under their control, and the fear that they
would absolutely subjugate the Anglo-Saxons was
imminent. Ethelwulf gave up the struggle in despair
and died. Ethelred fell in battle. And as the Greeks of
old in their terror cast around for the strongest man
they could find to repel the Persian invaders, and picked

on the boy Alexander, so did the Anglo-Saxons turn to Alfred, the gentle and silent. He was only twenty-three years old. In build he was slight and slender, but he had given token of his courage for four years, fighting with his brother. He had qualities that were closely akin to those of both Alexander and Cæsar. He had a cool, clear and vivid intellect and he had invincible courage. But he surpassed both of the men just named in that he had a tender, sympathetic heart.

The Danes were overconfident, and had allowed their discipline to relax. Alfred had at first evidently encouraged them in their idea that they had won, for he struck feebly and then withdrew his army to the marshes, where the Danish horsemen could not follow.

The Danes went into winter quarters, fat and feasting. Alfred made a definite plan for a campaign, drilled his men, prayed with them, and filled their hearts with the one idea that they were going forth to certain victory. And to victory they went. They fell upon the Danes with an impetuosity as unexpected as it was invincible, and before they could get into their armor, or secure their horses, they were in a rout. Every timid Engle and Saxon now took heart—it was the Lord's victory —they were fighting for home—the Danes gave way. This was not all accomplished quite as easily as I am writing it, but difficulties, deprivations and disaster only brought out new resources in Alfred. He was as serenely hopeful as was Washington at Valley Forge,

and his soldiers were just as ragged. He, too, like
Thomas Paine, cried, " These are the times that try
men's souls—be grateful for this crisis, for it will give
us opportunity to show that we are men." He had
aroused his people to a pitch where the Danes would
have had to kill them all, or else give way. As they
could not kill them they gave way. Napoleon at twenty-
six was master of France and had Italy under his heel,
and so was Alfred at the same age supreme in Southern
Britain—including Wessex and Mercia. He rounded up
the enemy, took away their weapons, and then held a
revival-meeting, asking everybody to come forward to
the mourners'-bench. There is no proof that he coerced
them into Christianity. They were glad to accept it.
Alfred seemed to have the persuasive power of the
Reverend Doctor Torrey. Guthrum, the Danish King,
who had come over to take a personal hand in the loot-
ing, was captured, baptized, and then Alfred stood
sponsor for him and gave him the name of Ethelstan.
He was made a bishop.

This acceptance of Christianity by the leaders of the
Danes broke their fierce spirit, and peace followed.
Alfred told the soldiers to use their horses to plow the
fields. The two armies that had fought each other now
worked together at road-making and draining the
marshes. Some of the Danes fled in their ships, but very
many remained and became citizens of the country. The
Danish names are still recognizable. Names beginning

with the aspirate, say Herbert, Hulett, Hubbard, Hubbs, Harold, Hancock, are Danish, and are the cause of that beautiful muddling of the " H " that still perplexes the British tongue, the rule governing which is to put it on where it is not needed and leave it off where it is. The Danes called the Engles, " Hengles," and the Engles called a man by the name of Henry, " Enry." ✠ ✠

In saving Wessex, Alfred saved England for the English people; for it was from Wessex, as a center, that his successors began the task of reconquering England from the Danes.

KING ALFRED

ITH the rule of Alfred begins the England that we know. As we call Herodotus the father of history, so could we, with equal propriety, call Asser, who wrote in the time of Alfred, the father of English history. The oldest English book is the " Life of Alfred " by Asser the monk.

That Asser was a dependent on his subject and very much in love with him, doubtless gave a very strong bias to the book. That it is right in the main, although occasionally wrong as to details, is proved by various corroborating records.

The king's word in Alfred's time was law, and Alfred proved his modesty by publicly proclaiming that a king was not divine, but only a man, and therefore a king's edicts should be endorsed by the people in Folkmoot. Here we get the genesis of popular government, and about the only instance that I can recall where a very strong man acting as chief ruler renounced a part of his power to the people, of his own accord. Kings usually have to be trimmed, and it is revolution that does the shearing. It is the rule that men do not relinquish power of their own accord—they have to be disannexed from it.

Alfred, however, knew the popular heart—he was very close to the common people. He had slept on the ground with his soldiers, fared at table with the swineherd's family, tilled the soil with the farmer folk. His heart went out to humanity. He did not overrate the average mind, nor did he underrate it. He had faith in mankind, and knew that at the last power was with the people. He did not say, " Vox populi, vox Dei," but he thought it. Therefore he set himself to educating the plain people. He prophesied a day when all grown men would be able to read and write, and when all would have an intelligent, personal interest in the government.

There have been periods in English history when Britain lagged woefully behind, for England has had kings who forgot the rights of mankind, and instead of seeking to serve their people, have battened and fattened upon them. They governed. George the Third thought that Alfred was a barbarian, and spoke of him with patronizing pity.

Alfred introduced the system of trial by jury, although the fact has been pointed out that he did not originate it. It goes back to the hardy Norseman who acknowledged no man as master, harking back to a time when there was no law, and to a people whose collective desire was supreme. In fact, it has its origin in " Lynch Law," or the rule of the Vigilantes. From a village turning loose on an offender and pulling him limb from limb, a degree of deliberation comes in and a committee of twelve are selected to investigate the deed and report their verdict.

The jury system began with pirates and robbers, but it is no less excellent on that account, and we might add that freedom also began with pirates and robbers,

for they were the people who cried, " We acknowledge
no man as master."

The early Greeks had trials by jury—Socrates was
tried by a jury of five hundred citizens.

But let the fact stand that Alfred was the man who
first introduced the jury system into England. He had
absolute power. He was the sole judge and ruler, but
on various occasions he abdicated the throne and said:
" I do not feel able to try this man, for as I look into
my heart I see that I am prejudiced. Neither will I
name men to try him, for in their selection I might also
be prejudiced. Therefore let one hundred men be called,
and from these let twelve be selected by lot, and they
shall listen to the charges and weigh the defense, and
their verdict shall be mine."

We sometimes say that English Common Law is built
on the Roman Law, but I can not find that Alfred ever
studied the Roman Law, or ever heard of the Justinian
Code, or thought it worth while to establish a system
of jurisprudence. His government was of the simplest
sort. He respected the habits, ways and customs of the
common people, and these were the Common Law. If
the people had a footpath that was used by their
children and their parents and their grandparents, then
this path belonged to the people, and Alfred said that
even the King could not take it from them.

This deference to the innocent ways, habits and natural
rights of the people mark Alfred as supremely great,

---

because a great man is one great in his sympathies. Alfred had the imagination to put himself in the place of the lowly and obscure.

The English love of law, system and order dates from Alfred. The patience, kindliness, good-cheer and desire for fair play were his, plus. He had poise, equanimity, unfaltering faith and a courage that never grew faint. He was as religious as Cromwell, as firm as Washington, as stubborn as Gladstone. In him were combined the virtues of the scholar and patriot, the efficiency of the man of affairs with the wisdom of the philosopher. His character, both public and private, is stainless, and his whole life was one of enlightened and magnanimous service to his country.

N the age of Augustus there was one study that was regarded as more important than all others, and this was rhetoric, or the art of the rhetor. The rhetor was a man whose business it was to persuade or convince.

The public forum has its use in the very natural town-meeting, or the powwow of savages. But in Rome it had developed and been refined to a point where the public had no voice, although the boasted forum still existed. The forum was monopolized by the professional orators hired by this political clique or that.

It was about like the political " forum " in America today

The greatest man in Rome was the man who could put up the greatest talk. So all Roman mammas and matrons had their boys study rhetoric. The father of Seneca had a school of oratory where rich Roman youths were taught to mouth in orotund and gesticulate in curves. He must have been a pretty good teacher, for he had two extraordinary sons, one of whom is mentioned in the Bible, and a most exemplary daughter. ¶ Oratory as an end we now regard as an unworthy art. The first requisite is to feel deeply—to have a message —and then if you are a person of fair intelligence and in good health, you 'll impress your hearers. But to hire out to impress people with another's theme is to be a pettifogger, and the genus pettifogger has nearly had his day.

History moves in circles. The Chicago Common Council, weary of rhetoric, has recently declined to listen to paid attorneys; but any citizen who speaks for himself and his neighbors can come before the Council and state his case.

Chief Justice Fuller has given it as his opinion that there will come a day in America when damage-cases will be taken care of by an automatic tribunal, without the help of lawyers. And as a man fills out a request for a money-order at the Post-Office, so will he file his claim for damages, and it will have attention. The contingent fee will yet be a misdemeanor. Also, it will be possible for plain citizens to be able to go before a Court of Equity and be heard without regard to law and precedent and attorney's quillets and quibbles, which so often hamper justice. Justice should be cheap and easy, instead of costly and complex.

Evidently the Chief Justice had in mind the usages in the time of King Alfred, when the barrister was an employee of the court, and his business was to get the facts and then explain them to the King in the fewest possible words.

Alfred considered a paid advocate, or even a counselor, as without the pale, and such men were never allowed at court. If the barrister accepted a fee from a man suing for justice, he was disbarred.

Finally, however, the practise of feeing in order to renew the zeal of a barrister grew so that it had to be tolerated, because things we can't suppress we license, and a pocket was placed on each barrister's back between his shoulders where he could not reach it without taking off his gown, and into this pocket clients were allowed slyly to slip such gratuities as they could afford ✄ ✄

But the general practise of the client paying the barrister, instead of the court, was not adopted for several hundred years later, and then it was regarded as an expeditious move to keep down litigation and punish the client for being fool enough not to settle his own troubles.

In England the rudimentary pocket still survives, like the buttons on the back of a coat, which were once used to support the sword-belt.

In America we have done away with wigs and gowns for attorneys, but attorneys are still regarded as attaches of the court, even though one-half of them, according to Judge DeCourcy of Boston, are engaged most of the time in attempts to bamboozle and befog the judge and jury and defeat the ends of justice. Likewise, we still use the word " Court," signifying the place where lives royalty, even for the dingy office of a country J. P., where sawdust spittoons are the bric-a-brac and patent-office reports loom large, and justice is dispensed with. We now also commonly call the man " the Court."

LFRED was filled with a desire to educate, and to this end organized a school at the Ox Ford, where his friend Asser taught. This school was the germ of the University of Oxford. Attached to this school was a farm, where the boys were taught how to sow and plant and reap to the best advantage. Here they also bred and raised horses and cattle, and the care of livestock was a part of the curriculum. It was the first College of Agriculture. ¶ It comes to us as somewhat of a surprise to see how we are now going back to simplicity, and the agricultural college is being given the due and thoughtful consideration which it deserves. Twenty years ago our agricultural college was considered more or less of a joke, but now that which adds greatly to the wealth of the nation, and the happiness and well-being of the people, is looked upon as worthy of our support and highest respect.

Up to the time of Alfred, England had no navy. For the government to own ships seemed quite preposterous, since the people had come to England to stay, and were not marauders intent on exploitation and conquest, like the Norsemen.

But after Alfred had vanquished the Danes and they had settled down as citizens, he took their ships, refitted them, built more and said: " No more marauders shall land on these shores. If we are threatened we will meet the enemy on the sea."

In a few years along came a fleet of marauding Norse.
The English ships on the lookout gave the alarm, and
England's navy put out to meet them. The enemy
were taken by surprise, and the fate that five hundred
years later was to overtake the Spanish Armada, was
theirs " "

From that time to this, England has had a navy that
has gradually grown in power.

Let no one imagine that peace and rest came to Alfred.
His life was a battle, for not only did he have to fight
the Danes, but he had to struggle with ignorance,
stupidity and superstition at home. To lead men out of
captivity is a thankless task. They always ask when
you take away their superstition, " What are you
going to give us in return? " They do not realize that
superstition is a disease, and that to give another disease in return is not nice, necessary or polite.

KING ALFRED

LFRED died, at the age of fifty-two, worn out with his ceaseless labors of teaching, building, planning, inventing and devising methods and means for the betterment and benefit of his people. ¶ After his death, the Danes were successful, and Canute became King of England. But he was proud to be called an Englishman, and declared he was no longer a Dane.

And so England captured him.

Then came the Norman William, claiming the throne by right of succession, and successfully battling for it; but the English people reckoned the Conqueror as of their own blood—their kith and kin—and so he was. He issued an edict forbidding any one to call him or his followers " Norman," " Norse " or " Norsemen," and declared there was a United England. And so he lived and died an Englishman; and after him no ruler, these nine hundred years, has ever sat on the throne of the Engles by right of conquest.

Both Canute and William recognized and prized the worth of Alfred's rule. The virtues of Alfred are the virtues that have made it possible for the Teutonic tribes to girdle the globe. It was Alfred who taught the nobility of industry, service, education, patience, loyalty, persistence, and the faith and hope that abide. By pen, tongue, and best of all by his life, Alfred taught the truths which we yet hold dear. And by this sign shall ye conquer!

148

ERASMUS

We see not a few mortals who, striving to emulate this divine virtue with more zeal than success, fall into a feeble and disjointed loquacity, obscuring the subject and burdening the wretched ears of their hearers with a vacant mass of words and sentences crowded together beyond all possibility of enjoyment. And writers who have tried to lay down the principles of this art have gained no other result than to display their own poverty while expounding abundance.

—Erasmus on " Preaching "

ERASMUS

ERASMUS

ERASMUS was born in Fourteen Hundred Sixty-six, and died in Fifteen Hundred Thirty-six. No thinker of his time influenced the world more. He stood at a pivotal point, and some say he himself was the intellectual pivot of the Renaissance ☙ ☙

The critics of the times were unanimous in denouncing him—which fact recommends him to us.

Several Churchmen, high in power, live in letters for no other reason than because they coupled their names with that of Erasmus by reviling him. Let the critics take courage—they may outwit oblivion yet, even though they do nothing but carp. Only let them be wise, and carp, croak, cough, cat-call and sneeze at some one who is hitching his wagon to a star. This way immortality lies. Erasmus was a monk who flocked by himself, and found diversion in ridiculing monkery. Also, he was the wisest man of his day. Wisdom is the distilled essence of intuition, corroborated by experience. Learning is something else. Usually, the learned man is he who has delved deep and soared high. But few there be who dive, that fish the murex up. Among those who soar, the ones who come back and tell us of what they have seen, are few. Like Lazarus, they say nothing.

ERASMUS

Erasmus had a sense of humor. Humor is a life-preserver and saves you from drowning when you jump off into a sea of sermons. A theologian who can not laugh is apt to explode—he is very dangerous. Erasmus, Luther, Beecher, Theodore Parker, Roger Williams, Joseph Parker—all could laugh. Calvin, Cotton Mather and Jonathan Edwards never gurgled in glee, nor chortled softly at their own witticisms—or those of others.

Erasmus smiled. He has been called the Voltaire of his day. What Rousseau was to Voltaire, Luther was to Erasmus. Well did Diderot say that Erasmus laid the egg which Luther hatched. Erasmus wrote for the educated, the refined, the learned—Luther made his appeal to the plain and common mind.

Luther split the power of the Pope. Erasmus thought it a calamity to do so, because he believed that strife of sects tended to make men lose sight of the one essential in religion—harmony—and cause them simply to struggle for victory. Erasmus wanted to trim the wings of the papal office and file its claws—Luther would have destroyed it. Erasmus considered the Church a very useful and needful organization—for social reasons. It tended to regulate life and conduct and made men " decentable." It should be a school of ethics, and take a leading part in every human betterment. Man being a gregarious animal, the congregation is in the line of natural desire. The excuse for gathering together is religion—let them gather. The Catholic Church is not

152

two thousand years old—it is ten thousand years old
and goes back to Egypt. The birth of Jesus formed
merely a psychosis in the Church's existence.

Here he parted company with Luther, who was a
dogmatist and wanted to debate his ninety-five theses.
Erasmus laughed at all religious disputations and called
them mazes that led to cloudland. Very naturally,
people said he was not sincere, since the mediocre mind
never knows that only the paradox is true. Hence
Erasmus was hated by Catholics and denounced by
Protestants.

The marvel is that the men with fetters and fagots did
not follow him with a purpose. Fifty years later he
would have been snuffed out. But at that time Rome
was so astonished to think that any one should criticize
her that she lost breath. Besides, it was an age of
laughter, of revolt, of contests of wit, of love-bouts and
love-scrapes, and the monks who lapsed were too many
to discipline. Everybody was busy with his own affairs.
Happy time!

Erasmus was part and parcel of the Italian Renaissance.
Over his head blazes, in letters that burn, the unforgetable date, Fourteen Hundred Ninety-two. He was a
part of the great unrest, and he helped cause the great
unrest. Every great awakening, every renaissance, is an
age of doubt. An age of conservatism is an age of moss,
of lichen, of rest, rust and ruin. We grow only as we
question. As long as we are sure that the present order

is perfect, we button our collars behind, a thing which Columbus, Luther, Melanchthon, Erasmus, Michelangelo, Leonardo and Gutenberg, who all lived at this one time, never did. The year of Fourteen Hundred Ninety-two, like the year Seventeen Hundred Seventy-six, was essentially " infidelic," just as the present age is constructively iconoclastic. We are tearing down our barns to build greater. The railroadman who said, " I throw an engine on the scrap-heap every morning before breakfast," expressed a great truth. We are discarding bad things for good ones, and good things for better ones.

ERASMUS

OTTERDAM has the honor of being the birthplace of Erasmus. A storm of calumny was directed at him during his life concerning the irregularity of his birth. "He had no business to be born at all," said a proud prelate, as he gathered his robes close around his prebendal form. But souls knock at the gates of life for admittance, and the fact that a man exists is proof of his right to live. The word "illegitimate" is not in the vocabulary of God. If you do not know that, you have not read His instructive and amusing works.

The critics variously declared the mother of Erasmus was a royal lady, a physician's only daughter, a kitchen-wench, a Mother Superior—all according to the prejudices preconceived. In one sense she was surely a Mother Superior—let the lies neutralize one another ⚜ The fact is, we do not know who the mother of Erasmus was. All we know is that she was the mother of Erasmus. Here history halts. Her son once told Sir Thomas More that she was married to a luckless nobody a few months after the birth of her first baby, and amid the cares of raising a goodly brood of nobodies on a scant allowance of love and rye-bread, she was glad to forget her early indiscretions. Not so the father. The debated question of whether a man really has any parental love is answered here.

The father of Erasmus was Gerhard von Praet, and the child was called Gerhard Gerhards—or the son of

155

Gerhard. The father was a man of property and held office under the State. At the time of the birth of the illustrious baby, Gerhard von Praet was not married, and it is reasonable to suppose that the reason he did not wed the mother of his child was because she belonged to a different social station. In any event the baby was given the father's name, and every care and attention was paid the tiny voyager. This father was as foolish as most fond mothers, for he dreamed out a great career for the motherless one, and made sundry prophecies ✠ At six years of age the child was studying Latin, when he should have been digging in a sand-pile. At eight he spoke Dutch and French, and argued with his nurse in Greek as to the value of buttermilk.

In the meantime the father had married and settled down in honorable obscurity as a respectable squire. Another account has it that he became a priest. Anyway, the little maverick was now making head alone in a private school.

When the lad was thirteen the father died, leaving a will in which he provided well for the child. The amount of property which by this will would have belonged to our hero when he became of age would have approximated forty thousand dollars.

Happily, the trustees of the fund were law-wolves. They managed to break the will, and then they showed the court that the child was a waif, and absolutely devoid of legal rights of any and every kind. He was then

156

committed to an orphan asylum to be given " a right religious education." It 's a queer old world, Terese, and what would have become of Gerhard Gerhards had he fallen heir to his father's titles and estate, no man can say. He might have accumulated girth and become an honored burgomaster. As it was he became powder-monkey to a monk, and scrubbed stone floors and rushed the growler for cowled and pious prelates.

Then he did copying for the Abbe, and proved himself a boy from Missouri Valley.

He was small, blue-eyed, fair-haired, slender, slight, with a long nose and sharp features. " With this nose," said Albrecht Durer, many years later, "he successfully hunted down everything but heresy."

At eighteen he became a monk and proudly had his flaxen poll tonsured. His superior was fond of him, and prophesied that he would become a bishop or something. ¶ Children do not suffer much, nor long. God is good to them. They slide into an environment and accept it. This child learned to dodge the big bare feet of the monks—got his lessons, played a little, worked his wit against their stupidity, and actually won their admiration—or as much of it as men who are alternately ascetics and libertines can give.

It was about this time that the lad was taunted with having no name. " Then I 'll make one for myself," was his proud answer.

Having entered now upon his novitiate, he was allowed

to take a new name, and being dead to the world, the old one was forgotten.

They called him Brother Desiderius, or the Desired One. He then amended this Latin name with its Greek equivalent, Erasmus, which means literally the Well-Beloved. As to his pedigree, or lack of it, he was needlessly proud. It set him apart as different. He had half-brothers and half-sisters, and these he looked upon as strangers. When they came to see him, he said, " There is no relationship between souls save that of the spirit."

¶ His sense of wit came in when he writes to a friend: " Two parents are the rule; no parents the exception; a mother but no father is not uncommon; but I had a father and never had a mother. I was nursed by a man, and educated by monks, all of which shows that women are more or less of a superfluity in creation. God Himself is a man. He had one son, but no daughters. The cherubim are boys. All of the angels are masculine, and so far as Holy Writ informs us, there are no women in heaven." ✠ ✠

That it was a woman, however, to whom Erasmus wrote this, lets him out on the severity of the argument. He was a joker. And while women did not absorb much of his time, we find that on his travels he often turned aside to visit with intellectual women—no other kind interested him, at all.

158

ERASMUS

O belong to a religious order is to be owned by it. You trade freedom for protection. The soul of Erasmus revolted at life in a monastery. He hated the typical monks—their food, their ways of life, their sophistry, their stupidity. To turn glutton and welcome folly as a relief from religion, he said, was the most natural thing in the world, when men had once started in to lead an unnatural life. Good food, daintily served, only goes with a co-ed mental regimen. Men eat with their hands, out of a pot, unless women are present to enforce the decencies. Women alone are a little more to be pitied than men alone, if 't were possible.

Through emulation does the race grow. Sex puts men and women on their good behavior.

Man's desire for power has caused him to enslave himself. Writes Erasmus, " In a monastery, no one is on his good behavior, except when there are visitors, but I am told that this is so in families."

The greasy, coarse cooking brought on a nice case of dyspepsia for poor Erasmus—a complaint from which he was never free as long as he lived. His system was too fine for any monastic general trough, but he found a compensation in having his say at odd times and sundry. At one time we hear of his printing on a card this legend, " If I owned hell and a monastery, I would sell the monastery and reside in hell." Thereby did Erasmus supply General Tecumseh Sherman the germ of a famous orphic. Sherman was a professor in a college at Baton Rouge before the War, and evidently had moused in the Latin classics to a purpose.

Connected with the monastery where Erasmus lived was a printing-outfit. Our versatile young monk learned the case, worked the ink-balls, manipulated the lever, and evidently dispelled, in degree, the monotony of the place by his ready pen and eloquent tongue. When he wrote, he wrote for his ear. All was tested by reading the matter aloud. At that time great authors were not so wise or so clever as printers, and it fell to the lot of Erasmus to improve upon the text of much of the copy that was presented.

Erasmus learned to write by writing; and among modern prose-writers he is the very first who had a distinct literary style. His language is easy, fluid, suggestive. His paragraphs throw a shadow, and are pregnant with meaning beyond what the lexicon supplies. This is genius—to be bigger than your words.

If Erasmus had been possessed of a bit more patience and a jigger of diplomacy, he would have been in line for a bishopric. That thing which he praised so lavishly, Folly, was his cause of failure and also his friend.

At twenty-six he was the best teacher and the most clever scholar in the place. Also, he was regarded as a thorn in the side of the monkery, since he refused to take it seriously. He protested that no man ever became a monk of his own accord—he was either thrust into a

religious order by unkind kinsmen or kicked into it by
Fate ❧ ❧

And then comes the Bishop of Cambray, with an attack
of literary scabies, looking for a young religieux who
could correct his manuscript. The Bishop was going to
Paris after important historical facts, and must have a
competent secretary. Only a proficient Latin and Greek
scholar would do. The head of the monastery recom-
mended Erasmus, very much as Artemus Ward vol-
unteered all of his wife's relatives for purposes of war.
❡ Andrew Carnegie once, when about to start for
Europe, said to his ironmaster, Bill Jones, " I am never
so happy or care-free, Bill, as when on board ship,
headed for Europe, and the shores of Sandy Hook fade
from sight."

And Bill solemnly replied, " Mr. Carnegie, I can truthfully say for myself and fellow-workers, that we are
never so happy and care-free as when you are on board
ship, headed for Europe."

Very properly Mr. Carnegie at once raised Bill's salary
five thousand a year.

The Carthusian Brothers parted with Erasmus in pretended tears, but the fact was they were more relieved
than bereaved.

And then began the travels of Erasmus.

The Bishop was of middle age, with a dash of the
cavalier in his blood, which made him prefer a saddle
to the cushions of a carriage. And so they started away

on horseback, the Bishop ahead, followed at a discreet distance by Erasmus, his secretary; and ten paces behind with well-loaded panniers, rode a servant as rear-guard.

To be free and face the world and on a horse! Erasmus lifted up his heart in a prayer of gratitude. He said that it was the first feeling of thankfulness he had ever experienced, and it was the first thing which had ever come to him worth gratitude.

And so they started for Paris.

Erasmus looked back and saw the monastery, where he had spent ten arduous years, fade from view.

It was the happiest moment he had ever known. The world lay beyond.

ERASMUS

HE Bishop of Cambray introduced Erasmus to a mode of life for which he was eminently fitted. It consisted in traveling, receiving honors, hospitality and all good things in a material way, and giving his gracious society in return. Doors flew open on the approach of the good Bishop. Everywhere he went a greeting was assured. He was a Churchman—that was enough. Erasmus shared in the welcomes, for he was handsome in face and figure, had a ready tongue, and could hold his own with the best ❧

Europe was then dotted with monasteries, nunneries and other church institutions. Their remains are seen there yet—one is really never out of sight of a steeple. But the exclusive power of the Church is gone, and in many places there are only ruins where once were cloisters, corridors, chapels, halls and gardens teeming with life and industry.

The "missions" of California were founded on the general plan of the monasteries of Europe. They afforded a lodging for the night—a resting-place for travelers— and were a radiatory center of education—at least all of the education that then existed.

In California these "missions" were forty miles apart —one day's journey. In France, Italy and Germany they were, say, ten miles apart. Between them, trudged or rode on horseback or in carriages, a picturesque array of pilgrims, young and old, male and female. To go anywhere and be at home everywhere, this was the

163

happy lot of a church dignitary. ¶ The parts in church institutions were interchangeable; and by a system of migration, life was made agreeable, and reasonable honesty was assured. I have noticed that certain Continental banking institutions, with branches in various cities, keep their cashiers rotating. The idea was gotten from Rome. Rome was very wise—her policies were the crystallizations of the world-wisdom of centuries. The church-militant battle-cry, " The world for Christ," simply means man's lust for ownership, with Christ as an excuse. If ever there was a man-made institution, it is the Church. To control mankind has been her desire, and the miracle is that, with a promise of heaven, a threat of hell, and a firm grip on temporal power—social and military—she was ever induced partially to loosen her grip. To such men as Savonarola, Luther and Erasmus, do we owe our freedom. These men cared more for truth than for power, and their influence was to disintegrate the ankylosis of custom and make men think. And a thought is mental dynamite. No wonder the Church has always feared and hated a thinker! ॐ ॐ

The Bishop of Cambray was not a thinker. Fenelon, who was later to occupy his office, was to make the bishopric of Cambray immortal. Conformists die, but heretics live on forever. They are men who have redeemed the cross and rendered the gallows glorious.

164

ERASMUS

ND so the Bishop of Cambray and his little light-haired secretary fared forth to fame and fortune—the Bishop to be remembered because he had a secretary, and the secretary to be remembered because he grew into a great teacher ✼ ✼

At each stopping-place the Bishop said mass—the workers, students and novitiates quitting their tasks to hear the words of encouragement from the lips of the great man. Occasionally Erasmus was pushed forward to say a few words, by the Bishop, who had to look after his own personal devotions. The assembled friends liked the young man—he was so bright and witty and free from cant. They even laughed out loud, and so, often two smiles were made to grow where there were no smiles before.

Leisurely they rode—stopping at times for several days at places where the food and drink were at their best, and the society sulphide. At nunneries and monasteries were always guest-chambers for the great, and they were usually occupied.

Thus it was that every church-house was a sort of university, depending of course on the soul-size of the Superior or Abbe. These constant journeyings and pilgrimages served in lieu of the daily paper, the Western Union Telegraph, and the telephone. Things have slipped back, I fear me, for now Mercury merely calls up his party on the long-distance, instead of making a personal visit—the Angel Gabriel as well. We save time, but we miss the personal contact.

The monastic impulse was founded on a human need. Like most good things, it has been sadly perverted; but the idea of a sanctuary for stricken souls—a place of refuge, where simplicity, service and useful endeavor rule—will never die from out the human heart. The hospice stands for hospitality, but we have now only a hotel and a hospital.

The latter stands for iodoform, carbolic acid and formaldehyde; the former often means gold, glitter, gluttony and concrete selfishness, with gout on one end, paresis at the other and Bright's Disease between.

The hospice was a part of the monastery. It was a home for the homeless. There met men of learning—men of wit—men of brains and brawn. You entered and were at home. There was no charge—you merely left something for the poor.

Any man who has the courage, and sufficient faith in humanity to install the hospice system in America will reap a rich reward. If he has the same faith in his guests that Judge Lindsey has in his bad boys, he will succeed; but if he hesitates, defers, doubts, and begins to plot and plan, the Referee in Bankruptcy will beckon.

The early universities grew out of the monastic impulse. Students came and went, and the teachers were a part of a great itinerancy. Man is a migratory animal. His evolution has come about through change of environ-

ment. Transplantation changes weeds into roses, and
the forebears of all the products of our greenhouses and
gardens once grew in hedgerows or open fields, choked
by unkind competition or trampled beneath the feet of
the heedless.

The advantage of university life is in the transplantation. Get the boy out of his home environment; sever
the cord that holds him to his " folks "; let him meet
new faces, see new sights, hear new sermons, meet new
teachers, and his efforts at adjustment will work for
growth. Alexander Humboldt was right—one year at
college is safer than four. One year inspires you—four
may get you pot-bound with pedant prejudice.

The university of the future will be industrial—all may
come and go. All men will be university men, and thus
the pride in an imaginary proficiency will be diluted
to a healthful attenuation. To work and to be useful—
not merely to memorize and recite—will be the only
initiation ৯ ৯

The professors will be interchangeable, and the rotation
of intellectual crops will work for health, harmony and
effectiveness.

The group, or college, will be the unit, not the family.
The college was once a collection of men and women
grouped for a mutual intellectual, religious or economic
good ৯ ৯

To this group or college idea will we return.

Man is a gregarious animal, and the Christ-thought of

giving all, and receiving all, some day in the near future will be found practical. The desire for exclusive ownership must be sloughed.

Universities devoted to useful work—art in its highest sense: head, hand and heart—will yet dot the civilized world. The hospice will return higher up the scale, and the present use of the word "hospitality" will be drowned in its pink tea, choked with cheese-wafers, rescued from the nervous clutch of the managing mama, and the machinations of the chaperone. A society built on the sands of silliness must give way to the universal university, and the strong, healthful, helpful, honest companionship and comradeship of men and women prevail ❧ ❧

ERASMUS

THE objective point of the Bishop was the University of Paris.

Here in due time, after their lingering ride from Holland, the Bishop and his secretary arrived. They settled down to literary work; and in odd hours the beauty and wonder of Paris became familiar to Erasmus. The immediate task completed, the Bishop proposed going home, and thought, of course, his secretary was a fixture and would go with him. But Erasmus had evolved ideas concerning his own worth. He had already collected quite a little circle of pupils about him, and these he held by his glowing personality. At this time the vow of poverty was looked upon lightly. And anyway, poverty is a comparative term. There were monks who always trudged afoot with staff and bag, but not so our Erasmus. He was Bishop of the Exterior ❧ ❧

The Bishop of Cambray, on parting with Erasmus, thought so much of him that he presented him with the horse he rode.

Erasmus used to take short excursions about Paris, taking with him a student and often two, as servants or attendants. Teaching then was mostly on an independent basis, each pupil picking his tutors and paying them direct.

Among other pupils whom Erasmus had at Paris was a young Englishman by the name of Lord Mountjoy. A great affection arose between these two, and when

Lord Mountjoy returned to England he was accompanied by Erasmus.

At London, Erasmus met on absolute equality many of the learned men of England. We hear of his dining at the house of the Lord Mayor of London, and there meeting Sir Thomas More and crossing swords with that worthy in wordy debate.

Erasmus seems to have carried the " New Humanism " into England. It has been said that the world was discovered in Fourteen Hundred Ninety-two, but Man was not discovered until Seventeen Hundred Seventy-six. This is hardly literal truth, since in Fourteen Hundred Ninety-two, there was a theologico-scientific party of young men in all of the European Universities who were reviving the Greek culture, and with it arose the idea of the dignity and worth of Man. To this movement Erasmus brought the enthusiasm of his nature. Perhaps he did as much as any other to fan the embers which grew into a flame called " The Reformation."

He constantly ridiculed the austerities, pedantry, priggishness and sciolism of the old-time Churchmen, and when a new question came up, he asked, " What good is there in it? "

Everything was tested by him in the light of commonsense. What end does it serve and how is humanity to be served or benefited by it?

Thus the good of humanity, not the glory of God, was the shibboleth of this rising party.

170

ERASMUS

Erasmus gave lectures and taught at Cambridge, Oxford and London.

Italy had been the objective point of his travels, but England had, for a time, turned him aside. In the year Fifteen Hundred, Erasmus landed at Calais, saddled his horse, and started southward, visiting, writing, teaching, lecturing, as he went. The stimulus of meeting new people and seeing new scenes, all tended toward intellectual growth.

The genus monk made mendicancy a fine art, and Erasmus was heir to most of the instincts of the order. His associations with the laity were mostly with the nobility or those with money. He was not slow in asking for what he wanted, whether it was a fur-lined cloak, a saddle, top riding-boots, a horse, or a prayer-book. He made no apologies—but took as his divine right all that he needed. And he justified himself in taking what he needed by the thought that he gave all he had. He supplied Sir Thomas More the germ of " Utopia," for Erasmus pictured again and again an ideal society where all would have enough, and none suffer from either want or surfeit—a society in which all would be at home wherever they went.

Had Erasmus seen fit to make England his home, his head, too, would have paid the forfeit, as did the head that wrote " Utopia." What an absurd use to make of a head—to separate it from the man's body!

Italy received Erasmus with the same royal welcome

that England had supplied. Scholars who knew the Greek and Roman classics were none too common. Most monks stopped with the writings of the saints, as South Americans balk at long division.

Erasmus could illumine an initial, bind a book, give advice to printers, lecture to teachers, give lessons on rhetoric and oratory, or entertain the ladies with recitations from the Iliad and the Odyssey.

So he went riding back and forth, stopping at cities and towns, nunneries and monasteries, until his name became a familiar one to every scholar of England, Germany and Italy. Scholarly, always a learner, always a teacher, gracious, direct, witty, men began to divide on an Erasmus basis. There were two parties: those for Erasmus and those against him.

In Fifteen Hundred Seventeen, came Luther with his bombshells of defiance. This fighting attitude was far from Erasmus—his weapons were words. Between bouts with prelates, Luther sent a few thunderbolts at Erasmus, accusing him of vacillation and cowardice. Erasmus replied with dignity, and entered into a lengthy dispute with Melanchthon, Luther's friend, on the New Humanism which was finding form in revolution ✠ ✠

Erasmus prophesied that by an easy process of evolution, through education, the monasteries would all become schools and workshops. He would not destroy them, but convert them into something different. He fell into disfavor with the Catholics, and was invited by Henry the Eighth to come to England and join the new religious regime. But this English Catholicism was not to the liking of Erasmus. What he desired was to reform the Church, not to destroy it or divide it.

His affairs were becoming critical: monasteries where he had once been welcomed now feared to have him come near, lest they should be contaminated and entangled. It was rumored that warrants of arrest were out. He was invited to go to Rome and explain his position ✄ Erasmus knew better than to acknowledge receipt of the letter. He headed his horse for Switzerland, the land of liberty. At Basel he stopped at the house of Froben, the great printer and publisher. He put his horse in the barn, unsaddled him, and said, " Froben, I 've come to stay." ✄ ✄

ERASMUS

WAS mousing around the other day in a book that is somewhat disjointed and disconnected, and yet interesting—" The Standard Dictionary "—when I came across the word " scamp." It is a handy word to fling, and I am not sure but that it has been gently tossed once or twice in my direction. Condemnation is usually a sort of subtle flattery, so I 'm not sad. To scamp means to cut short, to be superficial, slipshod, careless, indifferent—to say, " Let 'er go, who cares—this is good enough! " If anybody ever was a stickler for honest work, I am that bucolic party. I often make things so fine that only one man out of ten thousand can buy them, and I have to keep 'em myself.

You know that, when you get an idea in your head, how everything you read contains allusions to the same thing. Knowledge is mucilaginous. Well, next day after I was looking up that pleasant word " scamp," I was reading in the Amusing Works of Erasmus, when I ran across the word again, but spelled in Dutch, thus, " schamp." Now Erasmus was a successful author, and he was also the best authority on paper, inks, bindings, and general bookmaking in Italy, Holland or Germany. Being a lover of learning, and listening to the lure of words, he never wallowed in wealth. But in his hunt for ideas he had a lot of fun. Kipling says, " There is no hunt equal to a man hunt." But Kip is wrong—to chase a thought is twice the sport. Erasmus chased ideas, and

174

very naturally the preachers chased Erasmus—out of England, through France, down to Italy and then he found refuge at Basel with Froben, the great Printer and Publisher.

Up in Frankfort was a writer-printer, who, not being able to answer the arguments of Erasmus, called him bad names. But this gentle pen-pusher in Frankfort, who passed his vocabulary at Froben's proofreader, Erasmus in time calls a " schamp," because he used cheap paper, cheap ink and close margins. Soon after, the word was carried to England and spelled " scamp " —a man who cheats in quality, weight, size and count. But the first use merely meant a printer who scamps his margins and so cheats on paper. I am sorry to see that Erasmus imitated his enemies and at times was ambidextrous in the use of the literary stinkpot. His vocabulary was equal to that of Muldoon. Erasmus refers to one of his critics as a " scenophylax-stikken," and another he calls a " schnide enchologion-schistosomus." And perhaps they may have been—I really do not know.

¶ But as an authority on books Erasmus can still be read. He it was who fixed the classic page margin— twice as wide at the top as on the inside; twice as wide at the outside as the top; twice as wide at the bottom as at the side. And any printer who varies from this displays his ignorance of proportion. Erasmus says, " To use poor paper marks the decline of taste, both in printer and in patron." After the death of Erasmus,

ERASMUS

Froben's firm failed because they got to making things cheap. " Compete in quality, not in price," was the working motto of Erasmus.

All of the great bookmaking centers languished when they began to scamp. That worthy wordissimus at Frankfort who called Erasmus names gave up business and then the ghost, and Erasmus wrote his epitaph, and thus supplied Benjamin Franklin an idea—" Here lies an old book, its cover gone, its leaves torn, the worms at work on its vitals."

The wisdom of doing good work still applies, just as it did in the days of Erasmus.

Erasmus proved a very valuable acquisition to Froben. He became general editor and literary adviser of this great publishing-house, which was then the most important in the world.

Besides his work as editor, Erasmus also stood sponsor for numerous volumes which we now know were written by literary nobodies, his name being placed on the title-page for commercial reasons.

At that time and for two hundred years later, the matter of attributing a book to this man or that was considered a trivial affair. Piracies were prevalent. All printers revised the work of classic authors if they saw fit, and often they were specially rewarded for it by the Church. It was about this time that some one slipped that paragraph into the works of Josephus about Jesus. The "Annals " of Tacitus were similarly doctored, if in fact they were not written entire, during the Sixteenth Century. It will be remembered that the only two references in contemporary literature to Jesus are those in Josephus and Tacitus, and these the Church proudly points to yet.

During the last few years of his life Erasmus accumulated considerable property. By his will he devised that this money should go to educate certain young men and women, grandchildren and nephews and nieces of his old friend, Johann Froben. He left no money for masses, after the usual custom of Churchmen, and during his last illness was not attended by a priest. For several years before his death he made no confessions and very seldom attended church service. He said, " I am much more proud of being a printer than a priest."

A statue of Erasmus in bronze adorns one of the public squares in Rotterdam, and Basel and Freiburg have honored themselves, and him also, in like manner.

¶ As a sample of the subtle and keen literary style of Erasmus, I append the following from " In Praise of Folly:"

The happiest times of life are youth and old age, and this for no reason but that they are the times most completely under the rule of folly, and least controlled by wisdom. It is the child's freedom from wisdom that makes it so charming to us; we hate a precocious child. So women owe their charm, and hence their power, to their " folley," that is, to their obedience to the impulse. But if, perchance, a woman wants to be thought wise, she only succeeds in being doubly a fool, as if one should train a cow for the prize-ring, a thing wholly against Nature. A woman will be a woman, no matter what mask she wear, and she ought to be proud of her folly and make the most of it.

Is not Cupid, that first father of all religion, is not he stark blind, that he can not himself distinguish of colors, so he would make us as mope-eyed in judging falsely of all love concerns, and wheedle us into a thinking that we are always in the right? Thus every Jack sticks to his own Jill; every tinker esteems his own trull; and the hobnailed suitor prefers Joan the milkmaid before any of milady's daughters. These things are true, and are ordinarily laughed at, and yet, however ridiculous they seem, it is hence only that all societies receive their cement and consolidation.

Fortune we still find favoring the blunt, and flushing the forward; strokes smooth up fools, crowning all their undertakings with success; but wisdom makes her followers bashful, sneaking and timorous, and therefore you commonly see that they are reduced to hard shifts; must grapple with poverty, cold and hunger; must lie recluse, despised, and unregarded; while fools roll in money, are advanced to dignities and offices, and in a word have the whole world at command. If any one thinks it happy to be a favorite at court, and to manage the disposal of places and preferments, alas, this happiness is so far from being attainable by wisdom, that the very suspicion of it would put a stop to advancement. Has any man a mind to raise himself a good estate? Alas, what dealer in the world would ever get a farthing, if he be so wise as to scruple at perjury, blush at a

178

lie, or stick at a fraud and overreaching? ¶ It is the public charter of all divines, to mold and bend the sacred oracles till they comply with their own fancy, spreading them (as Heaven by its Creator) like a curtain, closing together, or drawing them back, as they please. Thus, indeed, Saint Paul himself minces and mangles some citations he makes use of, and seems to wrest them to a different sense from what they were first intended for, as is confessed by the great linguist, Saint Hieron. Thus when that apostle saw at Athens the inscription of the altar, he draws from it an argument for the proof of the Christian religion; but leaving out great parts of the sentence, which perhaps if fully recited might have prejudiced his cause, he mentions only the last two words, namely, " To the Unknown God "; and this, too, not without alteration, for the whole inscription runs thus: " To the Gods of Asia, Europe, and Africa, to all Foreign and Unknown Gods." ¶ 'T is an imitation of the same pattern, I will warrant you, that our young divines, by leaving out four or five words in a place and putting a false construction on the rest, can make any passage serviceable to their own purpose; though from the coherence of what went before, or follows after, the genuine meaning appears to be either wide enough, or perhaps quite contradictory to what they would thrust and impose upon it. In which knack the divines are grown now so expert that the lawyers themselves begin to be jealous of an encroachment on what was formerly their sole privilege and practise. And indeed what can they despair of proving, since the forementioned commentator did upon a text of Saint Luke put an interpretation no more agreeable

to the meaning or the place than one contrary quality
is to another.

But because it seemed expedient that man, who was born
for the transaction of business, should have so much wisdom as should fit and capacitate him for the discharge
of his duty herein, and yet lest such a measure as is requisite for this purpose might prove too dangerous
and fatal, I was advised with for an antidote, and prescribed this infallible receipt of taking a wife, a creature
so harmless and silly, and yet so useful and convenient,
as might mollify and make pliable the stiffness and
morose humor of man. Now that which made Plato
doubt under what genus to rank woman, whether
among brutes or rational creatures, was only meant to
denote the extreme stupidness and Folly of that sex, a
sex so unalterably simple that for any one of them to
thrust forward and reach at the name of wise, is but to
make themselves the more remarkable fools, such an
endeavor being but a swimming against the stream,
nay, the turning the course of Nature, the bare attempting whereof is as extravagant as the effecting of it is
impossible: for as it is a trite proverb, that an ape will
be an ape, though clad in purple, so a woman will be a
woman, that is, a fool, whatever disguise she takes up.
And yet there is no reason women should take it amiss
to be thus charged, for if they do but rightly consider,
they will find to Folly they are beholden for those
endowments wherein they so far surpass and excel
Man; as first for their unparalleled beauty, by the charm
whereof they tyrannize over the greatest of tyrants;
for what is it but too great a smatch of wisdom that
makes men so tawny and thick-skinned, so rough and

180

prickly-bearded, like an emblem of winter or old age,
while women have such dainty, smooth cheeks, such a
low, gentle voice, and so pure a complexion, as if Nature
had drawn them for a standing pattern of all symmetry
and comeliness? Besides, what greater or juster aim
and ambition have they than to please their husbands?
In order whereunto they garnish themselves with paint,
washes, curls, perfumes, and all other mysteries of
ornament; yet, after all, they become acceptable to them
only for their Folly. Wives are always allowed their
humor, yet it is only in exchange for titillation and
pleasure, which indeed are but other names for Folly;
as none can deny, who consider how a man must dandle,
and kittle, and play a hundred little tricks for his help-
mate ✂ ✂

But now some blood-chilled old men, that are more for
wine than wenching, will pretend that in their opinion
the greatest happiness consists in feasting and drinking.
Grant it be so; yet certainly in the most luxurious
entertainments it is Folly must give the sauce and relish
to the daintiest delicacies; so that if there be no one of
the guests naturally fool enough to be played upon by
the rest, they must procure some comical buffoon, that
by his jokes and flouts and blunders shall make the
whole company split themselves with laughing; for to
what purpose were it to be stuffed and crammed with
so many dainty bits, savory dishes, and toothsome
rarities, if after all this epicurism, the eyes, the ears,
and the whole mind of man, were not so well foisted
and relieved with laughing, jesting, and such like diver-
tisements, which, like second courses, serve for the pro-
moting of digestion? And as to all those shoeing-horns

of drunkenness, the keeping every one his man, the throwing high jinks, the filling of bumpers, the drinking two in a hand, the beginning of mistresses' healths; and then the roaring out of drunken catches, the calling in a fiddler, the leading out every one his lady to dance, and such like riotous pastimes—these were not taught or dictated by any of the wise men of Greece, but of Gotham rather, being my invention, and by me prescribed as the best preservative of health: each of which, the more ridiculous it is, the more welcome it finds. And indeed, to jog sleepingly through the world, in a dumpish, melancholy posture, can not properly be said to live ❧ ❧

BOOKER T. WASHINGTON

There is something in human nature which always makes people reward merit, no matter under what color of skin merit is found. I have found, too, that it is the visible, the tangible, that goes a long way in softening prejudices. The actual sight of a good house that a Negro has built is ten times more potent than pages of discussion about a house that he ought to build, or perhaps could build. The individual who can do something that the world wants done will, in the end, make his way regardless of his race.

—*Booker T. Washington*

BOOKER T. WASHINGTON

BOOKER T. WASHINGTON

HIS is a story about a Negro. The story has the peculiarity of being true. The man was born a slave in Virginia. His mother was a slave, and was thrice sold in the market-place. This man is Booker T. Washington ⚉ ⚉

The name Booker was a fanciful one given to the lad by playmates on account of his love for a certain chance dog-eared spelling-book. Before this he was only Mammy's Pet. The T. stood for nothing, but later a happy thought made it Taliaferro. ¶ Most Negroes, fresh from slavery, stood sponsor to themselves, and chose the name Washington; if not this, then Lincoln, Clay or Webster.

This lad when but a child, being suddenly asked for his name, exclaimed, "Washington," and stuck to it. ¶ The father of this boy was a white man; but children always take the status of the mother, so Booker T. Washington is a Negro, and proud of it, as he should be, for he is standard by performance, even if not by pedigree ⚉ ⚉

This Negro's father is represented by the sign *x*. By remaining in obscurity the fond father threw away his one chance for immortality. We do not even know his name, his social position, or his previous condition of

185

turpitude. We assume he was happily married and respectable. Concerning him legend is silent and fable dumb. As for the child, we are not certain whether he was born in Eighteen Hundred Fifty-eight or Eighteen Hundred Fifty-nine, and we know not the day or the month. There were no signs in the East.

The mother lived in a log cabin of one room, say ten by twelve. This room was also a kitchen, for the mother was cook to the farmhands of her owner. There were no windows and no floor in the cabin save the hard-trodden clay. There were a table, a bench and a big fireplace. There were no beds, and the children at night simply huddled and cuddled in a pile of straw and rags in the corner. Doubtless they had enough food, for they ate the crumbs that fell from the rich man's table—who, by the way, was n't so very rich.

One of the earliest recollections of Black Baby Booker was of being awakened in the middle of the night by his mother to eat fried chicken. Imagine the picture—it is past midnight. No light in the room save the long, flickering streaks that dance on the rafters. Outside the wind makes mournful, sighing melody. In the corner huddled the children, creeping close together with intertwining arms to get the warmth of each little half-naked body.

The dusky mother moves swiftly, deftly, half-frightened at her task.

She has come in from the night with a chicken! Where

186

did she get it? Hush! Where do you suppose oppressed colored people get chickens?

She picks the bird—prepares it for the skillet—fries it over the coals. And then when it is done just right, Maryland style, this mother full of mother-love, an ingredient which God never omits, shakes each little piccaninny into wakefulness, and gives him the forbidden dainty—drumstick, wishbone, gizzard, white meat, or the part that went through the fence last—anything but the neck.

Feathers, bones, waste are thrown into the fireplace, and what the village editor calls the " devouring element " hides all trace of the crime. Then all lie down to sleep, until the faint flush of pink comes into the East, and jocund day stands tiptoe on the mountain-tops.

THIS ex-slave remembers a strange and trying time, when all of the colored folk on the plantation were notified to assemble at the " big house." They arrived and stood around in groups, waiting and wondering, talking in whispers. The master came out, and standing on the veranda read from a paper in a tremulous voice. Then he told them that they were all free, and shook hands with each. Everybody cried. However, they were very happy in spite of the tears, for freedom to them meant heaven— a heaven of rest. Yet they bore only love towards their former owners.

Most of them began to wander—they thought they had to leave their old quarters. In a few days the wisest came back and went to work just as usual. Booker T.'s mother quit work for just half a day.

But in a little while her husband arrived—a colored man to whom she had been married years before, and who had been sold and sent away. Now he came and took her and the little monochrome brood, and they all started away for West Virginia, where they heard that colored men were hired to work in coalmines and were paid wages in real money.

It took months and months to make the journey. They carried all their belongings in bundles. They had no horses—no cows—no wagon—they walked. If the weather was pleasant they slept out of doors; if it rained they sought a tobacco-shed, a barn, or the friendly side of a straw-stack. For food they depended on a little cornmeal they carried, with which the mother made pone-cakes in the ashes of a campfire. Kind colored people on the way replenished the meal-bag, for colored people are always generous to the hungry and needy if they have anything to be generous with. Then Providence sent stray, ownerless chickens their way, at times, just as the Children of Israel were fed on quails in the wilderness. Once they caught a 'possum—and there was a genuine banquet, where the children ate until they were as tight as drums.

Finally they reached the promised land of West Virginia, and at the little village of Malden, near Charleston, they stopped, for here were the coal mine and the salt-works where colored men were hired and paid in real money. ¶ Booker's stepfather found a job, and he also found a job for little Booker. They had nothing to live on until pay-day, so the kind man who owned the mine allowed them to get things at the store on credit. This was a brand-new experience—and no doubt they bought a few things they did not need, for prices and values were absolutely out of their realm. Besides, they did not know how much wages they were to get, neither could they figure the prices of the things they bought. At any rate, when pay-day came they were still in debt, so they saw no real money—certainly little Booker at this time of his life never did.

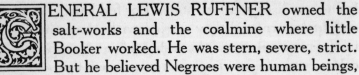ENERAL LEWIS RUFFNER owned the salt-works and the coalmine where little Booker worked. He was stern, severe, strict. But he believed Negroes were human beings, and there were those then who disputed the proposition. ¶ Ruffner organized a night-school for his helpers, and let a couple of his bookkeepers teach it. At this time there was not a colored person in the neighborhood who could spell cat, much less write his name. A few could count five. Booker must have been about ten years old when one day he boasted a bit of his skill in mathematics. The foreman told him to count the loads of coal as they came out of the mine. The boy started in bravely, " One—two—three—four—dere goes one, dere goes anoder, anoder, anoder, anoder, anoder! "

The foreman laughed.

The boy was abashed, then chagrined. " Send me to the night-school and in a month I 'll show you how to count! " ⚜ ⚜

The foreman wrote the lad an order which admitted him to the night-school.

But now there was another difficulty—the boy worked until nine o'clock at night, the last hour's work being to sweep out the office. The night-school began at nine o'clock and it was two miles away.

The lad scratched his head and thought and thought. A great idea came to him—he would turn the office clock ahead half an hour. He could then leave at nine o'clock,

190

and by running part of the way could get to school at exactly nine o'clock.

The scheme worked for two days, when one of the clerks in the office said that a spook was monkeying with the clock. They tried the plan of locking the case, and all was well.

Booker must have been about twelve years old, goin' on thirteen, when one day as he lay on his back in the coalmine, pushing out the broken coal with his feet, he overheard two men telling of a very wonderful school where colored people were taught to read, write and cipher—also, how to speak in public. The scholars were allowed to work part of the time to pay for their board. ¶ The lad crawled close in the darkness and listened to the conversation. He caught the names " Hampton " and "Armstrong." Whether Armstrong was the place and Hampton was the name of the man, he could not make out, but he clung to the names.

Here was a school for colored people—he would go there! That night he told his mother about it. She laughed, patted his kinky head, and indulged him in his dream ✤ ✤

She was only a poor black woman; she could not spell ab, nor count to ten, but she had a plan for her boy— he would some day be a preacher.

This was the very height of her imagination—a preacher! Beyond this there was nothing in human achievement. The night-school came after a day of fourteen hours' work. Little Booker sat on a bench, his feet dangling about a foot from the floor. As he sat there one night trying hard to drink in knowledge, he went to sleep. He nodded, braced up, nodded again, and then pitched over in a heap on the floor, to the great amusement of the class, and his own eternal shame.

The next day, however, as he was feeling very sorrowful over his sad experience, he heard that Mrs. Ruffner wanted a boy for general work at the big house.

Here was a chance. Mrs. Ruffner was a Vermont Yankee, which meant that she had a great nose for dirt, and would not stand for a " sassy nigger." Her reputation had gone abroad, and of how she pinched the ears of her " help," and got them up at exactly a certain hour, and made them use soap and water at least once a day, and even compelled them to use a toothbrush; all this was history, well defined.

Booker said he could please her, even if she was a Yankee. He applied for the job and got it, with wages fixed at a dollar a week, with a promise of twenty-five cents extra every week, if he did his work without talking back and breaking a tray of dishes.

192

ENIUS! No hovel is safe from it!" says
Whistler ✄ ✄

Genius consists in doing the right thing without being told more than three times.

Booker silently studied the awful Yankee woman to
see what she really wanted. He finally decided that she
desired her servants to have clean skins, fairly neat
clothing, do things promptly, finish the job and keep
still when they had nothing to say.

He set himself to please her—and he did.

She loaned him books, gave him a lead-pencil, and
showed him how to write with a pen without smearing
his hands and face with ink.

He told her of his dream and asked about Armstrong
and Hampton. She told him that Armstrong was the
man and Hampton the place.

At last he got her consent to leave and go to Hampton.
¶ When he started she gave him a comb, a toothbrush,
two handkerchiefs and a pair of shoes. He had been
working for her for a year, and she thought, of course,
he saved his wages. He never told her that his money
had gone to keep the family, because his stepfather had
been on a strike and therefore out of work.

So the boy started away for Hampton. It was five hundred miles away. He did n't know how far five hundred
miles is—nobody does unless he has walked it.

He had three dollars, so he gaily paid for a seat in the
stage. At the end of the first day he was forty miles

from home and out of money. He slept in a barn, and a colored woman handed him a ham-bone and a chunk of bread out of the kitchen-window, and looked the other way.

He trudged on east—always and forever east—towards the rising sun.

He walked weeks—months—years, he thought. He kept no track of the days. He carried his shoes as a matter of economy.

Finally he sold the shoes for four dollars to a man who paid him ten cents cash down, and promised to pay the rest when they should meet at Hampton. Nearly forty years have passed and they have never met.

On he walked—on and on—east, and always forever east ❧ ❧

He reached the city of Richmond, the first big city he had ever seen. The wide streets—the sidewalks—the street-lamps entranced him. It was just like heaven. But he was hungry and penniless, and when he looked wistfully at a pile of cold fried chicken on a street-stand and asked the price of a drumstick, at the same time telling he had no money, he discovered he was not in heaven at all. He was called a lazy nigger and told to move on.

Later he made the discovery that a " nigger " is a colored person who has no money.

He pulled the piece of rope that served him for a belt a little tighter, and when no one was looking, crawled

194

under a sidewalk and went to sleep, disturbed only by the trampling overhead.

When he awoke he saw he was near the dock, where a big ship pushed its bowsprit out over the street. Men were unloading bags and boxes from the boat. He ran down and asked the mate if he could help. " Yes! " was the gruff answer.

He got in line and went staggering under the heavy loads ✄ ✄

He was little, but strong, and best of all, willing, yet he reeled at the work.

" Have you had any breakfast? Yes, you liver-colored boy—you, I say, have you had your breakfast? " ✄

" No, sir," said the boy; " and no supper last night nor dinner yesterday! "

" Well, I reckoned as much. Now you take this quarter and go over to that stand and buy you a drumstick, a cup of coffee and two fried cakes! "

The lad did n't need urging. He took the money in his palm, went over to the man who the night before had called him a lazy nigger, and showing the silver, picked out his piece of chicken.

The man hastened to wait on him, and said it was a fine day and hoped he was well.

RRIVING at Hampton, this colored boy, who had tramped the long, weary miles, stood abashed before the big brick building which he knew was Hampton Institute.

He was so little—the place was so big—by what right could he ask to be admitted?

Finally he boldly entered, and in a voice meant to be firm, but which was very shaky, said, " I am here!" and pointed to the bosom of his hickory shirt.

The Yankee woman motioned him to a chair. Negroes coming there were plentiful. Usually they wanted to live the Ideal Life. They had a call to preach—and the girls wanted to be music-teachers.

The test was simple and severe: would they and could they do one useful piece of work well?

Booker sat and waited, not knowing that his patience was being put to the test.

Then Miss Priscilla, in a hard, Neill Burgess voice, " guessed " that the adjoining recitation-room needed sweeping and dusting. She handed Booker a broom and dust-cloth, motioned to the room, and went away.

Oho! Little did she know her lad. The colored boy smiled to himself—sweeping and dusting were his specialties— he had learned the trade from a Yankee woman from Vermont! He smiled.

Then he swept that room—moved every chair, the table, the desk. He dusted each piece of furniture four times. He polished each rung and followed around the

196

baseboard on hands and knees. ¶ Miss Priscilla came back—pushed the table around and saw at once that the dirt had not been concealed beneath it. She took out her handkerchief and wiped the table top, then the desk ✒ ✒

She turned, looked at the boy, and her smile met his half-suppressed triumphant grin.

" You 'll do," she said.

BOOKER T. WASHINGTON

ENERAL SAMUEL C. ARMSTRONG, the founder of Hampton Institute, and the grandfather of Tuskegee, was a white man who fought the South valiantly and well.

He seems about the only man in the North who, at the close of the war, clearly realized that the war had just begun—that the real enemies were not subdued, and that these enemies were ignorance, superstition and incompetence.

The pitiable condition of four million human beings, flung from slavery into freedom, thrown upon their own resources, with no thought of responsibility, and with no preparation for the change, meant for them only another kind of slavery.

General Armstrong's heart went out to them—he desired to show them how to be useful, helpful, self-reliant, healthy. For the whites of the South he had only high regard and friendship. He, of all men, knew how they had suffered from the war—and he realized also that they had fought for what they believed was right. In his heart there was no hate. He resolved to give himself—his life—his fortune—his intellect—his love—his all, for the upbuilding of the South. He saw with the vision of a prophet that indolence and pride were the actual enemies of white and black alike. The blacks must be taught to work—to know the dignity of human labor—to serve society—to help themselves by helping others. He realized that there are no menial tasks—that

198

all which serves is sacred. ¶ And this is the man who sowed the seeds of truth in the heart of the nameless black boy—Booker Washington. Armstrong's shibboleth, too, was, " With malice toward none, but with charity for all, let us finish the work God has given us to do."

BOOKER T. WASHINGTON

DO not know very much about this subject of education, yet I believe I know as much about what others know about it as most people. I have visited the principal colleges of America and Europe, and the methods of Preparatory and High Schools are to me familiar. I know the night-schools of the cities, the " Ungraded Rooms," the Schools for Defectives, the educational schemes in prisons, the Manual-Training Schools, the New Education (first suggested by Socrates) as carried out by G. Stanley Hall, John Dewey, and dozens of other good men and women in America. I am familiar with the School for the Deaf at Malone, New York, and the School for the Blind at Batavia, where even the sorely stricken are taught to be self-sufficient, self-supporting and happy. I have tumbled down the circular fire-escape at Lapeer with the inmates of the Home of Epileptics, and heard the shouts of laughter from lips that never laughed before. I have seen the Jewish Manual Training School of Chicago transform Russian refugees into useful citizens—capable, earnest and excellent. I know a little about Swarthmore, Wellesley, Vassar, Radcliffe, and have put my head into West Point and Annapolis, and had nobody cry, " Genius! "

Of Harvard, Yale and Princeton I know something, having done time in each. I have also given jobs to graduates of Oxford, Cambridge and Heidelberg, to my sorrow and their chagrin. This does not prove that

200

graduates of the great universities are, as a rule, out of work, or that they are incompetent. It simply means that it is possible for a man to graduate at these institutions and secure his diploma and yet be a man who has nothing the world really wants, either in way of ideas or services.

The reason that my " cum laude " friends did not like me, and the cause of my having to part with them—getting them a little free transportation from your Uncle George—was not because they lacked intelligence, but because they wanted to secure a position, while I simply offered them a job.

They were like Cave-of-the-Winds of Oshkosh, who is an ice-cutter in August, and in winter is an out-of-door horticulturist—a hired man is something else.

As a general proposition, I believe this will not now be disputed: the object of education is that a man may benefit himself by serving society.

To benefit others, you must be reasonably happy: there must be animation through useful activity, good-cheer, kindness and health—health of mind and health of body. And to benefit society you must also have patience, persistency, and a firm determination to do the right thing, and to mind your own business so that others, too, may mind theirs. Then all should be tinctured with a dash of discontent with past achievements, so you will constantly put forth an effort to do more and better work.

201

When what you have done in the past looks large to you, you have n't done much today.

So there you get the formula of Education: health and happiness through useful activity—animation, kindness, good-cheer, patience, persistency, willingness to give and take, seasoned with enough discontent to prevent smugness, which is the scum that grows over every stagnant pond.

Of course no college can fill this prescription—no institution can supply the ingredients—all that the college can do is to supply the conditions so that these things can spring into being. Plants need the sunlight—mushrooms are different.

The question is, then, what teaching concern in America supplies the best quality of actinic ray?

And I answer, Tuskegee is the place, and Booker Washington is the man.

" What! " you exclaim. " The Ideal School a school for Negroes, instituted by a Negro, where only Negroes teach, and only Negroes are allowed to enter as students? " ₰ ₰

And the answer is, " Exactly so."

At Tuskegee there are nearly two thousand students, and over one hundred fifty teachers. There are two classes of students—" day-school " and "night-school" students. The night-school students work all day at any kind of task they are called upon to do. They receive their board, clothing and a home—they pay

202

no tuition, but are paid for their labor, the amount being placed to their credit, so when fifty dollars is accumulated they can enter as " day students."

The " day students " make up the bulk of the scholars. Each pays fifty dollars a year. These all work every other day at manual labor or some useful trade.

Tuskegee has fully twice as many applicants as it can accommodate; but there is one kind of applicant who never receives any favor. This is the man who says he has the money to pay his way, and wishes to take the academic course only. The answer always is: " Please go elsewhere—there are plenty of schools that want your money. The fact that you have money will not exempt you here from useful labor."

This is exactly what every college in the world should say.

¶ The Tuskegee farm consists of about three thousand acres. There are four hundred head of cattle, about five hundred hogs, two hundred horses, great flocks of chickens, geese, ducks and turkeys, and many swarms of bees. It is the intention to raise all the food that is consumed on the place, and to manufacture all supplies. There are wagon-shops, a sawmill, a harness-shop, a shoe-shop, a tailor-shop, a printing-plant, a model laundry, a canning establishment. Finer fruit and vegetables I have never seen, and the thousands of peach, plum and apple trees, and the vast acreage of berries that have been planted, will surely some day be a goodly source of revenue ✵ ✵

The place is religious, but not dogmatically so—the religion being merely the natural safety-valve for emotion. At Tuskegee there is no lacrimose appeal to confess your sins—they do better—they forget them.

I never heard more inspiring congregational singing, and the use of the piano, organ, orchestra and brass band are important factors in the curriculum. In the chapel I spoke to an audience so attentive, so alert, so receptive, so filled with animation, that the whole place looked like a vast advertisement for Sozodont.

No prohibitive signs are seen at Tuskegee. All is affirmative, yet it is understood that some things are tabu— tobacco, for instance, and strong drink, of course ✄ We have all heard of Harvard Beer and Yale Mixture, but be it said in sober justice, Harvard runs no brewery, and Yale has no official brand of tobacco. Yet Harvard men consume much beer, and many men at Yale smoke. And if you want to see the cigarette-fiend on his native heath, you'll find him like the locust on the campus at Cambridge and New Haven. But if you want to see the acme of all cigarette-bazaars, just ride out of Boylston Street, Boston, any day at noon, and watch the boys coming out of the Institute of Technology. ¶ I once asked a Tech Professor if cigarette-smoking was compulsory in his institution. "Yes," he replied; "but the rule is not strictly enforced, as I know three students who do not smoke."

Tuskegee stands for order, system, cleanliness, industry,

courtesy and usefulness. There are no sink-holes around the place, no " back yards." Everything is beautiful, wholesome and sanitary. All trades are represented. The day is crammed so full of work from sunrise to sunset that there is no time for complaining, misery or faultfinding—three things that are usually born of idleness. At Tuskegee there are no servants. All of the work is done by the students and teachers—everybody works—everybody is a student, and all are teachers ℀ We are all teachers, whether we will it or not—we teach by example, and all students who do good work are good teachers.

When the Negro is able to do skilled work, he ceases to be a problem—he is a man. The fact that Alexandre Dumas was a Negro does not count against him in the world's assize.

The old-time academic college, that cultivated the cerebrum and gave a man his exercise in an indoor gymnasium, or not at all, has ruined its tens of thousands. To have top—head and no lungs—is not wholly desirable. The student was made exempt from every useful thing, just as the freshly freed slave hoped and expected to be, and after four years it was often impossible for him to take up the practical lessons of life. He had gotten used to the idea of one set of men doing all the work and another set of men having the culture. To a large degree he came to regard culture as the aim of life. And when a man begins to pride himself upon his

205

culture, he has n't any to speak of. Culture must be merely incidental, and to clutch it is like capturing a butterfly: you do not secure the butterfly at all—you get only a grub.

Let us say right here that there is only one way in which a Negro, or a white man, can ever make himself respected. Statute law will not do it; rights voted him by the State are of small avail; making demands will not secure the desired sesame. If we ever gain the paradise of freedom it will be because we have earned it —because we deserve it. A make-believe education may suffice for a white man—especially if he has a rich father, but a Negro who has to carve out his own destiny must be taught order, system, and quiet, per-sistent, useful effort.

A college that has its students devote one-half their time to actual, useful work is so in line with common-sense that we are amazed that the idea had to be put into execution by the ex-slave as a life-saver for his disenfranchised race. Our great discoveries are always accidents: we work for one thing and get another. I expect that the day will come, and erelong, when the great universities of the world will have to put the Tuskegee Idea into execution in order to save themselves from being distanced by the Colored Race.

If life were one thing and education another, it might be all right to separate them. Culture of the head over a desk, and indoor gymnastics for the body, are not the

ideal, and that many succeed in spite of the handicap
is no proof of the excellence of the plan. Ships that go
around the world accumulate many barnacles, but
barnacles as a help to the navigator are an iridescent
dream ❧ ❧

A little regular manual labor, rightly mixed with the
mental, eliminates draw-poker, highballs, brawls, broils,
Harvard Beer, Yale Mixture, Princeton Pinochle,
Chippee dances, hazing, roistering, rowdyism and the
bulldog propensity. The Heidelberg article of cocked
hat and insolent ways is not produced at Tuskegee. At
Tuskegee there is no place for those who lie in wait for
insults and regard scrapping as a fine art. As for college
athletics at the Orthodox Universities, only one man
out of ten ever does anything at it anyway—the college
man who needs the gymnasium most is practically
debarred from everything in it and serves as a laughing-
stock whenever he strips. Coffee, cocaine, bromide,
tobacco and strong drink often serve in lieu of exercise
and ozone, and Princeton winks her woozy eye in
innocency ❧ ❧

Freedom can not be bestowed—it must be achieved.
Education can not be given—it must be earned. Lincoln
did not free the slaves—he only freed himself. The
Negroes did not know they were slaves, and so they
had no idea of what freedom meant. Until a man wants
to be free, each kind of freedom is only another form of
slavery. Booker Washington is showing the colored man

how to secure a genuine freedom through useful activity.
To get freedom you must shoulder responsibility.

If college education were made compulsory by the State,
and one-half of the curriculum consisted of actual,
useful manual labor, most of our social ills would be
solved, and we would be well out on the highway
towards the Ideal City.

Without animation, man is naught—nothing is accomplished, nothing done. People who inspire other people
have animation plus.

And animation plus is ecstacy. In ecstasy the spirit
rushes out, runs over and saturates all. Oratory is an
ecstasy that inundates the hearer and makes him ride
upon the crest of another's ideas.

Art is born of ecstasy—art is ecstasy in the concrete.
Beautiful music is ecstasy expressed in sound, regulated
into rhythm, cadence and form. " Statuary is frozen
music," said Heine.

A man who is not moved into ecstasy by ecstasy is
hopeless. A people that has not the surging, uplifting,
onward power that ecstasy gives, is decadent—dead ఆ
The Negro is easily moved to ecstasy. Very little musical
training makes him a power in song. At Tuskegee the
congregational singing is a feature that, once heard, is
never to be forgotten. Fifteen hundred people lifting
up their hearts in an outburst of emotion—song!
Fifteen hundred people of one mind, doing anything in
unison—do you know what it means? Ecstasy is

essentially a matter of sex. In art and religion sex can not be left out of the equation. The simple fact that in forty years the Negro race in America has increased from four million to ten million tells of their ecstasy as a people. " Only happy beings reproduce themselves," says Darwin. Depress your animal and it ceases to breed; so there are a whole round of animals that do not reproduce in captivity. But in slavery or freedom the Negro sings, and reproduces—he is not doomed nor depressed—his soul arises superior to circumstance ⚘

Without animation, education is impossible. And the problem of the educator is to direct this singing, flowing, moving spirit of the hive into useful channels.

Education is simply the encouragement of right habits— the fixing of good habits until they become a part of one's nature, and are exercised automatically.

The man who is industrious by habit is the only man who wins. The man who is not industrious except when driven to it, or when it occurs to him, accomplishes little ⚘ ⚘

Man gets his happiness by doing: and work to a slave is always distasteful. The power of mimicry and imitation is omitted—the owner does not work—the strong man does not work. Ergo—to grow strong means to cease work. To be strong means to be free—to be free means no work!

It has been a frightfully bad education that the Negro has had—work distasteful, and work disgraceful! And the slave-owner suffered most of all, for he came to regard work as debasing.

And now a Negro is teaching the Negro that work is beautiful—that work is a privilege—that only through willing service can he ever win his freedom. Architecture is fixed ecstasy, inspired always by a strong man who gives a feeling of security. Athens was an ecstasy in marble ✣ ✣

Tuskegee is an ecstasy in brick and mortar.

Don't talk about the education of the Negro! The experiment has really never been tried, except spasmodically, of educating either the whites or the blacks in the South—or elsewhere.

A Negro is laying hold upon the natural ecstasy of the Negro, and directing it into channels of usefulness and excellence. Can you foretell where this will end—this formation of habits of industry, sobriety and continued, persistent effort towards the right?

Booker Washington, child of a despised race, has done and is doing what the combined pedagogic and priestly wisdom of ages has failed to do. He is the Moses who by his example is leading the children of his former oppressors out into the light of social, mental, moral and economic freedom.

I am familiar in detail with every criticism brought against Tuskegee. On examination these criticisms all reduce themselves down to three:

1. A vast sum of money has been collected by Booker

Washington for his own aggrandizement and benefit.
2. Tuskegee is a show-place where all the really good work is done by picked men from the North.
3. Booker Washington is a tyrant, a dictator and an egotist. ¶ If I were counsel for Tuskegee—as I am not—I would follow the example of the worthy accusers, and submit the matter without argument. Booker Washington can afford to plead guilty to every charge; and he has never belittled himself by answering his accusers. ¶ But let the facts be known, that this man has collected upward of six million dollars, mostly from the people of the North, and has built up the nearest perfect educational institution in the world.

It is probably true that many of his teachers and best workers are picked people—but they are Negroes, and were selected by a Negro. The great general reveals his greatness in the selection of his generals: it was the marshals whom Napoleon appointed who won for him his victories; but his spirit animated theirs, and he chose them for this one reason—he could dominate them. He infused into their souls a goodly dash of his own enthusiasm.

Booker Washington is a greater general than Napoleon. For the Tuskegee idea no Waterloo awaits. And as near as I can judge, Booker Washington's most noisy critics are merely camp-followers.

That the man is a tyrant and a dictator there is no doubt. He is a beneficent tyrant, but a tyrant still, for he always, invariably, has his own way in weighty matters—in trivialities others can have theirs. And as for dictatorship, the man who advances on chaos and transforms it into cosmos is perforce a dictator and an egotist *&* *&*

Booker Washington believes he is in the right, and he makes no effort to conceal the fact that he is on earth. In him there is no disposition to run and peep about, and find himself a dishonorable grave. All live men are egotists, and they are egotists just in proportion as they have life. Dead men are not egotists. Booker Washington has life in abundance, and through him I truly believe runs the spirit of Divinity, if ever a living man had it. A man like this is the instrument of Deity.

Tuskegee Institute has applications ahead all the time, from all over America, for competent colored men and women who can take charge of important work and do it. Dressmakers, housekeepers, cooks, farmers, stockmen, builders, gardeners, are in demand. The world has never yet had enough people to bear its burdens.

Recently we have heard much of the unemployed, but a very little search will show that the people out of work are those of bad habits, which make them unreliable and untrustworthy. The South, especially, needs the willing worker and the practical man. And best of all the South knows it, and stands ready to pay for the service.

¶ A few years ago there was a fine storm of protest from Northern Negroes to the effect that Booker Washington

was endeavoring to limit the Negro to menial service—
that is, thrust him back into servility. The first ambition of the Negro was to get an education so that he
might become a Baptist preacher. To him, education
meant freedom from toil, and of course we do not have
to look far to see where he got the idea. Then when
Tuskegee came forward and wanted to make black-
smiths, carpenters and brick-masons out of black men,
there was a cry, " If this means education, we will none
of it—treason, treason! " It was assumed that the Negro
who set other Negroes to work was not their friend.
This phase of the matter requires neither denial nor
apology. We smile and pass on.

In Eighteen Hundred Seventy-seven, the Negro was
practically disenfranchised throughout the South, by
being excluded from the primaries. He had no recognized
ticket in the field. For both the blacks and the whites
this has been well. To most of the blacks freedom
meant simply exemption from work. So there quickly
grew up a roistering, turbulent, idle and dangerous
class of black men who were used by the most ambitious
of their kind for political ends. To preserve the peace of
the community, the whites were forced to adopt heroic
measures, with the result that we now have the disenfranchised Negro.

Early in the Eighties, Booker Washington realized that,
politically, there was no hope for his race. He saw,
however, that commerce recognized no color line. We

would buy, sell and trade with the black man on absolute equality. Life-insurance companies would insure
him, banks would receive his deposits, and if honest and
competent, would loan him money. If he could shoe a
horse, we waived his complexion; and in every sort and
kind of craftsmanship he stood on absolute equality
with the whites. The only question ever asked was,
" Can you do the work? "

And Booker Washington set out to help the Negro win
success for himself by serving society through becoming
skilled in doing useful things. And so it became Head,
Hand and Heart. The manual was played off against
the intellectual.

But over and beyond the great achievement of Booker
Washington in founding and carrying to a successful
issue the most complete educational scheme of this age,
or any other, stands the man himself. He is one without
hate, heat or prejudice. No one can write on the lintels
of his doorpost the word, " Whim." He is half-white,
but calls himself a Negro. He sides with the disgraced
and outcast black woman who gave him birth, rather
than with the respectable white man who was his sire.
¶ He rides in the Jim Crow cars, and on long trips, if it
is deemed expedient to use a sleeping-car, he hires the
stateroom, so that he may not trespass or presume upon
those who would be troubled by the presence of a
colored man. Often in traveling he goes for food and
shelter to the humble home of one of his own people.

214

At hotels he receives and accepts, without protest or resentment, the occasional contumely of the inferior whites—whites too ignorant to appreciate that one of God's noblemen stands before them. For the whites of the South he has only words of kindness and respect ; the worst he says about them is that they do not understand. His modesty, his patience, his forbearance, are sublime. He is a true Fabian—he does what he can, like the royal Roycroft opportunist that he is. Every petty annoyance is passed over; the gibes and jeers and the ingratitude of his own race are forgotten. " They do not understand," he calmly says. He does his work. He is respected by the best people of North and South. He has the confidence of the men of affairs—he is a safe man.

THOMAS ARNOLD

Let me mind my own personal work; keep myself pure and zealous and believing; laboring to do God's will in this fruitful vineyard of young lives committed to my charge, as my allotted field, until my work be done.

—*Thomas Arnold*

THOMAS ARNOLD

THOMAS ARNOLD

THOMAS ARNOLD was born in Seventeen Hundred Ninety-five, and died in Eighteen Hundred Forty-two. His life was short, as men count time, but he lived long enough to make for himself a name and a fame that are both lasting and luminous. Though he was neither a great writer nor a great preacher, yet there were times when he thought he was both. He was only a schoolteacher. However, he was an artist in schoolteaching, and art is not a thing—it is a way. It is the beautiful way—the effective way.

Schoolteachers have no means of proving their prowess by conspicuous waste, and no time to convince the world of their excellence through conspicuous leisure; consequently, for histrionic purposes, a schoolteacher's cosmos is a plain, slaty gray. Schoolteachers do not wallow in wealth nor feed fat at the public trough. No one ever accuses them of belonging to the class known as the predatory rich, nor of being millionaire malefactors. They have to do their work every day at certain hours and dedicate its results to time.

For many years Thomas Arnold has been known as the father of his son. Several great men have been thus overshadowed. The father of Disraeli, for instance, was favored by fame and fortune, until his gifted son moved into the limelight, and after that Pater shone mostly in a reflected glory. Jacopo Bellini was the greatest painter in Venice until his two sons, Gian and Gentile, surpassed him, and history writes him down as the father of the Bellinis. Lyman Beecher was regarded as America's greatest preacher until Henry Ward moved the mark up a few notches. The elder Pitt was looked upon as a genuine statesman until his son graduated into the Cabinet, and then " the terrible cornet of horse " became known as the father of Pitt. Now that both are dust, and we are getting the proper perspective, we see that " the great commoner " was indeed a great man, and so they move down the corridors of time together, arm in arm, this father and son. That excellent person who carried the gripsacks of greatness so long that he thought the luggage was his own, Major James B. Pond, launched at least one good thing. It was this: " Matthew Arnold gave fifty lectures in America, and nobody ever heard one of them; those in his audience who could no longer endure the silence slipped quietly out." ⚬ ⚬

Matthew Arnold was a critic and writer who, having secured a tuppence worth of success through being the son of his father, and thus securing the speaker's eye, finally got an oratorical bee in his bonnet and went a-barnstorming. He cultivated reserve and indifference, both of which he was told were necessary factors of success in a public speaker. ¶ And this is true. But they will not make an orator, any more than long hair, a peculiar necktie, and a queer hat will float a poet on the tide of time safely into the Hall of Fame.

Matthew Arnold cultivated repose, but instead of convincing the audience that he had power, he only made them think he was sleepy. Major Pond, having lived much with orators, and thinking the trick easy, tried oratory on his own account, and succeeded as well as did Matthew Arnold. No one ever heard Major Pond: his voice fell over the footlights, dead, into the orchestra; only those with opera-glasses knew he was talking ✄ But to be unintelligible is not a special recommendation. Men may be moderate for two reasons—through excess of feeling and because they are actually dull.

Matthew Arnold has slipped back into his true position —that of a man of letters. The genius is a man of affairs. Humanity is the theme, not books. Books are usually written about the thoughts of men who wrote books. Books die and disintegrate, but humanity is an endless procession, and the souls that go marching on are those who fought for freedom, not those who speculate on abstrusities ✄ ✄

The credential of Thomas Arnold to immortality is not that he was the father of Matthew and eight other little Arnolds, but it lies in the fact that he fought for a wider horizon in life through education. He lifted his voice for liberty. He believed in the divinity of the child, not in its depravity. Arnold of Rugby was a teacher of teachers, as every great teacher is. The pedagogic world is now going back to his philosophy, just as in statesmanship we are reverting to Thomas Jefferson. These men who spoke classic truth, not transient—truth that fits in spite of fashion, time and place—are the true prophets of mankind. Such was Thomas Arnold!

THOMAS ARNOLD

F Thomas Arnold had been just a little bigger, the world probably would never have heard of him, for an interdict would have been placed upon his work. The miracle is that, as it was, the Church and the State did not snuff him out. ¶ He stood for sweet reasonableness, but unintentionally created much opposition. His life was a warfare. Yet he managed to make himself acceptable to a few; so for fourteen years this head master of a preparatory school for boys lived his life and did his work. He sent out his radiating gleams, and grew straight in the strength of his spirit, and lived out his life in the light. ¶ His sudden death sanctified and sealed his work before he was subdued and ironed out by the conventions ৺ ৺

Happy Arnold! If he had lived, he might have met the fate of Arnold of Brescia, who was also a great teacher. Arnold of Brescia was a pupil of Abelard, and was condemned by the Church as a disturber of the peace for speaking in eulogy of his master. Later, he attacked the profligacy of the idle prelates, as did Luther, Savonarola and all the other great church-reformers. When ordered into exile and silence, he still protested his right to speak. He was strangled on order of the Pope, his body burned, and the ashes thrown into the Tiber. The Baptists, I believe, claim Arnold of Brescia as the forerunner of their sect, and certain it is that he was of the true Roger Williams type.

223

THOMAS ARNOLD

Thomas Arnold, too, was filled with a passion for right-eousness. His zeal for the upright, manly life constituted his strength. Of course he would not have been executed, as was Arnold of Brescia—the times had changed—he would simply have been shelved, poohpoohed, deprived of his living and socially Crapseyized. Death saved him —aged forty-seven—and his soul goes marching on!

HE parents of Thomas Arnold belonged to the great Middle Class—that class which Disraeli said never did any thinking on its own account, but to the best of its ability deferred to and imitated the idle rich in matters of religion, education and politics.

Doctor Johnson maintained that if members of the Middle Class worked hard and economized, it was in the hope that they might leave money and name for their children and make them exempt from all useful effort ✄ ✄

" To indict a class," said Burke, " is neither reasonable nor right." But certain it is that a vast number of fairly intelligent people in England and elsewhere regard the life of the " aristocracy " as very desirable and beautiful.

To this end they want their boys to become clergymen, lawyers, doctors or army officers.

" Only two avenues of honor are open to aspiring youth in England," said Gladstone—" the Army and the Church." ✄ ✄

The father of Thomas Arnold was Collector of Customs at Cowes, Isle of Wight. Holding this petty office under the Government, with a half-dozen men at his command, we can easily guess his caliber, habits, belief and mode of life. He was respectable; and to be respectable, a Collector of Customs must be punctilious in Church matters, in order to be acceptable to Church people, for

225

of such is the Kingdom of Heaven. The parents of Thomas Arnold very naturally centered their ambitions for him on the Church, as he was not very strong.

When the child was only six years old, the father died from " spasm of the heart." At this time the boy had begun to take Latin, and his education was being looked after by a worthy governess, who daily drilled his mental processes and took him walking, leading him by the hand. On Sundays he wore a wide, white collar, shiny boots and a stiff hat. The governess cautioned him not to soil his collar, nor to get mud on his boots. ¶ In later years he told how he looked covetously at the boys who wore neither hats nor boots, and who did not have a governess.

His mother had a fair income, and so this prim, precise, exact and crystallized mode of education was continued. Out of her great love for her child, the mother sent him away from home when he was eight years old. Of course there were tears on both sides; but now a male man must educate him, and women were to be dropped out of the equation—this that the evil in the child should be curbed, his spirit chastened, and his mind disciplined.

The fact that a child rather liked to be fondled by his mother, or that his mother cared to fondle him, was proof of total depravity on the part of both.

The Reverend Doctor Griffiths, who took charge of the boy for two years, was certainly not cruel, but at the same time he was not exactly human. In Nature we never hear of a she-lion sending her cubs away to be looked after by a denatured lion. It is really doubtful whether you could ever raise a lion to lionhood by this method. Some goat would come along and butt the life out of him, even after he had evolved whiskers and a mane ❧ ❧

After two years with Doctor Griffiths, young Arnold was sent to Manchester, where he remained in a boys' boarding-house from his tenth to his fourteenth year. To the teachers here—all men—he often paid tribute, but uttered a few heretical doubts as to whether discipline as a substitute for mother-love was not an error of pious but overzealous educators.

At sixteen years of age he was transferred to Corpus Christi College at Oxford. In Eighteen Hundred Fifteen, being then twenty years of age, he was elected a Fellow of Oriel College, and there he resided until he was twenty-four ❧ ❧

He was a prizeman in Latin, Greek and English, and was considered a star scholar—both by himself and by others. Ten years afterwards he took a backward glance, and said: "At twenty-two I was proud, precise, stiff, formàl, uncomfortable, unhappy, and unintentionally made everybody else unhappy with whom I came in contact. The only people I really mixed with were those whose lives were dedicated to the ablative."

¶ When twenty-four he was made a deacon and used

227

to read prayers at neighboring chapels, for which service he was paid five shillings. Being now thrown on his own resources, he did the thing a prizeman always does: he showed others how. As a tutor he was a success: more scholars came to him than he could really take care of. But he did not like the work, since all the pupil desired, and all the parents desired, was that he should help the backward one get his marks, and glide through the eye of a needle into pedagogic paradise ꝸ At twenty-six he was preaching, teaching and writing learned essays about things he did not understand. ¶ From this brief sketch it will be seen that the early education of Thomas Arnold was of the kind and type that any fond parent of the well-to-do Middle Class would most desire. He had been shielded from all temptations of the world; he could do no useful thing with his hands; his knowledge of economics—ways and means—was that of a child; of the living present he knew little, but of the dead past he assumed and believed he knew much.

It was purely priestly, institutional education. It was the kind of education that every well-to-do Briton would like to have his sons receive. It was, in short, England's Ideal ꝸ ꝸ

THOMAS ARNOLD

UGBY GRAMMAR SCHOOL was endowed in Sixteen Hundred Fifty-three by one Laurence Sherif, a worthy grocer. The original gift was comparatively small, but the investment being in London real estate, has increased in value until it yields now an income of about thirty-five thousand dollars a year.

In the time of Arnold there were about three hundred pupils. It is not a large school now; there are high schools in a hundred cities of America that surpass it in many ways.

Rugby's claim to special notice lies in its traditions— the great men who were once Rugby boys, and the great men who were Rugby teachers. Also, in the fact that Thomas Hughes wrote a famous story called, " Tom Brown at Rugby."

Rugby Grammar School was one hundred twenty-five years old when Sir Joshua Reynolds commissioned Lord Cornwallis to go to America and fetch George Washington to England, that Sir Joshua might paint his portrait.

For a hundred years prior to the time of Arnold, there had not been a perceptible change in the methods of teaching. The boys were herded together. They fought, quarreled, divided into cliques; the big boys bullied the little ones. Fagging was the law; so the upper forms enslaved the lower ones. There was no home life, and the studies were made irksome and severe, purposely,

229

as it was thought that pleasant things were sinful.
¶ If any better plan could have been devised to make
study absolutely repulsive, so the student would
shun it as soon as he was out of school, we can not
guess it.

The system was probably born of inertia on the part of
the teachers. The pastor who pushes through his prescribed services, with mind on other things, and thus
absolves his conscience for letting his congregation go
drifting straight to Gehenna, was duplicated in the
teacher. He did his duty—and nothing more.

Selfishness, heartlessness and brutality manipulated the
birch. Head was all; heart and hand nothing. This was
schoolteaching. As a punishment for failure to memorize
lessons, there were various plans to disgrace and dis-
courage the luckless ones. Standing in the corner with
face to the wall, and the dunce-cap, had given place to
a system of fines, whereby " ten lines of Vergil for
failure to attend prayers," and ten more for failure to
get the first, often placed the boy in hopeless bankruptcy. If he was a fag, or slave of a higher-form boy,
cleaning the other's boots, scrubbing stairs, running on
foolish and needless errands, getting cuffs and kicks by
way of encouragement, he saw his fines piling up and
no way ever to clear them off and gain freedom by
promotion ᔥ ᔥ

Viewed from our standpoint, the thing has a ludicrous
bouffe air that makes us smile. But to the boy caught in

the toils it was tragic. To work and evolve in an environment of such brutality was impossible to certain temperaments. Success lay in becoming calloused and indifferent. If the boy of gentle habits and slight physical force did not sink into mental nothingness, he was in danger of being bowled over by disease and death ॐ ॐ

Indeed, the physical condition of the pupils was very bad: smallpox, fevers, consumption, and breaking out with sores and boils, were common.

Thomas Arnold was thirty-three years old when he was called as head master to Rugby. He was married, and babies were coming along with astonishing regularity. He had taken priestly orders and was passing rich on one hundred pounds a year. Poverty and responsibiltiy had given him ballast, and love for his own little brood had softened his heart and vitalized his soul.

As a writer and speaker he had made his presence felt at various college commencements and clergymen's meetings. He had challenged the brutal, indifferent, lazy and so-called disciplinary methods of teaching.

And so far as we know, he is the first man in England to declare that the teacher should be the foster-parent of the child, and that all successful teaching must be born of love ॐ ॐ

The well-upholstered conservatives twiddled their thumbs, coughed, and asked: " How about the doctrine of total depravity? Do you mean to say that the child

231

should not be disciplined? What does Solomon say about the use of the rod? Does the Bible say that the child is good by nature?"

But Thomas Arnold could not explain all he knew. Moreover, he did not wish to fight the Church—he believed in the Church—to him it was a divine institution. But there were methods and practises in the Church that he would have liked to forget.

"My sympathies go out to inferiority," he said. The weakling often needed encouragement, not discipline. The bad boy must be won, not suppressed.

In one of these conferences of clergymen, Arnold said: ¶ " I once chided a pupil, a little, pale, stupid boy— undersized and seemingly half-sick—for not being able to recite his very simple lesson. He looked up at me and said with a touch of spirit: ' Sir, why do you get angry with me? Do you not know I am doing the best I can?'" ✄ ✄

One of the clergymen present asked Arnold how he punished the boy for his impudence.

And Arnold replied: " I did not punish him—he had properly punished me. I begged his pardon."

The idea of a teacher begging the pardon of a pupil was a brand-new thing.

Several clergymen present laughed—one scowled—two sneezed. But a Bishop, shortly after this, urged the name of Thomas Arnold as master of Rugby, and added to his recommendation this line: " If elected to the

office he will change the methods of schoolteaching in
every public school in England."
The ayes had it, and Arnold was called to Rugby. The
salary was so-so, the pupils between two and three
hundred in number—many were home on sick-leave—
the Sixth Form was in charge.

THOMAS ARNOLD

THE genius of Arnold was made manifest, almost as soon as he went to Rugby, by the way in which he managed the boys who bullied the whole school, and what is worse, did it legally. ¶ Fagging was official.

The Sixth Form was composed of thirty boys who stood at the top, and these boys ran the school. They were boys who, by reason of their size, strength, aggressiveness and mental ability, got the markings that gave them this autocratic power. They were now immune from authority—they were free. In a year they would gravitate to the University.

We can hardly understand now how a bully could get markings through his bullying propensities; but a rudimentary survival of the idea may yet be seen in big football-players, who are given good marks, and very gentle mental massage in class. If the same scholars were small and skinny, they would certainly be plucked.

The faculty found freedom in shifting responsibility for discipline to the Sixth Form.

Read the diary of Arnold, and you will be amazed on seeing how he fought against taking from the Sixth Form the right to bodily chastise any scholar in the school that the king of the Sixth Form declared deserved it ⚜ ⚜

If a teacher thought a pupil needed punishment, he turned the luckless one over to the Sixth Form. Can we

234

now conceive of a system where the duty of certain scholars was to whip other scholars? Not only to whip them, but to beat them into insensibility if they fought back? ✺ ✺

Such was schoolteaching in the public schools of England in Eighteen Hundred Thirty.

Against this brutality there was now a growing sentiment—a piping voice bidding the tide to stay!

But now that Arnold was in charge of Rugby, he got the ill-will of his directors by declaring that he did not intend to curtail the powers of the Sixth Form—he proposed to civilize it. To try out the new master, the Sixth Form, proud in their prowess, sent him word that if he interfered with them in any way, they would first " bust up the school," and then resign in a body. Moreover, they gave it out that if any pupil complained to the master concerning the Sixth Form, the one so complaining would be taken out by night and drowned in the classic Avon.

There were legends among the younger boys of strange disappearances, and these were attributed to the swift vengeance of " The Bloody Sixth."

Above the Sixth Form there was no law.

Every scholar took off his hat to a " Sixth." A Sixth uncovered to nobody, and touched his cap only to a teacher ✺ ✺

And custom had become so rooted that the Sixth Form was regarded as a sort of police necessity—a caste which served the school just as the Army served the Church. To reach the Sixth Form were paradise—it meant liberty and power—liberty to do as you pleased, and power to punish all who questioned your authority ⚜

To uproot the power of the Sixth Form was the intent of a few reformers in pedagogics.

There were two ways to deal with the boys of the Sixth —fight them or educate them.

Arnold called the Rugby Sixth together and assured them that he could not do without their help. He needed them: he wanted to make Rugby a model school, a school that would influence all England—would they help him?

The dogged faces before him showed signs of interest. He continued, without waiting for their reply, to set before them his ideal of an English Gentleman. He persuaded them, melted them by his glowing personality, shook hands with each, and sent them away.

The next day he again met them in the same intimate way, and one of the boys made bold to assure him that if he wanted anybody licked—pupils or teachers—they stood ready to do his bidding.

He thanked the boy, but assured him that he was of the opinion that it would not be necessary to do violence to any one; he was going to unfold to them another way— a new way, which was very old, but which as yet England had not tried.

236

THOMAS ARNOLD

HE great teacher is not the one who imparts the most facts—he is the one who inspires by supplying a nobler ideal.

Men are superior or inferior just in the ratio that they possess certain qualities. Truth, honor, frankness, health, system, industry, kindliness, good-cheer and a spirit of helpfulness are so far beyond any mental acquisition that comparisons are not only odious, but absurd ✄ ✄

Arnold inspired qualities, and in this respect his work at Rugby forms a white milestone on the path of progress in pedagogy.

To an applicant for a position as teacher, Arnold wrote:

What I want is a man who is a Christian and a gentleman, an active man, and one who has commonsense, and understands boys. I do not so much care about scholarship, as he will have immediately under him the lowest forms in the school, but yet, on second thought, I do care about it very much, because his pupils may be in the highest forms; and besides, I think that even the elements are best taught by a man who has a thorough knowledge of the matter. However, if one must give way, I prefer activity of mind and an interest in his work to high scholarship; for the one may be acquired far more easily than the other. I should wish it also to be understood that the new master may be called upon to take boarders in his house, it being my intention for the future to require this of all masters as I see occasion, that so in time the school-barracks may die a natural death. With this to offer, I think I

237

have a right to look rather high for the man whom
I fix upon, and it is my great object to get here a society
of intelligent, gentlemanly and active men, who may
permanently keep up the character of the school, and
if I were to break my neck tomorrow, carry it on.

¶ Ideas are in the air, and great inventions are worked
out in different parts of the world at the same time.
Rousseau had written his "Emile," but we are not aware
that Arnold ever read it.

And if he had, he probably would have been shocked,
not inspired, by its almost brutal frankness. The French
might read it—the English could not.

Pestalozzi was working out his ideas in Switzerland, and
Froebel, an awkward farmer lad in Germany, was
dreaming dreams that were to come true. But Thomas
Arnold caught up the threads of feeling in England and
expressed them in the fabric of his life.

His plans were scientific, but his reasons, unlike those of
Pestalozzi, will not always stand the test of close analy-
sis. Arnold was true to the Church, but he found it
convenient to forget much for which the Church stood.
He went back to a source nearer the fountainhead. All
reforms in organized religion lie in returning to the
primitive type. The religion of Jesus was very simple;
that of a modern church dignitary is very complex. One
can be understood; the other has to be explained and
expounded, and usually several languages are required.

¶ Arnold would have his boys evolve into Christian

238

gentlemen. And his type of English gentleman he did not get out of books on theology—it was his own composite idea. But having once evolved it, he cast around to justify it by passages of Scripture. This was beautiful, too, but from our standpoint it wasn't necessary ᛋ From his it was.

A gentleman to him was a man who looked for the best in other people, and not for their faults; who overlooked slights; who forgot the good he had done; who was courteous, kind, cheerful, industrious and clean inside and out; who was slow to wrath, fervent in spirit, serving the Lord. And the " Lord "to Arnold was embodied in Church and State.

Arnold used to say that schoolteaching should not be based upon religion, but it should be religion. And to him religion and conduct were one.

That he reformed Rugby through the Sixth Form is a fact. He infused into the big boys the thought that they must help the little ones; that for a first offense a lad must never be punished; that he should have the matter fully explained to him, and be shown that he should do right because it is right, and not for fear of punishment ᛋ ᛋ

The Sixth Form was taught to unbend its dignity and enter into fellowship with its so-called inferiors. To this end Arnold set the example of playing cricket with the " scrubs." ᛋ He never laughed at a poor player nor at a poor scholar. He took dull pupils into his own house, and insisted that his helpers, the other teachers, should do the same. He showed the Sixth Form how much better it was to take the part of the weak, and stop bullying the lower forms, than to set the example of it in the highest. Before Arnold had been at Rugby a year, the Sixth Form had resolved itself into a Reception Committee that greeted all newcomers, got them located, introduced them to the other boys, showed them the sights, and looked after their wants like big brothers or foster-fathers.

Christianity to Arnold was human service. In his zeal to serve, to benefit, to bless, to inspire, he never tired ❧ Such a disposition as this is contagious. In every big business or school, there is one man's mental attitude that animates the whole institution. Everybody partakes of it. When the leader gets melancholia, the shop has it—the whole place becomes tinted with ultramarine. The best helpers begin to get out, and the honeycombing process of dissolution is on.

A school must have a soul, just as surely as a shop, a bank, a hotel, a store, a home, or a church has to have. When an institution grows so great that it has no soul—simply a financial head and a board of directors—dry-rot sets in and disintegration in a loose wrapper is at the door.

This explains why the small colleges are the best, when they are: there is a personality about them, an animating spirit that is pervasive and preservative.

240

THOMAS ARNOLD

Thomas Arnold was not a man of vast learning, nor could one truthfully say he had a surplus of intellect; but he had soul, plus. He never sought to save himself. He gave himself to the boys of Rugby. His heart went out to them, he believed in them—and he believed them even when they lied, and he knew they lied. He knew that humanity was sound at heart; he believed in the divinity of mankind, and tried hard to forget the foolish theology that taught otherwise.

Like Thomas Jefferson, who installed the honor system in the University of Virginia, he trusted young men. He made his appeal to that germ of goodness which is in every human soul. In some ways he anticipated Ben Lindsey in his love for the boy, and might have conjured forth from his teeming brain the Juvenile Court, and thus stopped the creation of criminals, had his life not been consumed in a struggle with stupidity and pedantry gone to seed that cried to him, " Oh, who ever heard of such a thing as that! "

¶ The Kindergarten utilizes the propensity to play; and Arnold utilizes the thirst for authority. Altruism is flavored with a desire for approbation.

The plan of self-government by means of utilizing the Sixth Form was quite on the order of our own " George Junior Republic." " A school," he said, " should be self-governing and cleanse itself from that which is harmful." And again he says: " If a pupil can gratify his natural desire for approbation by doing that which

is right, proper and best, he will work to this end instead
of being a hero by playing the rowdy. It is for the
scholars to set the seal of their approval on character,
and they will do so if we as teachers speak the word.
If I find a room in a tumult, I blame myself, not the
scholars. It is I who have failed, not they. Were I what
I should be, every one of my pupils would reflect my
worth. I key the situation, I set the pace, and if my
soul is in disorder, the school will be in confusion."
¶ Nothing is done without enthusiasm. It is heart that
wins, not head, the round world over. And yet head
must systematize the promptings of the heart. Arnold
had a way of putting soul into a hand-clasp. His pupils
never forgot him. Wherever they went, no matter how
long they lived, they proclaimed the praises of Arnold
of Rugby. How much this earnest, enthusiastic, loving
and sincere teacher has influenced civilization, no man
can say. But this we know, that since his day there has
come about a new science of teaching. The birch has
gone with the dunce-cap. The particular cat-o'-nine-
tails that was burned in the house of Thomas Arnold
as a solemn ceremony, when the declaration was made,
"Henceforth I know my children will do right !" has
found its example in every home of Christendom ✖
We no longer whip children. Schools are no longer
places of dread, pain and suffering, and we as teachers
are repeating with Friedrich Froebel the words of the
Nazarene, "Suffer little children to come unto me,

and forbid them not, for of such is the Kingdom of Heaven."

Also, we say with Thomas Arnold: " The boy is father to the man. A race of gentlemen can only be produced by fostering in the boy the qualities that make for health, strength and a manly desire to bless, benefit and serve the race."

FRIEDRICH FROEBEL

The purpose of the Kindergarten is to provide the necessary and natural help which poor mothers require who have to be about their work all day, and must leave their children to themselves. The occupations pursued in the Kindergarten are the following: free play of a child by itself; free play of several children by themselves; associated play under the guidance of a teacher; gymnastic exercises; several sorts of handiwork suited to little children; going for walks; learning music, both instrumental and vocal; learning the repetition of poetry; story-telling; looking at really good pictures; aiding in domestic occupations; gardening.

—Froebel

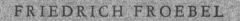

FRIEDRICH FROEBEL

FRIEDRICH FROEBEL

FRIEDRICH FROEBEL

RIEDRICH FROEBEL was born in a Thuringian village, April Twenty-first, Seventeen Hundred Eighty-two. His father was pastor of the Lutheran Church. When scarcely a year old his mother died. Erelong a stepmother came to fill her place —but did n't. This stepmother was the kind we read about in the " Six Best Sellers." ✖️ Her severity, lack of love, and needlessly religious zeal served the future Kindergartner a dark background on which to paint a joyous picture. Froebel was educated by antithesis. His home was the type etched so unforgetably by Colonel Ed. Howe in his " Story of a Country Town," which is n't bad enough to be one of the Six Best Sellers.

At the age of ten, out of pure pity, young Friedrich was rescued from the cuckoo's nest by an uncle who had a big family of his own and love without limit. There was a goodly brood left, so little Friedrich, slim, slender, yellow, pensive and sad, was really never missed. ¶The uncle brought the boy up to work, but treated him like a human being, answering his questions, even allowing him to have stick horses and little log houses and a garden of his own.

At fifteen his nature had begun to awaken, and the

uncle, harkening to the boy's wish, apprenticed him for two years to a forester. The young man's first work was to make a list of the trees in a certain tract and approximate their respective ages. The night before his work began he lay awake thinking of the fun he was going to have at the job. In after-years he told of this incident in showing that it was absurd to try to divorce work from play. ¶ The two years as forester's apprentice, from fifteen to seventeen, were really better for him than any university could have been. His step-mother's instructions had mostly been in the line of prohibition. From earliest babyhood he had been warned to " look out." When he went on the street it was with a prophecy that he would get run over by a cart, or stolen by the gypsies, or fall off the bridge and be drowned. The idea of danger had been dinged into his ears so that fear had become a part of the fabric of his nature. Even at fifteen, he took pains to get out of the woods before sundown to avoid the bears. At the same time his intellect told him there were no bears there. But the shudder habit was upon him ॐ Yet by degrees the work in the woods built up his body and he grew to be at home in the forest, both day and night. His duties taught him to observe, to describe, to draw, to investigate, to decide. Then it was trans-plantation, and perhaps the best of college life consists in taking the youth out of the home environment and supplying him new surroundings.

248

FRIEDRICH FROEBEL

Forestry in America is a brand-new science. To clear the ground has been our desire, and so to strip, burn and destroy, saving only such logs as appealed to us for "lumber," was the desideratum. But now we are seriously considering the matter of tree-planting and tree-preservation, and perhaps it would be well to ask ourselves if two years at forestry, right out of doors, in contact with Nature, wrestling with the world of wood, rock, plant and living things, would n't be better for the boy than double the time in stuffy dormitories and still more stuffy recitation-rooms—listening to stuffy lectures about things that are foreign to life ✄ I would say that a boy is a savage, but I do not care to give offense to fond mammas. To educate him in the line of his likes, as the race has been educated, seems sensible and right. How would Yellowstone Park answer for a National University, with Captain Jack Crawford, William Muldoon, John Burroughs, John Dewey, Stanley Hall and a mixture of men of these types, for a faculty ?

Froebel thought his two years in the forest saved him from consumption, and perhaps from insanity, for it taught him to look out, not in, and to lend a hand. At times he was a little too sentimental, as it was, and a trifle more of morbidity and sensitiveness would have ruined his life, absolutely.

The woods and God's great out-of-doors gave him balance and ballast, good digestion and sweet sleep o' nights.

FRIEDRICH FROEBEL

The two years past, he went to Jena, where he had an elder brother. This brother was a star scholar, and Friedrich looked up to him as a pleiad of pedagogy. He became a professor in a Jena preparatory school and then practised medicine; but he never had the misfortune to affront public opinion, and so oblivion lured and won him, and took him as her own.

At Jena poor Froebel did not make head. His preparatory work had n't prepared him. He floundered in studies too deep for one of his age, then followed some foolish advice and hired a tutor to help him along. Then he fell down, was plucked, got into debt, and also into the " carcer," where he boarded for nine weeks at the expense of the State.

In the carcer he did n't catch up with his studies, quite naturally, and the imprisonment almost broke his health. Had he been in the carcer for dueling, he would have emerged a hero. But debt meant that he had neither money nor friends. When he was given his release, as an economic move, he slipped away between two days and made his way to the Forestry Office, where he applied for a job as laborer. He got it. In a few days he was promoted to chief of apprentices ⚹ Forestry meant a certain knowledge of surveying, and this Froebel soon acquired. Then came map-making, and that was only fun. From map-making to architecture is but a step, and Froebel quit the woods to work as assistant to an architect at ten pounds a year and found. It was confining work, and a trifle more exacting than he had expected—it required a deal of mathematics, and mathematics was Froebel's short suit. Froebel was disappointed and so was his employer—when something happened. It usually does in books, and in life, always.

FRIEDRICH FROEBEL

ENIUS has its prototype. Before Froebel comes Pestalozzi, the Swiss, who studied theology and law, and then abandoned them both as futile to human evolution, and turned his attention to teaching. Pestalozzi was inspired by Jean Jacques Rousseau, and read his " Emile " religiously. To teach by natural methods and mix work and study, and make both play, was his theme. Pestalozzi believed in teaching out of doors, because children are both barbaric and nomadic—they want to go somewhere. His was the Aristotle method, as opposed to those of the closet and the cloister. But he made the mistake of saying that teaching should be taken out of the hands and homes of the clergy, and then the clergy said a few things about him.

Pestalozzi at first met with very meager encouragement. Only poor and ignorant people entrusted their children to his care, and some of the parents were actually paid in money for the services of the children. The thought that the children were getting an education and being useful at the same time was quite beyond their comprehension

Pestalozzi educated by stealth. At first he took several boys and girls of eight, ten or twelve years of age, and had them work with him in his garden. They cared for fowls, looked after the sheep, milked the cows. The master worked with them, and as they worked they talked. Going to and from their duties, Pestalozzi would

252

call their attention to the wild birds, and to the flowers, plants and weeds. They would draw pictures of things, make collections of leaves and flowers, and keep a record of their observations and discoveries. Through keeping these records they learned to read and write and acquired the use of simple mathematics. Things they did not understand they would read about in the books found in the teacher's library. But books were secondary and quite incidental in the scheme of study. When work seemed to become irksome they would all stop and play games. At other times they would sit and just talk about what their work happened to suggest. If the weather was unpleasant, there was a shop where they made hoes and rakes and other tools they needed. They also built bird-houses, and made simple pieces of furniture, so all the pupils, girls and boys, became more or less familiar with carpenter's and blacksmith's tools. They patched their shoes, mended their clothing, and at times prepared their own food.

Pestalozzi found that the number of pupils he could look after in this way was not more than ten. But to his own satisfaction, at least, he proved that children taught by his method surpassed those who were given the regular set courses of instruction. His chief difficulties lay in the fact that the home did not co-operate with the school, and that there was always a tendency to " return to the blanket."

Pestalozzi wrote accounts of his experiments and

emphasized his belief that we should educate through the child's natural activities; also that all growth should be pleasurable. His shibboleth was, "From within, out." He thought education was a development and not an acquirement.

One of Pestalozzi's little pamphlets fell into the hands of Friedrich Froebel, architect's assistant, at Frankfort ✠ ✠

Froebel was twenty-two years old, and Fate had tossed him around from one thing to another since babyhood. All of his experiences had been of a kind that prepared his mind for the theories that Pestalozzi expressed ✠ Besides that, architecture had begun to pall upon him. "Those who can, do; those who can't, teach." This was said in derision, but it holds a grain of truth ✠ Froebel had a great desire to teach. Now, in Frankfort there was a Model School or a school for teachers, of which one Herr Gruner was master. This school was actually carrying out some of the practical methods suggested by Pestalozzi. Quite by accident Gruner and Froebel met. Gruner wanted a teacher who could teach by the Pestalozzi methods. Froebel straightway applied to Herr Gruner for the position. He was accepted as a combination janitor and instructor and worked for his board and ten marks, or two and a half dollars a week. ¶ The good-cheer and enthusiasm of Froebel won Gruner's heart. Together they discussed Pestalozzi and his works, read all that he had written, and opened

up a correspondence with the great man. This led to
an invitation that Froebel should visit him at his farm-
school, near Yverdon, in Switzerland.

Gruner supplied Froebel the necessary money to replace
his very seedy clothes for something better, and the
young man started away. It was a walk of more than
two hundred miles, but youth and enthusiasm count
such a tramp as an enjoyable trifle. Froebel wore his
seedy clothes and carried his good ones, and so he
appeared before the master spick and span.

Pestalozzi was sixty years old at this time, and his
hopes for the " new method " were still high. He had
met opposition, ridicule and indifference, and had spent
most of his little fortune in the fight, but he was still
at it and resolved to die in the harness.

Froebel was not disappointed in Pestalozzi, and certainly Pestalozzi was delighted and a bit amused at
the earnestness of the young man. Pestalozzi was
working in a very economical way, but all the place
lacked Froebel, in his exuberant imagination, made good.
¶ Froebel found much, for he had brought much with
him ❧ ❧

FRIEDRICH FROEBEL

ROEBEL returned to Frankfort from his visit to Pestalozzi, full of enthusiasm, and that is the commodity without which no teacher succeeds. Gruner allowed him to gravitate. And soon Froebel's room was the central point of interest for the whole school. But trouble was ahead for Froebel.

He had no college degrees. His pedagogic pedigree was very short. He hoped to live down his university record, but it followed him. Gruner's school was under government inspection, and the gentlemen with double chins, who came from time to time to look the place over, asked who this enthusiastic young person was, and why had the worthy janitor and ex-forester been so honored by promotion ✠ ✠

In truth, during his life, Froebel never quite escaped the taunt that he was not an educated man. That is to say, no college had ever supplied him an alphabetic appendage. He had been a forester, a farmer, an architect, a guardian for boys and a teacher of women, but no institution had ever said officially he was fit to teach men. ¶ Gruner tried to explain that there are two kinds of teachers: people who are teachers by nature, and those who have acquired the methods by long study. The first, having little to learn, and a love for the child, with a spontaneous quality of giving their all, succeed best. ¶ But poor Gruner's explanation did not explain.

Then the matter was gently explained to Froebel, and

he saw that in order to hold a place as teacher he must acquire a past. "Time will adjust it," he said, and started away on a second visit to Pestalozzi. His plan was to remain with the master long enough so he could secure a certificate of proficiency.

Again Pestalozzi welcomed the young man, and he slipped easily into the household and became both pupil and teacher. His willingness to work—to do the task that lay nearest him—his good-nature, his gratitude, won all hearts.

At this time the plan of sending boys to college with a tutor who was both a companion and a teacher, was in vogue with those who could afford it. It will be remembered that William and Alexander von Humboldt received their early education in this way—going with their tutor from university to university, teacher and pupils entering as special students, getting into the atmosphere of the place, soaking themselves full of it, and then going on.

And now behold, through Gruner or Pestalozzi or both, a woman of wealth with three boys to educate applied to Froebel to come over into Macedonia and help her ✄ It was in Eighteen Hundred Seven that Froebel became tutor in the Von Holzhausen family. He was twenty-five years old, and this was his first interview with wealth and leisure. That he was hungry enough to appreciate it need not be emphasized.

He got goodly glimpses of Gottingen, Berlin, and was

long enough at Jena to rub the blot off the 'scutcheon. A stay at Weimar, in the Goethe country, completed the four years' course.

The boys had grown to men, and proved their worth in after-years; but whether they had gotten as much from the migrations as their teacher is very doubtful. He was ripe for opportunity—they had had a surfeit of it ⚞ ⚞

Then came war. The order to arms and the rush of students to obey their country's call caught Froebel in the patriotic vortex, and he enlisted with his pupils. ¶ His service was honorable, even if not brilliant, and it had this advantage: the making of two friends, companions in arms, who caught the Pestalozzian fever, and lived out their lives preaching and teaching " the new method."

These men were William Middendorf and Henry Langenthal. This trinity of brothers evolved a bond as beautiful as it is rare in the realm of friendship. Forty years after their first meeting, Middendorf gave an oration over the dead body of Froebel that lives as a classic, breathing the love and faith that endure ⚞ And then Middendorf turned to his work, and dared prison and disgrace by upholding the Kindergarten System and the life and example of his dear, dead friend. The Kindergarten Idea would probably have been buried in the grave with Froebel—interred with his bones—were it not for Middendorf and Langenthal.

FRIEDRICH FROEBEL

HE first Kindergarten was established in Eighteen Hundred Thirty-six, at Blankenburg, a little village near Keilhau. Froebel was then fifty-four years old, happily married to a worthy woman who certainly did not hamper his work, even if she did not inspire it. He was childless, that all children might call him father.

The years had gone in struggles to found Normal Schools in Germany after the Pestalozzian and Gruner methods. But disappointment, misunderstanding and stupidity had followed Froebel. The set methods of the clergy, accusations of revolution and heresy, tilts with pious pedants as to the value of dead languages, all combined with his own lack of business shrewdness, had wrecked his various ventures.

Froebel's argument that women were better natural teachers than men on account of the mother-instinct, brought forth a retort from a learned monk to the effect that it was indelicate if not sinful for an unmarried female, who was not a nun, to study the natures of children. ¶ Parents with children old enough to go to school would not entrust their darlings with the teaching experimenter —this on the advice of their pastors.

Middendorf and Langenthal were still with him, partners in the disgrace or failure, for none was willing to give up the fight for education by the natural methods. ¶ A great thought and a great word came to them, all at once—out on the mountainside!

FRIEDRICH FROEBEL

Begin with the children before the school age, and call it the Kindergarten!

Hurrah! They shouted for joy, and ran down the hill to tell Frau Froebel.

The schools they had started before had been called, "The Institution for Teaching According to the Pestalozzi Method and the Natural Activities of the Child," "Institution for the Encouragement and Development of the Spontaneous Activities of the Pupil," and "Friedrich Froebel's School for the Growth of the Creative Instinct Which Makes for a Useful Character."

A school with such names, of course, failed. No one could remember it long enough to send his child there—it meant nothing to the mind not prepared for it ⚄ What's in a name? Everything. Books sell or become dead stock on the name. Commodities the same. Railroads must have a name people are not afraid to pronounce. ¶ The officers of the law came and asked to see Froebel's license for manufacturing. Others asked as to the nature of his wares, and one dignitary called and asked, "Is Herr Pestalozzi in?"

The Kindergarten! The new name took. The children remembered it. Overworked mothers liked the word and were glad to let the little other-mothers take the children to the Kindergarten, certainly.

Froebel had grown used to disappointments—he was an optimist by nature. He saw the good side of everything, including failure.

260

He made the best of necessity. And now it was very clear to him that education must begin " a hundred years before the child is born." He would reach the home and the mother through the children. " It will take three generations to prove the truth of the Kindergarten Idea," he said.

And so the songs, the gifts, the games—all had to be invented, defended, tried and tried again. Pestalozzi had a plan for teaching the youth; now a plan had to be devised for teaching the child. Love was the keystone, and joy, unselfishness and unswerving faith in the Natural or Divine impulses of humanity crowned the structure.

FRIEDRICH FROEBEL

ROEBEL invented the schoolma'am. That is, he discovered the raw product and adapted it. He even coined the word, and it struck the world as being so very funny that we forthwith adopted it as a term of provincial pleasantry and quasi-reproach. The original term used was " school mother," but when it reached these friendly shores we translated it " schoolmarm." Then we tittered, also sneezed

Froebel died in Eighteen Hundred Fifty-two. His first Kindergarten was not a success until he was nearly sixty years old, but the idea had been perfecting itself in his mind more or less unconsciously for over thirty years

He had been thinking, writing, working, experimenting all these years on the subject of education, and he had become well-nigh discouraged. He had observed that six was the " school age." That is, no child could go to school until he was six years old—then his education began

But Froebel had been teaching in a country school and boarding 'round, and he had discovered that long before this the child had been learning by observing and playing, and that these were formative influences, quite as potent as actual school.

In the big families where Froebel boarded, he noticed that the older girls took charge of the younger ones. So, often a girl of ten, with dresses to her knees, carried one baby in her arms and two toddled behind her, and this child of ten was really the other-mother. The true mother worked in the fields or toiled at her housework, and the little other-mother took the children out to play and thus amused them while the mother worked ⚸ The desire of Froebel was to educate the race, but what are a few hours a day in a schoolroom with a totally unsympathetic home environment!

To reach and interest the mother in the problem of education was well-nigh impossible. Toil, deprivation, poverty, had killed all the romance and enthusiasm in her heart. She was the victim of arrested development; but the little other-mother was a child, impressionable, immature, and she could be taught. The home must co-operate with the school, otherwise all the school can teach will be forgotten in the home. Froebel saw, too, that often the little other-mother was so over-worked in the care of her charges that she was taken from school. Besides, the idea was abroad that education was mostly for boys, anyway.

And here Froebel stepped in and proved himself a law-breaker, just as Ben Lindsey was when he inaugurated the juvenile court and waived the entire established legal procedure, even to the omission of swearing his witnesses, and believed in the little truant even though he lied. Froebel told the little other-mothers to come to school anyway and bring the babies with them ⚸ And then he set to work showing these girls how to amuse, divert and teach the babies. And he used to say the babies taught him.

Some of these half-grown girls showed a rare adaptability as teachers. They combined mother-love and the teaching instinct ✄ Froebel utilized their services in teaching others in order that he might teach them ✄ He saw that the teacher is the one who gets the most out of the lessons, and that the true teacher is a learner. These girl teachers he called school-mothers, and thus was evolved the word and the person.

Froebel founded the first normal and model school for the education of women as teachers, and this was less than a hundred years ago.

The years went by and the little mothers had children of their own, and these children were the ones that formed the first actual, genuine kindergarten ✄ Also, these were the mothers who formed the first mothers' clubs ✄ And it was the success of these clubs that attracted the attention of the authorities, who could not imagine any other purpose for a club than to hatch a plot against the government.

Anyway, a system which taught that women were just as wise, just as good and just as capable as men—just as well fitted by nature to teach—would upset the clergy. If women can break into the school, they will also break into the church. Moreover, the encouragement of play was atrocious. Mein Gott, or words to that effect, play in a schoolroom! Why, even a fool

264

would know that that is the one thing that stood in the way of education, the one fly in the pedagogic ointment. If Mynheer Froebel would please invent a way to do away with play in schoolrooms, he would be given a pension.

The idea that children were good by nature was rank heresy. Where does the doctrine of regeneration come in, and how about being born again! The natural man is at enmity toward God. We are conceived in sin and born in iniquity. The Bible says it again and again ⚘ And here comes a man who thinks he knows more than all the priests and scholars who have ever lived, and fills the heads of fool women with the idea that they are born to teach instead of to work in the fields and keep house and wait on men.

Mein Gott in Himmel, the women know too much, already! If this thing keeps on, men will have to get off the earth, and women and children will run the world, and do it by means of play. Aha! What does Solomon say? Spare the rod and spoil the child. Aber nicht, say these girls.

This thing has got to stop before Germany becomes the joke of mankind—the cat-o'-nine-tails for anybody who uses the word kindergarten!

FRIEDRICH FROEBEL

UFFER little children to come unto me, and forbid them not, for of such is the Kingdom of Heaven." Had the man who uttered these words been given a little encouragement, he probably would have inaugurated a child-garden and provided a place and environment where little souls could have bloomed and blossomed. He was by nature a teacher, and his best pupils were women and children. Male men are apt to think they already know and so are immune from ideas.

Jerusalem, nineteen hundred years ago, was about where Berlin was in Eighteen Hundred Fifty. In both instances the proud priest and the aristocrat-soldier were supreme. And both were quite satisfied with their own mental attainments and educational methods. They were sincere. It was a very similar combination that crucified Jesus to that which placed an interdict on Friedrich Froebel, making the Kindergarten a crime, and causing the speedy death of one of the gentlest, noblest, purest men who have ever blessed this earth. ¶ Froebel was just seventy when he passed out. " His eye was not dimmed nor his natural force abated "— he was filled with enthusiasm and hope as never before. His ideas were spreading—success, at last, was at the door, he had interested the women and proved the fitness of women to teach—his mothers' clubs were numerous—love was the watchword. And in the midst of this flowering time, the official order came, without

266

FRIEDRICH FROEBEL

warning, apology or explanation, and from which there
was no appeal. The same savagery, chilled with fear,
that sent Richard Wagner into exile, crushed the life
and broke the heart of Friedrich Froebel. But these
names now are the pride and glory of the land that
once scorned them. Men who govern should be those
with a reasonable doubt concerning their own infalli-
bility, and an earnest faith in men, women and children.
To teach is better than to rule. We are all children in
the Kindergarten of God.

HYPATIA

Neo-Platonism is a progressive philosophy, and does not expect to state final conditions to men whose minds are finite. Life is an unfoldment, and the further we travel the more truth we can comprehend. To understand the things that are at our door is the best preparation for understanding those that lie beyond.

—*Hypatia*

HYPATIA

HYPATIA

HE father of Hypatia was Theon, a noted mathematician and astronomer of Alexandria. He would have been regarded as a very great man had he not been cast into the shadow by his daughter. Let male parents beware ✄ ✄

At that time, astronomy and astrology were one. Mathematics was useful, not for purposes of civil engineering, but principally in figuring out where a certain soul, born under a given planet, would be at a certain time in the future.

No information comes to us about the mother of Hypatia—she was so busy with housework that her existence is a matter of assumption or a priori reasoning; thus, given a daughter, we assume the existence of a mother ✄ ✄

Hypatia was certainly the daughter of her father. He was her tutor, teacher, playmate. All he knew he taught to her, and before she was twenty she had been informed by him of a fact which she had previously guessed—that considerable of his so-called knowledge was conjecture ✄ ✄

Theon taught his daughter that all systems of religion that pretend to teach the whole truth were to a great degree false and fraudulent. He explained to her that

271

his own profession of astronomy and astrology was only for other people. By instructing her in all religions she grew to know them comparatively, and so none took possession of her to the exclusion of new truth. To have a religion thrust upon you, and be compelled to believe in it or suffer social ostracism, is to be cheated of the right to make your own. In degree it is letting another live your life. A child does not need a religion until he is old enough to evolve it, and then he must not be robbed of the right of independent thinking by having a fully-prepared plan of salvation handed out to him. The brain needs exercise as much as the body, and vicarious thinking is as erroneous as vicarious exercise. Strength comes from personal effort. To think is natural, and if not intimidated or coerced the man will evolve a philosophy of life that is useful and beneficent ✄ Religious mania is a result of dwelling on a borrowed religion. If let alone no man would become insane on religious topics, for the religion he would evolve would be one of joy, laughter and love, not one of misery or horror. The religion that contemplates misery and woe is one devised by priestcraft for a purpose, and that purpose is to rule and rob. From the blunt ways of the road we get a polite system of intimidation which makes the man pay. It is robbery reduced to a system, and finally piously believed in by the robbers, who are hypnotized into the belief that they are doing God's service ✄ ✄

HYPATIA

"All formal dogmatic religions are fallacious and must never be accepted by self-respecting persons as final," said Theon to Hypatia. "Reserve your right to think, for even to think wrongly is better than not to think at all." ❧ ❧

Theon gave lectures, and had private classes in esoterics, wherein the innermost secrets of divinity were imparted. Also, he had a plan for the transmutation of metals and a recipe for perpetual youth. When he had nothing else to do, he played games with his daughter.

At twenty-one Hypatia had mastered the so-called art of Rhetoric, or the art of expression by vocal speech ❧ It will be remembered that the Romans considered rhetoric, or the art of the rhetor, or orator, as first in importance. To impress people by your personal presence they regarded as the gift of gifts.

This idea seems to have been held by the polite world up to the Italian Renaissance, when the art of printing was invented and the written word came to be regarded as more important than the spoken. One lives, and the other dies on the air, existing only in memory, growing attenuated and diluted as it is transferred. The revival of sculpture and painting also helped oratory to take its proper place as one of the polite arts, and not a thing to be centered upon to the exclusion of all else.

Theon set out to produce a perfect human being; and whether his charts, theorems and formulas made up a complete law of eugenics, or whether it was dumb luck, this we know: he nearly succeeded. Hypatia was five feet nine, and weighed one hundred thirty-five pounds. This when she was twenty. She could walk ten miles without fatigue; swim, row, ride horseback and climb mountains. Through a series of gentle calisthenics invented by her father, combined with breathing exercises, she had developed a body of rarest grace. Her head had corners, as once Professor O. S. Fowler told us that a woman's head must have, if she is to think and act with purpose and precision.

So having evolved this rare beauty of face, feature and bodily grace, combined with superior strength and vitality, Hypatia took up her father's work and gave lectures on astronomy, mathematics, astrology and rhetoric, while he completed his scheme for the transmutation of metals. Hypatia's voice was flute-like, and used always well within its compass, so as never to rasp or tire the organs. Theon knew the proper care of nose and throat, a knowledge which with us moderns is all too rare. Hypatia told of and practised the vocal ellipse, the pause, the glide, the slide and the gentle, deliberate tones that please and impress. That the law of suggestion was known to her was very evident, and certain it is that she practised hypnotism in her classes, and seemed to know as much about the origin of the mysterious agent as we do now, even though she never tagged or labeled it.

One very vital thought she worked out was, that the

young mind is plastic, impressionable and accepts without question all that it is told. The young receive their ideas from their elders, and ideas once impressed upon this plastic plate of the mind can not be removed &
Said Hypatia: "Fables should be taught as fables, myths as myths, and miracles as poetic fancies. To teach superstitions as truths is a most terrible thing. The child-mind accepts and believes them, and only through great pain and perhaps tragedy can he be in after-years relieved of them. In fact, men will fight for a superstition quite as quickly as for a living truth— often more so, since a superstition is so intangible you can not get at it to refute it, but truth is a point of view, and so is changeable."

Gradually, over the mind of the beautiful and gifted Hypatia, there came stealing a doubt concerning the value of her own acquirements, since these were "acquirements," and not evolutions or convictions gathered from experience, but things implanted upon her plastic mind by her father.

In this train of thought Hypatia had taken a step in advance of her father, for he seems to have had a dogmatic belief in a few things incapable of demonstration; but these things he taught to the plastic mind, just the same as the things he knew. Theon was a dogmatic liberal. Possibly the difference between an illiberal Unitarian and a liberal Catholic is microscopic.

Hypatia clearly saw that knowledge is the distilled

essence of our intuitions, corroborated by experience. But belief is the impress made upon our minds when we are under the spell of or in subjection to another ✠ These things caused the poor girl many unhappy hours, which fact, in itself, is proof of her greatness. Only superior people have a capacity for doubting.

Probably not one person in a million ever gets away far enough from his mind to take a look at it, and see the wheels go round. Opinions become ossified and the man goes through life hypnotizing others, never realizing for an instant that in youth he was hypnotized and that he has never been able to cast off the hypnosis ✠ This is what our pious friends mean when they say, " Give me the child until he is ten years old and you may have him afterward." That is, they can take the child in his plastic age and make impressions on his mind that are indelible. Reared in an orthodox Jewish family a child will grow up a dogmatic Jew, and argue you on the Talmud six nights and days together ✠ Catholic, Presbyterian, Baptist, the same. I once knew an Arapahoe Indian who was taken to Massachusetts when four years old. He grew up not only with New England prejudices, but with a New England accent, and saved his pennies to give to missionaries that they might " convert " the Red Men.

When the suspicion seized upon the soul of Hypatia that her mind was but a wax impression taken from her father's, she began to make plans to get away from him. Her efforts at explanations were futile, but when placed upon the general ground that she wished to travel, see the world and meet people of learning and worth, her father acquiesced and she started away on her journeyings. He wanted to go, too, but this was the one thing she did not desire, and he never knew nor could know why.

She spent several months at Athens, where her youth, beauty and learning won her entry into the houses of the most eminent. It was the same at Rome and in various other cities of Italy. Money may give you access to good society, but talent is always an open sesame. She traveled like a princess and was received as one, yet she had no title nor claim to nobility nor station. Beauty of itself is not a credential—rather it is an object of suspicion, unless it goes with intellect ๕ Hypatia gave lectures on mathematics; and there was a fallacy abroad then as there is now that the feminine mind is not mathematical. That the great men whom Hypatia met in each city were first amazed and then abashed by her proficiency in mathematics is quite probable. Some few male professors being in that peculiar baldheaded hypnotic state when feminine charms dazzle and lure, listened in rapture as Hypatia dissolved logarithms and melted calculi, and not understanding a word she said, declared that she was the goddess Minerva, reincarnated. Her coldness on near approach confirmed their suspicions.

HYPATIA

UST how long a time Hypatia spent upon her pilgrimage, visiting all of the great living philosophers, we do not know. Some accounts have it one year, others ten ✄ Probably the pilgrimages were extended over a good many years, and were not continuous. Several philosophers proved their humanity by offering to marry her, and a prince or two did likewise, we are credibly informed. To these persistent suitors, however, Hypatia gently broke the news that she was wedded to truth, which is certainly a pretty speech, even if it is poor logic. The fact was, however, that Hypatia never met a man whose mind matched her own, otherwise logic would have bolstered love, instead of discarding it ✄ Travel, public speaking and meeting people of note form a strong trinity of good things. The active mind is the young mind, and it is more than the dream of a poet which declares that Hypatia was always young and always beautiful, and that even Father Time was so in love with her that he refused to take toll from her, as he passed with his hourglass and scythe ✄ In degree she had followed the example of her great prototype, Plotinus, and had made herself master of all religions. She knew too much of all philosophies to believe implicitly in any. Alexandria was then the intellectual center of the world. People who resided there called it the hub of the universe. It was the meeting-place of the East and the West.

278

HYPATIA

And Hypatia, with her Thursday lectures, was the chief intellectual factor of Alexandria.

Her philosophy she called Neo-Platonism. It was Plato distilled through the psychic alembic of Hypatia. Just why the human mind harks back and likes to confirm itself by building on another, it would be interesting to inquire. To explain Moses; to supply a key to the Scriptures; to found a new School of Philosophy on the assumption that Plato was right, but was not understood until the Then and There, is alluring. And now the pilgrims came from Athens, and Rome, and the Islands of the Sea to sit at the feet of Hypatia.

279

HYPATIA

YPATIA was born in the year Three Hundred Fifty-five, and died in Four Hundred Fifteen. She exerted an influence in Alexandria not unlike that which Mrs. Eddy exerted in Boston. She was a person who divided society into two parts: those who regarded her as an oracle of light, and those who looked upon her as an emissary of darkness.

Strong men paid her the compliment of using immoderate language concerning her teaching. But whether they spoke ill or well of her matters little now. The point is this: they screeched, sneezed, or smiled on those who refused to acknowledge the power of Hypatia. Some professors of learning tried to waive her; priests gently pooh-poohed her; and some elevated an eyebrow and asked how the name was spelled. Others, still, inquired, " Is she sincere? "

She was the Ralph Waldo Emerson of her day. Her philosophy was Transcendentalism. In fact, she might be spoken of as the original charter member of the Concord School of Philosophy. Her theme was the New Thought, for New Thought is the oldest form of thought of which we know. Its distinguishing feature is its antiquity. Socrates was really the first to express the New Thought, and he got his cue from Pythagoras. ¶ The ambition of Hypatia was to revive the flowering-time of Greece, when Socrates and Plato walked arm in arm through the streets of Athens, followed by the greatest group of intellectuals the world has ever seen ⚓

280

HYPATIA

It was charged against Hypatia that Aspasia was her ideal, and that her ambition was to follow in the footsteps of the woman who was beloved by Pericles. If so, it was an ambition worthy of a very great soul. Hypatia, however, did not have her Pericles, and never married. That she should have had love experiences was quite natural, and that various imaginary romances should have been credited to her was also to be expected ✺ Hypatia was nearly a thousand years removed from the time of Pericles and Aspasia, but to bridge the gulf of time with imagination was easy. Yet Hypatia thought that the New Platonism should surpass the old, for the world had had the Age of Augustus to build upon. ¶ Hypatia's immediate prototype was Plotinus, who was born two hundred four years after Christ, and lived to be seventy. Plotinus was the first person to use the phrase " Neo-Platonism," and so the philosophy of Hypatia might be called " The New Neo-Platonism." ¶ To know but one religion is not to know that one ✺ In fact, superstition consists in this one thing—faith in one religion, to the exclusion of all others. To know one philosophy is to know none. They are all comparative, and each serves as a small arc of the circle. A man living in a certain environment, with a certain outlook, describes the things he sees; and out of these, plus what he imagines, is shaped his philosophy of life. If he is repressed, suppressed, frightened, he will not see very much, and what he does see will be out of focus.

281

HYPATIA

Spiritual strabismus and mental myopia are the results of vicarious peeps at the universe. All formal religions have taught that to look for yourself was bad. The peephole through the roof of his garret cost Copernicus his liberty, but it was worth the price.

Plotinus made a study of all philosophies—all religions. He traveled through Egypt, Greece, Assyria, India. He became an "adept", and discovered how easily the priest drifts into priestcraft, and fraud steps in with legerdemain and miracle to amend the truth. As if to love humanity were not enough to recommend the man, they have him turn water into wine and walk on the water.

¶Out of the labyrinth of history and speculation Plotinus returned to Plato as a basis or starting-point for all of the truth which man can comprehend. Plotinus believed in all religions, but had absolute faith in none. It will be remembered that Aristotle and Plato parted as to the relative value of poetry and science—science being the systematized facts of Nature. Plotinus comes in and says that both were right, and each was like every good man who exaggerates the importance of his own calling. In his ability to see the good in all things, Hypatia placed Plotinus ahead of Plato, but even then she says: "Had there been no Plato, there would have been no Plotinus; although Plotinus surpassed Plato, yet it is plain that Plato, the inspirer of Plotinus and so many more, is the one man whom philosophy can not spare. Hail, Plato!!"

282

HYPATIA

HE writings of Hypatia have all disappeared, save as her words come to us, quoted by her contemporaries. If the Essays of Emerson should all be swept away, the man would still live in the quotations from his pen, given to us by every writer of worth who has put pencil to paper during the last fifty years. So lives Sappho, and thus did Charles Kingsley secure the composite of the great woman who lives and throbs through his book. Legend pictures her as rarely beautiful, with grace, poise and power, plus. ¶ She was sixty when she died. History kindly records it forty-five—and all picture her as a beautiful and attractive woman to the last. The psychic effects of a gracefully-gowned first reader, with sonorous voice, using gesture with economy, and packing the pauses with feeling, have never been fully formulated, analyzed and explained. Throngs came to hear Hypatia lecture— came from long distances, and listened hungrily, and probably all they took away was what they brought, except a great feeling of exhilaration and enthusiasm. To send the hearer away stepping light, and his heart beating fast—this is oratory—which is n't so much to bestow facts, as it is to impart a feeling. This Hypatia surely did. Her theme was Neo-Platonism. " Neo " means new, and all New Thought harks back to Plato, who was the mouthpiece of Socrates. " Say what you will, you 'll find it all in Plato." Neo-Platonism is our New Thought, and New Thought is Neo-Platonism.

HYPATIA

There are two kinds of thought: New Thought and Secondhand Thought. New Thought is made up of thoughts you, yourself, think. The other kind is supplied to you by jobbers. The distinguishing feature of New Thought is its antiquity. Of necessity it is older than Secondhand Thought. All genuine New Thought is true for the person who thinks it. It only turns sour and becomes error when not used, and when the owner forces another to accept it. It then becomes a secondhand revelation. All New Thought is revelation, and secondhand revelations are errors half-soled with stupidity and heeled with greed.

Very often we are inspired to think by others, but in our hearts we have the New Thought; and the person, the book, the incident, merely remind us that it is already ours. New Thought is always simple; Secondhand Thought is abstruse, complex, patched, peculiar, costly, and is passed out to be accepted, not understood. That no one comprehends it is often regarded as a recommendation.

For instance, "Thou shalt not make unto thyself any graven image," is Secondhand Thought. The first man who said it may have known what it meant, but surely it is nothing to us. However, that does not keep us from piously repeating it, and having our children memorize it ⚘ ⚘

We model in clay or wax, and carve if we can, and give honors to those who do, and this is well. This

284

commandment is founded on the fallacy that graven images are gods, whatever that is. The command adds nothing to our happiness, nor does it shape our conduct, nor influence our habits. Everybody knows and admits its futility, yet we are unable to eliminate it from our theological system. It is strictly secondhand—worse, it is junk.

Conversely, the admonition, " Be gentle and keep your voice low," is New Thought, since all but savages know its truth, comprehend its import, and appreciate its excellence ✲ ✲

Dealers in Secondhand Thought always declare that theirs is the only genuine, and that all other is spurious and dangerous.

Dealers in New Thought say, " Take this only as it appeals to you as your own—accept it all, or in part, or reject it all—and in any event, do not believe it merely because I say so."

New Thought is founded on the laws of your own nature, and its shibboleth is, " Know Thyself."

Secondhand Thought is founded on authority, and its war-cry is, " Pay and Obey."

New Thought offers you no promise of paradise or eternal bliss if you accept it; nor does it threaten you with everlasting hell, if you don't. All it offers is unending work, constant effort, new difficulties; beyond each success is a new trial. Its only satisfactions are that you are allowing your life to unfold itself according to the laws of its nature. And these laws are divine, therefore you yourself are divine, just as you allow the divine to possess your being. New Thought allows the currents of divinity to flow through you unobstructed.

Secondhand Thought affords no plan of elimination; it tends to congestion, inflammation, disease and disintegration ৺ ৺

New Thought holds all things lightly, gently, easily—even thought. It works for a healthy circulation, and tends to health, happiness and well-being now and hereafter. It does not believe in violence, force, coercion or resentment, because all these things react on the doer. It has faith that all men, if not interfered with by other men, will eventually evolve New Thought, and do for themselves what is best and right, beautiful and true ৺ ৺

Secondhand Thought has always had first in its mind the welfare of the dealer. The rights of the consumer, beyond keeping him in subjection, were not considered. Indeed, its chief recommendation has been that " it is a good police system."

New Thought considers only the user. To " Know Thyself " is all there is of it.

When a creator of New Thought goes into the business of retailing his product, he often forgets to live it, and soon is transformed into a dealer in Secondhand Thought ৺ ৺

That is the way all purveyors in secondhand revelation

286

begin. In their anxiety to succeed, they call in the police. The blessing that is compulsory is not wholly good, and any system of morals which has to be forced on us is immoral. New Thought is free thought. Its penalty is responsibility. You either have to live it, or else lose it. Its reward is Freedom.

T was only a little more than a hundred years before the time of Hypatia that the Roman Empire became Christian. When Constantine embraced Christianity, all of his loyal subjects were from that moment Christians—Christians by edict, but Pagans by character, for the natures of men can not be changed by the passing of a resolution. From that time every Pagan temple became a Christian church, and every Pagan priest a Christian preacher.

Alexandria was under the rule of a Roman Prefect, or Governor. It had been the policy of Rome to exercise great tolerance in religious matters. There was a State Religion, to be sure, but it was for the nobility or those who helped make the State possible. To look after the thinking of the plain people was quite superfluous— they were allowed their vagaries.

The Empire had been bold, brazen, cruel, coercive in its lust for power, but people who paid were reasonably safe. And now the Church was coming into competition with the State and endeavoring to reduce spoliation to a system.

To keep the people down and under by mental suppression—by the engine of superstition—were cheaper and more effective than to employ force or resort to the old-time methods of shows, spectacles, pensions and costly diversions. When the Church took on the functions of the State, and sought to substitute the gentle Christ for Cæsar, she had to recast the teachings of Christ. Then for the first time coercion and love dwelt side by side. " Depart from me, ye cursed, into everlasting fire prepared for the devil and his angels," and like passages were slipped into the Scriptures as matters of wise expediency. This was continued for many hundred years, and was considered quite proper and legitimate. It was slavery under a more subtle form.

¶ The Bishop of Alexandria clashed with Orestes the Prefect. To hold the people under by psychologic methods was better than the old plans of alternate bribery and force—so argued the Bishop.

Orestes had come under the spell of Hypatia, and the Republic of Plato was saturating his mind.

" To rule by fettering the mind through fear of punishment in another world is just as base as to use force," said Hypatia in one of her lectures. Orestes sat in the audience and as she spoke the words he clapped his hands. The news was carried to the Bishop, who gently declared that he would excommunicate him.

Orestes sent word back that the Emperor should be informed of how this Bishop was misusing his office by making threats of where he could land people he did not like, in another world. Neither the Bishop nor the Prefect could unseat each other—both derived their power from the Emperor. For Orestes to grow interested in the teachings of Hypatia, instead of siding with the Bishop, was looked upon by the loyalists as little short of treason ✄ ✄

289

Orestes tried to defend himself by declaring that the policy of the Cæsars had always been one of great leniency toward all schools of philosophy. Then he quoted Hypatia to the effect that a fixed, formal and dogmatic religion would paralyze the minds of men and make the race, in time, incapable of thought ᴣᴣ Therefore, the Bishop should keep his place, and not try to usurp the functions of the police. In fact, it was better to think wrongly than not to think at all. We learn to think by thinking, and if the threats of the Bishop were believed at all, it would mean the death of science and philosophy.

The Bishop made answer by declaring that Hypatia was endeavoring to found a Church of her own, with Pagan Greece as a basis. He intimated, too, that the relationship of Orestes with Hypatia was very much the same as that which once existed between Cleopatra and Mark Antony. He called her " that daughter of Ptolemy," and by hints and suggestions made it appear that she would, if she could, set up an Egyptian Empire in this same city of Alexandria where Cleopatra once so proudly reigned.

The excitement increased. The followers of Hypatia were necessarily few in numbers. They were thinkers —and to think is a task. To believe is easy. The Bishop promised his followers a paradise of ease and rest. He also threatened disbelievers with the pains of hell. A promise on this side—a threat on that! Is it not a wonder that a man ever lived who put his honest thought against such teaching when launched by men clothed in almost absolute authority!

Hypatia might have lived yesterday, and her death at the hands of a mob was an accident that might have occurred in Boston, where a respectable company once threw a rope around the neck of a good man and ran him through streets supposed to be sacred to liberty and free speech.

A mob is made up of cotton waste, saturated with oil, and a focused idea causes spontaneous combustion. Let a fire occur in almost any New York State village, and the town turns wrecker, and loot looms large in the limited brain of the villager. Civilization is a veneer. ¶ When one sees emotionalism run riot at an evangelistic revival, and five thousand people are trooping through an undesirable district at midnight, how long, think you, would a strong voice of opposition be tolerated?

Hypatia was set upon by a religious mob as she was going in her carriage from her lecture-hall to her home. She was dragged to a near-by church with the intent of making her publicly recant, but the embers became a blaze, and the blaze became a conflagration, and the leaders lost control. The woman's clothes were torn from her back, her hair torn from her head, her body beaten to a pulp, dismembered, and then to hide all traces of the crime and distribute the guilt so no one

291

person could be blamed, a funeral-pyre quickly consumed the remains of what but an hour before had been a human being. Daylight came, and the sun's rays could not locate the guilty ones.

Orestes made a report of the affair, resigned his office, asked the Government at Rome to investigate, and fled from the city. Had Orestes endeavored to use his soldiery against the Bishop, the men in the ranks would have revolted. The investigation was postponed from time to time for lack of witnesses, and finally it was given out by the Bishop that Hypatia had gone to Athens, and there had been no mob and no tragedy. ¶ The Bishop nominated a successor to Orestes, and the new official was confirmed.

Dogmatism as a police system was supreme.

It continued until the time of Dante, or the Italian Renaissance. The reign of Religious Dogmatism was supreme for well-nigh a thousand years—we call it the Dark Ages.

SAINT BENEDICT

If any pilgrim monk come from distant parts, if with wish as a guest to dwell in the monastery, and will be content with the customs which he finds in the place, and do not perchance by his lavishness disturb the monastery, but is simply content with what he finds: he shall be received, for as long a time as he desires. If, indeed, he find fault with anything, or expose it, reasonably, and with the humility of charity, the Abbot shall discuss it prudently, lest perchance God had sent for this very thing. But, if he have been found gossipy and contumacious in the time of his sojourn as guest, not only ought he not to be joined to the body of the monastery, but also it shall be said to him, honestly, that he must depart. If he does not go, let two stout monks, in the name of God, explain the matter to him.

—*St. Benedict*

SAINT BENEDICT

ST. BENEDICT

AS the traveler journeys through Southern Italy, Sicily and certain parts of what was Ancient Greece, he will see broken arches, parts of viaducts, and now and again a single, beautiful column pointing to the sky. All about is the desert or solitary pastures, and only this white milestone, marking the path of the centuries and telling in its own silent, solemn and impressive way of a day that is dead.

In the Fifth Century a monk called Simeon the Syrian, and known to us as Simeon Stylites, having taken the vow of chastity, poverty and obedience, began to fear greatly lest he might not be true to his pledge. And that he might live absolutely beyond reproach, always in public view, free from temptation, and free from the tongue of scandal, he decided to live in the world, and still not be of it. To this end he climbed to the top of a marble column, sixty feet high, and there on the capstone he lived a life beyond reproach.

Simeon was then twenty-four years old.

The environment was circumscribed, but there was outlook, sunshine, ventilation—three good things. But beyond these the place had certain disadvantages. The capstone was a little less than three feet square, so

Simeon could not lie down. He slept sitting, with his head bowed between his knees, and indeed, in this posture he passed most of his time. Any recklessness in movement, and he would have slipped from his perilous position and been dashed to death upon the stones beneath ⚜ ⚜

As the sun arose he stood up, just for a few moments, and held his arms out in greeting, blessing and prayer. Three times during the day did he thus stretch his cramped limbs, and pray with his face to the East. At such times those who stood near shared in his prayers, and went away blessed and refreshed.

How did Simeon get to the top of the column?

Well, his companions at the monastery, a mile away, said he was carried there in the night by a miraculous power; that he went to sleep in his stone cell and awoke on the pillar. Other monks said that Simeon had gone to pay his respects to a fair lady, and in wrath God had caught him and placed him on high. The probabilities are, however, Terese, as viewed by an unbeliever, that he shot a line over the column with a bow and arrow and then drew up a rope ladder and ascended with ease. ¶ However, in the morning the simple people of the scattered village saw the man on the column. All day he stayed there. The next day he was still there.

The days passed, with the scorching heat of the midday sun, and the cool winds of the night.

Still Simeon kept his place.

296

ST. BENEDICT

The rainy season came on. When the nights were cold and dark, Simeon sat there with bowed head, and drew the folds of his single garment, a black robe, over his face ❦ ❦

Another season passed; the sun again grew warm, then hot, and the sand-storms raged and blew, when the people below almost lost sight of the man on the column. Some prophesied he would be blown off, but the morning light revealed his form, naked from the waist up, standing with hands outstretched to greet the rising sun. ¶ Once each day, as darkness gathered, a monk came with a basket containing a bottle of goat's milk and a little loaf of black bread, and Simeon dropped down a rope and drew up the basket.

Simeon never spoke, for words are folly, and to the calls of saint or sinner he made no reply. He lived in a perpetual attitude of adoration.

Did he suffer? During those first weeks he must have suffered terribly and horribly. There was no respite nor rest from the hard surface of the rock, and aching muscles could find no change from the cramped and perilous position. If he fell, it was damnation for his soul—all were agreed as to this.

But man's body and mind accommodate themselves to almost any condition. One thing at least, Simeon was free from economic responsibilities, free from social cares and intrusion. Bores with sad stories of unappreciated lives and fond hopes unrealized, never broke in

297

upon his peace. He was not pressed for time. No frivolous dame of tarnished fame sought to share with him his perilous perch. The people on a slow schedule, ten minutes late, never irritated his temper. His correspondence never got in a heap.

Simeon kept no track of the days, having no engagements to meet, or offices to perform, beyond the prayers at morn, midday and night.

Memory died in him, the hurts became calluses, the world-pain died out of his heart, to cling became a habit. Language was lost in disuse. The food he ate was minimum in quantity; sensation ceased, and the dry, hot winds reduced bodily tissue to a dessicated something called a saint—loved, feared and reverenced for his fortitude ✠ ✠

This pillar, which had once graced the portal of a pagan temple, again became a place of pious pilgrimage, and people flocked to Simeon's rock, so that they might be near when he stretched out his black, bony hands to the East, and the spirit of Almighty God, for a space, hovered close around.

So much attention did the abnegation of Simeon attract that various other pillars, marking the ruins of art and greatness gone, in that vicinity, were crowned by pious monks. Their thought was to show how Christianity had triumphed over heathenism. Imitators were numerous. About that time the Bishops in assembly asked, " Is Simeon sincere? " To test the matter of Simeon's

pride, he was ordered to come down from his retreat.
¶ As to his chastity, there was little doubt, and his
poverty was beyond question; but how about obedience
to his superiors?

The order was shouted up to him in a Bishop's voice
—he must let down his rope, draw up a ladder, and
descend ℁ ℁

Straightway Simeon made preparation to obey. And
then the Bishops relented and cried, " We have changed
our minds, and now order you to remain! "

Simeon lifted his hands in adoration and thankfulness
and renewed his lease.

And so he lived on and on and on—he lived on the top
of that pillar, never once descending, for thirty years.
¶ All of his former companions grew a-weary; one
by one they died, and the monastery-bells tolled their
requiem as they were laid to rest. Did Simeon hear the
bells and say, " Soon it will be my turn "?

Probably not. His senses had flown, for what good were
they! The young monk who now at eventide brought
the basket with the bottle of goat's milk and the loaf
of dry bread was born since Simeon had taken his place
on the pillar. " He has always been there," the people
said, and crossed themselves hurriedly.

But one evening when the young monk came with his
basket, no line was dropped from above. He waited and
then called aloud, but all in vain.

When sunrise came, there sat the monk, his face between

his knees, the folds of his black robe drawn over his head. But he did not rise and lift his hands in prayer. ¶ All day he sat there, motionless.

The people watched in whispered silence. Would he arise at sundown and pray, and with outstretched hands bless the assembled pilgrims?

But as they watched a vulture came sailing slowly through the blue ether, and circled nearer and nearer; and off on the horizon was another—and still another, circling nearer and nearer.

N humanity's march of progress there are a vanguard and a rearguard. The rearguard dwindles away into a mob of camp-followers, who follow for diversion and to escape starvation. Both the vanguard and the rearguard are out of step with the main body, and therefore both are despised by the many who make up the rank and file. ¶ And yet, out of pity, the main body supplies ambulances and "slum-workers," who aim to do "good"—but this good is always for the rearguard and the camp-followers, never for those who lead the line of march, and take the risk of ambush and massacre.

But this scorn of the vanguard has its recompense—often delayed, no doubt—but those who compose it are the only ones whom history honors and Clio crowns. If they get recognition in life, it is wrung tardily from an ungrateful and ungracious world. And this is the most natural thing in the world, and it would be a miracle if it were otherwise, for the very virtue of the vanguard consists in that their acts outrun human sympathy

Benedict was a scout of civilization. In his day he led the vanguard. He found the prosperous part of the world given over to greed and gluttony. The so-called religious element was in partnership with fraud, superstition, ignorance, incompetence, and an asceticism like that of Simeon Stylites, leading to nothing.

Men know the good and grow through experience. To

realize the worthlessness of place and position and of riches, you must have been at some time in possession of these. Benedict was born into a rich Roman family, in the year Four Hundred Eighty. His parents wished to educate him for the law, so he would occupy a position of honor in the State.

But at sixteen years of age, at that critical time when nerves are vibrating between manhood and youth, Benedict cut the umbilical domestic cord, and leaving his robes of purple and silken finery, suddenly disappeared, leaving behind a note which was doubtless meant to be reassuring and which was quite the reverse, for it failed to tell where his mail should be forwarded. He had gone to live with a hermit in the fastnesses of the mountains. He had desired to do something peculiar, strange, unusual, unique and individual, and now he had done it.

Back of it all was the Cosmic Urge, with a fair slip of a girl, and meetings by stealth in the moonlight; and then those orders from his father to give up the girl, which he obeyed with a vengeance.

Monasticism is a reversal or a misdirection of the Cosmic Urge. The will brought to bear in fighting temptation might be a power for good, if used in co-operation with Nature. But Nature to the priestly mind has always been bad. The worldly mind was one that led to ruin. To be good by doing good was an idea the monkish mind had not grasped. His way of being good was to

302

be nothing, do nothing—just resist. Successfully to fight temptation, the Oriental Monk regarded as an achievement ✄ ✄

One day, out on that perilous and slippery rock on the mountain-side, Benedict ceased saluting the Holy Virgin long enough to conceive a thought. It was this: To be acceptable to God, we must do something in the way of positive good for man. To pray, to adore, to wander, to suffer, is not enough. We must lighten the burdens of the toilers and bring a little joy into their lives. Suffering has its place, but too much suffering would destroy the race.

Only one other man had Benedict ever heard of, who put forth this argument, and that was Saint Jerome; and many good men in the Church regarded Saint Jerome as little better than an infidel. Saint Jerome was a student of the literature of Greece and Rome—" Pagan Books," they were called, " rivals of the Bible." Saint Anthony had renounced and denounced these books and all of the learning of Paganism. Saint Anthony, the father of Christian Monasticism, dwelt on the terrible evils of intellectual pride, and had declared that the joys of the mind were of a more subtle and devilish character than those of the flesh.

Anthony, assisted by inertia, had won the ear of the Church; and dirt, rags and idleness had come to be regarded as sacred things.

Benedict took issue with Anthony.

ST. BENEDICT

THE Monastic Impulse is a protest against the Cosmic Urge, or reproductive desire.

Necessarily, the Cosmic Urge is older than the Monastic Impulse; and beyond a doubt it will live to dance on the grave of its rival.

The Cosmic Urge is the creative instinct. It includes all planning, purpose, desire, hope, unrest, lust and ambition. In its general sense, it is Unfulfilled Desire. It is the voice constantly crying in the ears of success, "Arise and get thee hence, for this is not thy rest." It is the dissatisfaction with all things done—it is our Noble Discontent. In its first manifestation it is sex. In its last refinement it means the love of man and woman, with the love of children, the home-making sense, and an appreciation of art, music and science—which is love with seeing eyes—as natural results.

Deity creates through its creatures, of which man is the highest type. But man, evolving a small spark of intellect, sits in judgment on his Creator, and finds the work bad. Of all the animals, man is the only one so far known that criticizes his environment, instead of accepting it. And we do this because, in degree, we have abandoned intuition before we have gotten control of intellect & &

The Monastic Instinct is the disposition ever to look outside of ourselves for help. We expect the Strong Man to come and give us deliverance from our woes. All nations have legends of saviors and heroes who came

304

and set the captives free, and who will come again in greater glory and mightier power and even release the dead from their graves.

The Monastic Impulse is based on world-weariness, with disappointed love, or sex surfeit, which is a phase of the same thing, as a basis. Its simplest phase is a desire for solitude.

" Mon " means one, and monasticism is simply living alone, apart from the world. Gradually it came to mean living alone with others of a like mind or disposition.

¶ The clan is an extension of the family, and so is originally a monastic impulse. The Group Idea is a variant of monasticism, but if it includes men and women, it always disintegrates with the second generation, if not before, because the Cosmic Urge catches the members, and they mate, marry and swing the circle ❧ ❧

Ernst Haeckel has recently intimated his belief that monogamy, with its exclusive life, is a diluted form of monasticism. And his opinion seems to be that, in order to produce the noblest race possible, we must have a free society, with a State that reverences and respects maternity and pensions any mother who personally cares for her child.

Monasticism and enforced monogamy often carry a disrespect, if not a positive contempt, for motherhood, especially free motherhood. We breed from the worst, under the worst conditions, and as punishment God has

305

made us a race of scrubs. If we had deliberately set about to produce the worst, we could not do better. ¶ It will at once be seen that a penalized free motherhood is exactly like the Monastic Impulse—a protest and a revolt from the Cosmic Urge. Hence Ernst Haeckel, harking back to Schopenhauer, declares that we must place a premium upon parenthood, and the State must subsidize all mothers, visiting them with tenderness, gentleness, sanctity and respect, before we shall be able to produce a race of demigods.

The Church has aureoled and sainted the men and women who have successfully fought the Cosmic Urge. Emerson says, " We are strong as we ally ourselves with Nature, and weak as we fight against her or disregard her." Thus does Emerson place himself squarely in opposition to the Church, for the Church has ever looked upon Nature as a lure and a menace to holy living ✢ ✢

Now, is it not possible that the prevalency of the Monastic Impulse is proof that it is in itself a movement in the direction of Nature? Possibly its error lies in swinging out beyond the norm. A few great Churchmen have thought so. And the greatest and best of them, so far as I know, was Benedict. Through his efforts, monasticism was made a power for good, and for a time, at least, it served society and helped humanity on its way. ¶ That the flagellants, anchorites, or monks with iron collars, and Simeon Stylites living his life perched on a pillar, benefited the human race—no one would now argue. Simeon was simply trying to please God—to secure salvation for his soul. His assumption was that the world was base and bad. To be pure in heart you must live apart from it. His persistence was the only commendable thing about him, and this was the persistence of a diseased mind. It was beautiful just as the persistence of cancer is beautiful.

Benedict, while agreeing that the world was bad, yet said that our business was to make it better, and that everything we did which was done merely to save our own souls, was selfish and unworthy. He advocated that, in order to save our own souls, we should make it our business to save others. Also, to think too much about your own soul was to have a soul not worth saving. If this life is a preparation for another, as Simeon thought, he was not preparing himself for a world where we would care to go. The only heaven in which any sane man or woman, be he saint or sinner, would care to live, would be one whose inhabitants would be at liberty to obey the Cosmic Urge just as freely as the Monastic Impulse, and where one would be regarded as holy as the other. So thought Saint Benedict.

THERE is a natural law, well recognized and defined by men who think, called the Law of Diminishing Returns, sometimes referred to as the Law of Pivotal Points.

A man starts in to take systematic exercise, and he finds that his strength increases. He takes more exercise and keeps on until he gets " stale "—that is, he becomes sore and lame. He has passed the Pivotal Point and is getting a Diminishing Return.

In running a railroad-engine a certain amount of coal is required to pull a train of given weight a mile, say at the rate of fifty miles an hour. You double the amount of your coal, and simple folks might say you double your speed, but railroad men know better. The double amount of coal will give you only about sixty miles instead of fifty. Increase your coal and from this on you get a Diminishing Return. If you insist on eighty miles an hour, you get your speed at a terrific cost and a terrible risk.

Another case: Your body requires a certain amount of food—the body is an engine; food is fuel; life is combustion. Better the quality and quantity of your food, and up to a certain point you increase your strength. Go on increasing your food and you get death. Loan money at five per cent and your investment is reasonably secure and safe. Loan money at ten per cent and you do not double the returns; on the contrary, you have taken on so much risk. Loan money at twenty per cent

308

and you will probably lose it; for the man who borrows at twenty per cent does not intend to pay if he can help it ✍ ✍

The Law of Diminishing Returns was what Oliver Wendell Holmes had in mind when he said, " Because I like a pinch of salt in my soup is no reason I wish to be immersed in brine."

Churches, preachers and religious denominations are good things in their time and place, and up to a certain point. Whether for you the church has passed the Pivotal Point is for you yourself to decide. But remember this, because a thing is good up to a certain point, or has been good, is no reason why it should be perpetuated. The Law of Diminishing Returns is the natural refutation of the popular fallacy that because a thing is good you can not get too much of it.

It is this law that Abraham Lincoln had in mind when he said, " I object to that logic which seeks to imply that because I wish to make the negro free, I desire a black woman for a wife."

Benedict had spent five years in resistance before it dawned upon him that Monasticism carried to a certain point was excellent and fraught with good results, but beyond that it rapidly degenerated.

To carry the plan of simplicity and asceticism to its summit and not go beyond was now his desire.

To withdraw from society he felt was a necessity, for the petty and selfish ambitions of Rome were revolting.

309

But the religious life did not for him preclude the joys of the intellect. In his unshaven and unshorn condition, wearing a single garment of goatskin, he dared not go back to his home. So he proceeded to make himself acceptable to decent people. He made a white robe, bathed, shaved off his beard, had his hair cut, and putting on his garments, went back to his family. The life in the wilderness had improved his health. He had grown in size and strength and he now, in his own person, proved that a religious recluse was not necessarily unkempt and repulsive.

His people greeted him as one raised from the dead. Crowds followed him wherever he went. He began to preach to them and to explain his position.

Some of his old school associates came to him.

As he explained his position, it began more and more to justify itself in his mind. Things grow plain as we analyze them to others—by explaining to another the matter becomes luminous to ourselves.

To purify the monasteries and carry to them all that was good and beautiful in the classics, was the desire of Benedict. His wish was to reconcile the learning of the past with Christianity, which up to that time had been simply ascetic. It had consisted largely of repression, suppression and a killing-out of all spontaneous, happy, natural impulses.

Very naturally, he was harshly criticized, and when he went back to the cave where he had dwelt and tried to

310

teach some of his old companions how to read and write, they flew first at him, and then from him. They declared that he was the devil in the guise of a monk; that he wished to live both as a monk and as a man of the world—that he wanted to eat his cake and still keep it. By a sort of divine right he took control of affairs, and insisted that his companions should go to work with him, and plant a garden and raise vegetables and fruits, instead of depending upon charity or going without ✂ ✂

The man who insists that all folks shall work, be they holy or secular, learned or illiterate, always has a hard road to travel. Benedict's companions declared that he was trying to enslave them, and one of them brewed a poison and substituted it for the simple herb tea that Benedict drank. Being discovered, the man and his conspirators escaped, although Benedict offered to forgive and forget if they would go to work.

Benedict adhered to his new inspiration with a persistency that never relaxed—the voice of God had called to him that he must clear the soil of the brambles and plant gardens.

The thorn-bush through which he had once rolled his naked body, he now cut down and burned. He relaxed the vigils and limited the prayers and adorations to a few short exercises just before eating, sleeping and going to work. He divided the day into three parts— eight hours for work, eight hours for study, eight hours

for sleep. Then he took one-half hour from each of these
divisions for silent prayer and adoration. He argued
that good work was a prayer, and that one could pray
with his heart and lips, even as his hands swung the
ax, the sickle or the grub-hoe. All that Benedict required of others, he did himself, and through the daily
work he evolved a very strong and sturdy physique.
From the accounts that have come to us he was rather
small in stature, but in strength he surpassed any man
in his vicinity.

Miraculous accounts of his physical strength were
related, and in the minds of his simple followers he
was regarded as more than a man, which shows us that
the ideals of what a man should be, or might be, were
not high. We are told that near Benedict's first monastery there was a very deep lake, made in the time of
Nero by damming up a mountain stream. Along this
lake the brambles and vines had grown in great confusion. Benedict set to work to clear the ground from
this lake to his monastery, half a mile up the hillside.
One day a workman dropped an ax into the lake. Benedict smiled, his lips moved in prayer and the ax came
to the surface. The story does not say that Benedict
dived to the bottom and brought up the ax, which he
probably did. The next day the owner of the ax fell
into the water, and the story goes that Benedict walked
out on the water and brought the man in on his shoulders. We who do not believe that the age of miracles has

312

passed, can well understand how Benedict was an active, agile and strong swimmer, and that through the natural powers which he evolved by living a sane and simple life, he was able to perform many feats which peasants round about considered miraculous. Benedict had what has been called the Builder's Itch. He found great joy in planning, creating and constructing. He had an eye for architecture and landscape-gardening. He utilized the materials of old Roman temples to construct Christian churches, and from the same quarry he took stone and built a monastery. A Roman ruin had a lure for him. It meant building possibilities. He stocked the lake with fish, and then made catches that rivaled the parable of the loaves and fishes. Only the loaves of Benedict were made from the wheat he himself raised, and the people he fed were the crowds who came to hear him preach the gospel he himself practised—the gospel of work, moderation and the commonsense exercise of head, hand and heart.

ST. BENEDICT

TO Benedict came twelve disciples. But further applications becoming numerous, to meet the pressure Benedict kept organizing them into groups of twelve, appointing a superior over each group. In order to prove his sense of equality, he had but eleven besides himself in the monastery. He recognized that leadership was a necessity; but the clothes he wore were no better than, and the food he ate no different from, what the others had. Yet to enforce discipline, rules were made and instant obedience was exacted. Benedict took his turn at waiting on the table and doing the coarsest tasks.

Were it not for the commonsense methods of life, and the element of human service, the Christian monastery and probably Christianity itself would not have survived. The dogma of religion was made acceptable by blending it with a service for humanity. And even to this day the popular plan of proving the miracles of the Old Testament to have been actual occurrences is to point to the schools, hospitals and orphan asylums that Christian people have provided.

In the efforts of Benedict to combine the life of unselfish service with intellectual appreciation of classic literature, he naturally was misunderstood. Several times he came near having serious collisions with the authorities of the Church at Rome.

His preaching attracted the jealous attention of certain churchmen, but as he was not a priest, the Pope refused

to take notice of his supposed heresies. ¶ An effort was
made to compel him to become a priest, but Benedict
refused on the plea that he was not worthy. The fact
was, however, that he did not wish to be bound by the
rules of the Church.

In one sense, his was a religion inside a religion, and a
slight accident might have precipitated an opposition
denomination, just as the Protestant issue of Luther
was an accident, and the Methodism of the Wesleys,
another ⚶ ⚶

Several times the opposition, in the belief that Benedict
was an enemy of the Church, went so far as to try to
kill him. And once a few pious persons in Rome induced
a company of wanton women to go out to Benedict's
monastery and disport themselves through his beautiful
grounds. This was done with two purposes in view;
one was to work the direct downfall of the Benedictines,
with the aid of the trulls, and the other was to create a
scandal among the visitors, who would carry the un-
savory news back to Rome and supply the gossips
raw stock.

Benedict was so deeply grieved by the despicable trick
that he retired to his former home, the cave in the
hillside, and there remained without food for a month.
¶ But during this time of solitude his mind was busy
with new plans. He now founded Monte Cassino. The
site is halfway between Rome and Naples, and the white,
classic lines of the buildings can be seen from the

315

railroad. There on the crags, from out of a mass of green, has been played out for more than a thousand years the drama of religious life. Death by fire and sword has been the fate of many of the occupants. But the years went by, new men came, the ruins were repaired, and again the cloisters were trodden by pious feet of holy men. Goths, Lombards, Saracens, Normans, Spaniards, Teutons, and finally came Napoleon Bonaparte, who confiscated the property, making the place his home for a brief space. Later he relented and took it from the favorite upon whom he had bestowed it and gave it back to the Church. It then remained a Benedictine monastery until the edict of Eighteen Hundred Sixty-six, which, with the help of Massini and Garibaldi, made the monastery in Italy a thing of the past. The place is now a school—a school with a co-ed proviso. Thus passes away the glory of the world, in order that a greater glory shall appear.

Six hundred years before Benedict's day, on the site of the cloister of Monte Cassino stood a temple to Apollo, and just below was a grove sacred to Venus.

Two hundred years before Benedict's time the Goths had done their work so well that even the walls of the temple to Apollo were razed, and the sacred grove became the home of wild beasts.

To this deserted place came Benedict and eleven men, filled with a holy zeal to erect on this very spot an edifice worthy of the living God. Here the practical builder and the religious dreamer combined. If you are going to build a building, why not build upon the walls already laid and with blocks ready hewn and fashioned! ¶ The Monte Cassino monastery of Benedict rivaled in artistic beauty the temple that it replaced.

Man is a building animal, and the same Creative Energy that impelled the Greeks and later the Romans to plan, devise, toil and build, now played through the good monk Benedict. His desire to create was a form of the great Cosmic Urge, that lives eternally and is building in America a finer, better and nobler religion than the world has ever seen—a Religion of Humanity—a religion of which at times Benedict caught vivid passing glimpses, as one sees at night the landscape brilliantly illumined by the lightning's flash.

ST. BENEDICT

HE motto of Benedict was "Ecce Labora." These words were carved on the entrance to every Benedictine Monastery.

The monastic idea originated in the Orient, where Nature placed no special penalty on idleness. Indeed, labor may have been a curse in Asia. Morality is crystallized expediency, and both, as we are told, are matters of geography, as well as time.

And truth it is, that north of the Mediterranean idleness is the curse, not labor.

The rule of Benedict was not unlike that of the Shakers, for near every monastery was a nunnery. The association of men and women, although quite limited, was better for both than their absolute separation, as with the Trappists, who regard it as a sin even to look upon the face of a woman.

The thrift and industry of the Benedictines was worthy of Ann Lee and our friends at Lebanon. A man who works eight hours, with fair intelligence, and does not set out to make consumption and waste the business of his life, grows rich. Thoreau was right—an hour a day will support you. But Thoreau was wrong in supposing men work only to get food, clothing and shelter. To work only an hour a day is to evolve into a loafer. We work not to acquire, but to become.

The group idea, cemented by able leadership and a religious concept, is always successful. The Mormons, Quakers, Harmonyites, Economites, and the Oneida

318

Community, all grew very rich, and surpassed their neighbors not only in point of money, but in health, happiness, intelligence and general mental grasp.

Brook Farm failed for lack of a leader with business instinct; but as it was, it divided up among its members a rich legacy of spiritual and mental assets. In family life, or what is called " Society," there is a constant danger through rivalry, not in well-doing or in human service, but in conspicuous waste and conspicuous leisure. The religious rite of feet-washing is absolutely lost, both as a rite and as an idea. In truth, " good society " is essentially predatory in its instincts. In communal life, or the life of a group, service and not waste is the watchword. This must be so, since every group, at its beginning, is held together through the thought of service. To meet and unite on a basis of jealous rivalry and sharp practise is unthinkable, for these are the things that disintegrate the group.

It is an economic law that a group founded upon and practising the idea of each member giving all, wins all. Benedict's idea of " Ecce labora " made every Benedictine monastery a center of wealth. Work stops bickering, strife and undue waste. It makes for health and strength. The reward of work is not immunity from toil, but more work—an increased capacity for effort ✠ ✠

De Tocqueville gave this recipe for success: Subdue yourself—Devote yourself.

319

ST. BENEDICT

That is to say, subdue the ego to a point where it gets
its gratification in concentrating on unselfish service.
He who does this always succeeds, for not only is he
engaged upon a plan of life in which there is little competition, but he is working in line with a divine law,
the law of mutuality, which provides that all the good
you do to others, you do for yourself.

Benedictine monasticism leads straight to wealth and
great power. The Abbot of the group became a Baron.
" I took the vow of poverty, and it led to an income
of twenty thousand pounds a year. I took the vow of
obedience and find myself ruler of fifty towns and
villages." These are the words which Sir Walter Scott
puts into the mouth of an Abbot, who became a Baron
through the simple law of which I have hinted. And
in his novel of " The Abbot," Sir Walter gives a tragic
picture of how power and wealth can be lost as well as
won. Feudalism began with the rule of the monastery.
¶ Benedict was one of the world's great Captains of
Industry. And like all great entrepreneurs, he won
through utilizing the efforts of others. In picking his
Abbots, or the men to be " father " of each particular
group, he showed rare skill. These men learned from
him and he learned from them. One of his best men was
Cassiodorus, the man who evolved the scheme of the
scriptorium. " To study eight hours a day was not
enough," said Cassiodorus. " We should copy the great
works of literature so that every monastery shall have

320

a library as good as that which we have at Monte Cassino." He himself was an expert penman, and he set himself the task of teaching the monks how to write as well as how to read. " To write beautifully is a great joy to our God," he said.

Benedict liked the idea, and at once put it into execution. Cassiodorus is the patron saint of every maker of books who loves his craft.

The systematic work of the scriptorium originated in the brain of Cassiodorus, and he was appointed by Benedict to go from one monastery to another and inform the Abbot that a voice had come from God to Benedict saying that these precious books must be copied, and presented to those who would prize them.

Cassiodorus had been a secretary of state under the Emperor Theodoric, and he had also been a soldier. He was seventy years of age when he came under the influence of Benedict, through a chance visit to Monte Cassino. Benedict at first ordered him to take an ax and work with the servants at grubbing out underbrush and preparing a field for planting. Cassiodorus obeyed, and soon discovered that there was a joy in obedience he had before never guessed. His name was Brebantus Varus, but on his declaring he was going to remain and work with Benedict, he was complimented by being given the name of Cassiodorus, suggested by the word Cassinum or Cassino. Cassiodorus lived to be ninety-two, and was one of the chief factors, after

321

Benedict himself, in introducing the love of art and beauty among the Benedictines.

Near Monte Cassino was a nunnery presided over by Scholastica, the twin sister of Benedict.

Renan says that the kinship of Scholastica and Benedict was a spiritual tie, not one of blood. If so, we respect it none the less. Saint Gregory tells of the death of Benedict thus:

Benedict was at the end of his career. His interview with Totila took place in Five Hundred Forty-two, in the year which preceded his death; and from his earliest days of the following year, God prepared him for his last struggle, by requiring from him the sacrifice of the most tender affection he had retained on earth. The beautiful and touching incident of the last meeting of Benedict and his twin sister, Scholastica, is a picture long to remember. At the window of his cell, three days after her death, Benedict had a vision of his dear sister's soul entering heaven in the form of a snowy dove. He immediately sent for the body and placed it in a sepulcher which he had already prepared for himself, that death might not separate those whose souls had always been united in God.

The death of his sister was the signal of departure for himself. He survived her forty days. He announced his death to several of his monks, then far from Monte Cassino. A violent fever having seized him, he caused himself on the sixth day of his sickness to be carried to the chapel of Saint John the Baptist; he had before ordered the tomb in which his sister already slept to be opened.

322

ST. BENEDICT

There, supported in the arms of his disciples, he received
the holy Viaticum, then placing himself at the side of
the open grave, but at the foot of the altar, and with
his arms extended towards heaven, he died, standing,
muttering a last prayer. Such a victorious death became
that great soldier of God. He was buried by the side
of his beloved Scholastica, in a sepulcher made on the
spot where stood the altar of Apollo, which had been
replaced by another to our beloved Savior.

N the very year, and at the same time, that Justinian and Theodora were preparing the Justinian Code, Benedict was busy devising "The Monastic Rules." Benedict did not put his rules forth as final, but explained that they were merely expedient for their time and place. In this he was singularly modest. If one can divest himself of the thought that there was anything "holy" or "sacred" about these communal groups called "monasteries," and then read these rules, he will see that they were founded on a good knowledge of economics and a very stern commonsense.

Humanity was the same a thousand years ago that it is now. Benedict had to fight inertia, selfishness and incipient paranoia, just as does the man who tries to introduce practical socialism today. A few extracts from this very remarkable Book of Rules will show the shrewd Connecticut wisdom of Benedict. To hold the dowdy, indifferent, slipshod and underdone in their proper places, so they could not disturb or destroy the peace, policy and prosperity of the efficient, was the task of Benedict ✄ ✄

Benedict says: "Written and formal rules are necessary only because we are all faulty men, with a tendency towards selfishness and disorder. When men become wise, and also unselfish, there will be no need of rules and laws."

The Book of Rules by Benedict is a volume of more

than twenty thousand words. Its scope reveals an insight that will appeal to all who have had to do with socialistic experiments, not to mention the management of labor-unions. Benedict was one of the industrial leaders of the world. His life was an epoch, and his influence still abides.

MARY BAKER EDDY

The chief stones in the temple of Christian Science are to be found in the following postulates: that Life is God, good and not evil; that Soul is sinless, not to be found in the body; that Spirit is not and can not be materialized; that Life is not subject to death; that the spiritual real man has no consciousness of material life or death.
— *Mary Baker Eddy*

MARY BAKER EDDY

MARY BAKER EDDY

ET the fact be here stated that Mary Baker Eddy was the founder of Christian Science. This woman lived long and well.

She was alert, earnest, highly intelligent, receptive. She was ever discovering. We know this because she put out a new message every little while, or modified an old one, having come in the meantime into a position to get a nearer and clearer view of the fact. The last edition of " Science and Health " is a different book from the first one.

Christian Science is not a fixed, formed, fossilized, ossified structure. Possibly it may become so. But the probabilities are it will grow, expand, advance. Life and growth consist in eliminating dead matter and evolving new tissue. The institution, commercial, artistic, social, political, religious, that has ceased to grow has begun to disintegrate.

Christian Scientists do not flee the world, renouncing and denouncing it. As a people they are well, happy, hopeful, enthusiastic and successful. I am fairly well informed on the history of all great religions. In degree I know the character of intellect possessed by the folks who make or made up their membership. And my opinion is, that no religion that has ever existed contained

329

so large a percentage of intelligent people, competent, safe and sane, as does Christian Science. There is an adage to the effect that a prophet is not without honor save in his own country.

In the case of Mary Baker Eddy, the adage just quoted goes awry. Mrs. Eddy as long as she lived, retained the good-will of Concord, Boston and Brookline, where she chose to make her home. Very many of the leading men and women of each of these cities are Christian Scientists ✄ ✄

The Christian Science Church at Concord cost upwards of two hundred thousand dollars, and was the gift of Mrs. Eddy. Over the entrance, cut deep in granite, are the words, " Presented by Mary Baker Eddy, Discoverer and Founder of Christian Science." As to the argument that the truths of Christian Science have always been known and practised by a few, Mrs. Eddy issued her direct challenge. In all of her literature she set out the unqualified statement that she was " The Discoverer and the Founder." She was never apologetic; she assumed no modesty she did not feel; she spoke as one having authority, as did Moses of old, " Thus saith the Lord!" ¶ She entered into no joint debates; she did not answer back. This intense conviction which admits of no parley was one of the secrets of her power. For many years the Billingsgate Calendar was directed at her upon every possible occasion.

But Mrs. Eddy won out, and legislation and courts
330

were compelled to whistle in their hounds. Your right
to keep well in your own way is now fully recognized.
Doctors are not liable when they give innocent sweetened water and call it medicine, nor do we place Christian Scientists on trial if their patients die, any more
than we do the M. D.'s.

In fact, Mrs. Eddy influenced both of the so-called
sciences of medicine and theology. Even those who are
perfectly willing to deny her, and noisily discard her
tenets, are debtors to her.

Homeopathy modified the dose of all the Allopaths;
and Christian Science has attenuated the Hahneman-
nian theory of attenuations, it having been found that
the blank tablet often cures quite as effectively as the
one that is medicated. Christian Science does not shout,
rant, defy nor preach. It is poised, silent, sure, and the
flagellants, like the dervishes, are noticeable by their
absence ⚶ ⚶

The Reverend Billy Sunday is not a Christian Scientist.
The Christian Scientist does not cut into the grape;
specialize on the elevated spheroid; devote his energies
to bridge whist; cultivate the scandal microbe; join the
anvil chorus, nor shake the red rag of wordy warfare.
He is diligent in business, fervent in spirit, and accepts
what comes without protest, finding it good.

Mary Baker Eddy lived a human life. Through her
manifold experiences she gathered gear—she was a very
great and wise woman. She was so great that she kept

her own counsel, received no visitors, made no calls, had no Thursday, wrote no letters, and even never went to the church that she presented to her native town. Mrs. Eddy's step was ever light, her form erect —a slender, handsome, queenly woman. When she passed on, in December, Nineteen Hundred Ten, in her ninetieth year, she looked scarce more than sixty. Her face showed experience, but not extreme age. The day I saw her, a few years before her death, she was dressed all in white satin and looked like a girl going to a ball.

Her eyes were not dimmed nor her face wrinkled ✄ Her hat was a milliner's dream; her gloves came to the elbow and were becomingly wrinkled; her form was the form of Bernhardt. Her secretary stood by the carriage-door, his head bared. He did not offer his hand to the lady nor seek to assist her into the carriage. He knew his business—a sober, silent, muscular, bronzed, farmer-like man, who evidently saw everything and nothing ✄ ✄

He closed the carriage-door and took his seat by the side of the driver, who wore no livery. The men looked like brothers. The big, brown horses started slowly away; they wore no blinders nor check-reins—they, too, had banished fear. The coachman drove with a loose rein. The next day I waited in Concord to see Mrs. Eddy again. At exactly two-fifteen the big, brown, slow-going horses turned into Main Street. Drays pulled

332

in to the curb, automobiles stopped, people stood on the street corners, and some—the pilgrims—uncovered. ¶ Mrs. Eddy sat back in the carriage, holding in her white-gloved hands a big spray of apple-blossoms, the same half-smile of satisfaction on her face—the smile of Pope Leo the Thirteenth. The woman was a veritable queen, and some of her devotees, not without reason, called her the Queen of the World.

Some doubtless prayed to her—and may yet, for that matter. Mrs. Eddy was married three times. First, to Colonel George W. Glover, an excellent and worthy man, who was the father of her only child, a son. On the death of Glover, the child was taken by Glover's mother and secreted so effectually that his mother did not see him until he was thirty-four years old, and the father of a family.

Her second husband was Daniel Patterson, who was not only a rogue but also a fool—a flashy one, who turned the head of a lone, lorn young widow, who certainly was not infallible in judgment. In two years the wife got a divorce from him, on the grounds of cruelty and desertion, at Salem, Massachusetts. Her third marital venture was Doctor Asa G. Eddy, a practising physician—a man of much intelligence and worth. From him Mrs. Eddy learned that the Science of Medicine was not much of a science after all. Mrs. Eddy used to say that her husband was her first convert; certain it is that Dr. Eddy gave up his practise to assist his wife in putting before the world the unreality of disease. That he did not fully grasp the idea is shown by the fact that he died of pneumonia. This, however, did not shake the faith of Mrs. Eddy in the doctrine that sickness was an error of mortal mind. For a good many years Mrs. Eddy drove the memory of her two good husbands tandem, hitched by a hyphen, thus: Mary Baker Glover-Eddy. Many a woman has joined her own name to that of her husband, but what woman ever before so honored the two men she had loved by coupling their names! Getting married is a bad habit, Mrs. Eddy would probably have said, but you have to get married to find it out.

In Eighteen Hundred Seventy-nine, Mrs. Eddy organized the First Church of Christ, Scientist, in Boston, and became its pastor. In Eighteen Hundred Eighty-one, being then sixty years of age, she founded the Massachusetts Metaphysical College, in Boston. For fifteen years she had been speaking in public, affirming that health was our normal condition and that as a man thinketh in his heart, so is he. From her forty-fifth to her sixtieth year she was glad to speak for what was offered, although I believe that even then she had discarded the good old priestly plan of taking up a collection. The Metaphysical College was started to prepare students for teaching Mrs. Eddy's doctrines.

The business ability of the woman was shown in thus organizing and allowing no one to teach who was not duly prepared. These students were obliged to pay a good stiff tuition, which fact made them appreciative. In turn they went out and taught; all students paid the tidy sum of one hundred dollars for the lessons, which fee was later cut to fifty. Salvation may be free, but Christian Science costs money. The theological genus piker, with his long, wrinkled, black coat, his collar buttoned behind, and his high hat, has been eliminated ✄ ✄

Mrs. Eddy was manager of the best-methodized institution in the world, save only the Roman Catholic Church and the Standard Oil Company. How many million copies of "Science and Health" have been sold, no man can say. What percentage of the money from the lessons went to Mrs. Eddy, only an Armstrong Committee could ascertain, and really it was nobody's business but hers.

That Mrs. Eddy had some very skilful helpers goes without saying. But here is the point—she selected them, and reigned supreme. That the student who paid fifty dollars got his money's worth, I have no doubt. Not that he understood the lessons, but he received a feeling of courage and a oneness with the whole which caused health to flow through his veins and his heart to beat with joy. The lesson might have been to him a jumble of words, but he lived in hopes that he would soon grow to a point where the lines were luminous ✄ In the meantime, all he knew was that whereas he was once lame he could now walk. Even the most bigoted and prejudiced now agree that the cures of Christian Science are genuine. People who think they have trouble have it, and it is the same with pain. Imagination is the only sure-enough thing in the world. Mrs. Eddy's doctrines abolish pain and therefore abolish poverty, for poverty, in America at least, is a disease. Mrs. Eddy's chief characteristics were:

First, Love of Beauty as manifest in bodily form, dress and surroundings.

Second, A zeal for system, order and concentrated effort on the particular business she undertakes.

Third, A dignity, courage, self-sufficiency and self-respect that comes from a belief in her own divinity

Fourth, An economy of time, money, materials, energy and emotion that wastes nothing, but which continually conserves and accumulates.

Fifth, A liberality, when advisable, which is only possible to those who also economize.

Sixth, Yankee shrewdness, great commonsense, all flavored with a dash of mysticism and indifference to physical scientific accuracy.

In other words, Christian Science is a woman's science —she knows! And it is good because it is good—this is a science sound enough for anybody—I guess so! Christian Science is scientific, but not for the reasons that its promoters maintain. Male Christian Scientists do not growl and kick the cat.

MARY BAKER EDDY

Women Christian Scientists do not nag. Christian Scientists do not have either the grouch or the meddler's itch. Among them there are no dolorosos, grumperinos or beggars. They respect all other denominations, having a serene faith that all will yet see the light—that is to say, adopt their doctrines. The most radical among old-school doctors could not deny that Mrs. Eddy's own life was conducted on absolutely scientific lines. She never answered the telephone, never fussed nor fumed ✠ ✠

She hired big, safe people and paid them a big wage. She gave her coachman fifty dollars a week, and her cook in proportion, and thus secured people who gave her peace. She went to bed with the birds and awoke with the dawn. At seven o'clock she was at her desk, dictating answers to the very few letters her secretary deemed it advisable she should see. She had breakfast at nine o'clock—ate anything she liked, taking her time and fletcherizing. After breakfast she worked upon her manuscripts until it was time for the daily ride.

At four o'clock she dined—two meals a day being the rule. If, however, she cared to dissipate a little and eat three meals a day, she was not afraid to do so.

She knew her horses and cows and sheep by name, and gave requests as to their care, holding that the laws of mind obtain as to dumb animals the same as man. Dogs she did not care for, and if she ever had an aversion it would have been cats. Her servants she called " My helpers." Christian Scientists very naturally believe in the equality of the sexes. When girl babies are born to them they bless God, just the same as when boy babies are born. In truth they bless God for everything, for to them all is beautiful and all is good. Paid preachers they do not have; they do not believe in priests or certain men who are nearer to God than others. All have access to Eternal Truth, and thus is the ecclesiastic excluded. To eliminate the theological middleman is well, and as for the Church itself, surely Mrs. Eddy eliminated it also; for she never entered a church, or at least not more than once a year, and then it was only in deference to the architect. A Church! Is it necessary? For herself Mrs. Eddy said, No.

But as for others, she said, Yes, a church is good for those who need it. Mrs. Eddy was the most successful author in the world, or, indeed, that the world has ever seen. No other writer ever made so much money as she, none is more devoutly read.

Shakespeare, with his fortune of a quarter of a million dollars, fades into comparative failure; and Arthur Brisbane, with his salary of seventy-five thousand a year, is an office-boy compared with this regal woman, who gave fifty thousand dollars a year for good roads.

MARY BAKER EDDY

THE valuable truths and distinguishing features of Christian Science are not to be found in Mrs. Eddy's books, but in Mrs. Eddy's life. She was a much bigger woman than she was a writer. Emerson says that every great institution is the lengthened shadow of a single man. Every great business enterprise has a soul—one man's spirit animates, pervades and tints the whole. You can go into any hotel or store, and behold! the nature or character of the owner or manager is everywhere proclaimed ✣ You do not have to see the man, and the bigger the institution the less need is there for the man to show himself. His work proclaims him, just as a farmer's livestock all moo, whinny and squeal his virtues— or lack of them. As a boy of ten I learned to know all of our neighbors by their horses. The horses of a drunkard, blanketless, hungry, shivering, outside of the village tavern, do they not proclaim the poor, despised owner within? ✣ ✣

You can walk through the passenger-coaches of a train made up at a terminal and read the character unmistakably of the general passenger-agent. The soul of John Wesley ran through Methodism and made it what it was. The Lutheranism of Luther yet lives; Calvinism the same; and the soul of John Knox still goes marching on, carrying the Presbyterian banner. ¶ Every religion partakes of the nature of its founder, until this religion is mixed with that of another and its character lost, as happened to the religion of Christ when it was launched by Paul and was finally fused with Paganism by the Roman Emperor, Constantine. ¶ Christian Science is as yet the lengthened shadow of Mary Baker Eddy. Her own immediate, personal pupils are still teaching, and her life and characteristics impressed upon them are given out to each and all. Every phase of life is solved by answering the question, "What would Mrs. Eddy do?" Mrs. Eddy's ideas about dress, housekeeping, business, food, health, the management of servants, the care of children—all are blended into a composite, and this composite is the Christian Scientist as we see and know him.

The fact that Mrs. Eddy was methodical, industrious, economical, persevering, courageous, hopeful, helpful, neat in her attire and smiling, makes all Christian Scientists exactly so. She did not play cards and indulge in the manifold silliness of so-called good society, and neither do they. Indeed, that one thing which has been referred to as "the plaster-of-Paris smile," the one feature in Christian Science to which many good people object, is the direct legacy of Mrs. Eddy to her pupils. "Science and Health" says nothing about it; no edict has been put forth recommending it; but all good Christian Scientists take it on—the smile that refuses to vacate the premises. And to some it is certainly very becoming. Mrs. Eddy's self-reliant, silent, smiling personality has given the key to conduct for the hundreds of thousands of people who love her and revere her memory ❧ ❧

Mrs. Eddy was a rare good listener. She did not argue. Once upon a time, indeed, she was guilty of waving the red flag of wordy warfare; but the passing of the years brought her wisdom, and then her only answer to impatience was the quiet smile. As for eating, her table always had enough, but it stopped short of surfeit; the service was dainty, and all these things are now seen in the homes of Christian Scientists. Always in the home of a good Christian Scientist the bathroom is as complete as the library, and both are models of good housekeeping, seemingly always in order for the inspection committee ❧ ❧

Mrs. Eddy did not say much about hot water, soap and clean towels; but the idea, regardless of the nonexistence of matter, is fixed in the consciousness of every Christian Scientist that absolute bodily cleanliness, fresh linen and fresh air are not only next to godliness, but elements of it. All of which you could never work out of " Science and Health with Key to the Scriptures " in a lifetime of study, any more than you could mine and smelt the Westminster Catechism out of the Bible ❧

The vital truths of right living come to us as a precious heritage from the character of this great woman. She, herself, perhaps may not have known this; but before she wrote her book and formulated her religion, she lived her life. Her book was an endeavor to explain her

341

life, and as her life grew better, stronger and more refined, she changed her book. Her book reacted on her life, and the person who got the most good out of " Science and Health " was Mary Baker Eddy herself ✠

" Science and Health " is mystical and beautifully human. The author's oar often fails to catch the water. For instance, she tries to show that animal magnetism, spiritualism, mental science, theosophy, agnosticism, pantheism and infidelity are all bad things and opposed to the science of " true being."

This statement presupposes that animal magnetism, infidelity, theosophy and agnosticism are specific entities or things, whereas they are only labels that are clapped quite indiscriminately on empty casks or full ones; and the contents of the casks may be sea-water or wine, and are really unknown to both mortal and divine mind, whatever these things are. Theosophists like Annie Besant, Spiritualists like Alfred Russel Wallace, Agnostics like Huxley and Ingersoll, are very noble and beautiful people. They are good neighbors and useful citizens.

" Science and Health " is an attempt to catch and hold in words the secrets of an active, honest, healthful, seeking, restless, earnest life, and as such is more or less of a failure ✠ ✠

Our actions are right, but our reasons seldom are ✠ Christian Science as a plan of life, embodying the great yet simple virtues, is beautiful. " Science and Health with Key to the Scriptures" does not explain the Scriptures. The book, as an attempt to explain and crystallize truth, is a failure. It ranks with that great mass of literature, written and copied at such vast pains and expense, bearing the high-sounding title, "Writings of the Saints."

MARY BAKER EDDY

LL publishers are familiar with inspired manuscripts. Such work always has one thing in
common—unintelligibility. Good literature is
lucid to the average mind. In fact, that is
its distinguishing feature. We understand what the
man means. No able writer uses the same word over
and over with varying sense. Alfred Henry Lewis and
William Marion Reedy use the mortal mind, and their
work is understandable. You can sit in judgment on
their conclusions and weigh, sift and decide for yourself.
They make an appeal to your intellect.

But you can not sit in judgment on " Science and
Health," because its language is not the language we
use in our common, every-day intercourse with one
another. It speaks of Christ as a person, a principle,
a spirit, a motive; as " Truth "; as one who was born
of one parent or no parents; who lived, died, or never
lived, never was born, and can not die.

Metaphysics is an attempt to explain a thing and
thereby evade the trouble of understanding it. You
throw the burden of proof on the other fellow—and
make him believe he does not comprehend because he
is too stupid. This is not fair!

Language is simply an agreement between people that
certain vocal sounds, or written symbols, shall stand
for certain ideas, thoughts or things. Inspired writers
string intelligent words together in an unintelligent
manner, and thereby give the reader an opportunity

344

to read anything into them that his preconceived thoughts may dictate. Metaphysical gibberish is a rudimentary survival of the practise of reading to the people in a dead language. The doctors continue the plan by writing prescriptions in Latin.

I once worked in a studio where the boys scraped their palette-knives on a convenient board. One day we took the board out and had it framed under glass, with a double, deep-shadow box. We gave it the best place in the studio and labeled it, " A Sunset at Sea—an Impression in Monochrome.'

The picture attracted much attention and great admiration from certain symbolists. It also created so much controversy that we were obliged to take it down in the interests of amity.

To assume that God inspired the Scriptures, and did the work so ill that, after more than two thousand years, it was necessary to inspire another person to make a " Key " to them, is hardly worthy of our serious attention. If God, being all-wise, all-powerful and all-loving, turns author, why does He produce work so muddy that it requires a " Key"?

Individuals may use a code that requires a " Key," because they wish to keep their matter secret from others. There may be for them a penalty on truth, but why Deity should write in a secret language, and then wait two thousand years before making the matter plain, and then to one single woman in Boston, is incomprehensible. What the world wants now is a Key to " Science and Health." In reading a book, the question that interests us is not, " Is it inspired ? " but, " Is it true ? "

Mrs. Eddy's ranks are recruited almost entirely from Orthodox Christianity. On page six hundred eight of " Science and Health," pocket edition of Nineteen Hundred Six, a lawyer gives testimony to the good he has gotten from Christian Science, and explains that he has long been a member of the Episcopal Church. He is delighted to know that he has not had to relinquish any of his old faith, but has simply kept the old and added to it the new.

This explains, in great degree, the popularity of Christian Science. People cling to the religious superstitions into which they were born. Mrs. Eddy's recruits were not from theosophy, spiritualism, agnosticism, unitarianism, universalism or infidelity. You can't give a freethinker a book with a statement of what he must find in it ✂ ✂

He has acquired the habit of thinking for himself ✂ Mrs. Eddy had no faith in Darwin, Spencer or Haeckel. She quoted Moses, Jesus and Paul to disprove the evolutionists, sat back and smiled content, innocently unaware that citations from Scriptures are in no sense proof to free minds. All of the Bible she wished to waive, she did. The cruelty and bestiality of Jehovah were nothing to her. Her " Key " does not unlock the

346

secrets of Deuteronomy and Leviticus, nor does it shed light on the doctrines of eternal punishment, the vicarious atonement, or the efficacy of baptism as a saving ordinance ✄ ✄

Explanations about mortal mind, divine mind and human mind, citing specific errors of the human mind, with a calm codicil to the effect that the human mind has no existence, are not what you might call illuminating literature. The stuff is simply "inspired." Mrs. Eddy was very wise in not allowing her "readers" or followers to sermonize or explain her writings. These writings are simply to be read. And so the hearers sit steeped in mist and wrapped in placidity, returning to their work rested and refreshed, without being influenced in any way, save by the soothing calm of forceful fog and mental vacuity.

The rest and relief from all thought is good. The related experiences of Christian Scientists are the things that convince and carry weight, not "Science and Health." "Science and Health" was made to sell. It was not given to you to be understood: it was to be bought and believed. If you doubt any portion of it, at once you are told that this is the work of your mortal mind, which is filled with error. Good Christian Scientists do not try to understand "Science and Health"— they just accept and believe it. "It is inspired," they say, "so it must be true—you will know when you are worthy to know."

347

And so we see our old friend Intellectual Tyranny come back in another form, not with cowl and cape, but tricked out with feminine finery and jewelry and gems that lure and dazzle. There is one thing quite as valuable as health, and that is intellectual integrity. To say, " Oh, 'Science and Health' is certainly inspired— just see how old Mrs. Johnson was cured of the rheumatism!" is not reasoning.

And it has given the scoffers excuse for calling it woman's logic. Such reasoning is on the plane of, " Why, Jesus must have been the only begotten son of God, born of a virgin, for if you don't believe it, just see the hospitals, orphan asylums and homes for the aged that Christianity has built!" Mrs. Johnson was surely cured of the rheumatism all right, but that does not prove that Mrs. Eddy is correct in her claim that Eve was made from Adam's rib; that agamogenesis is a fact in Nature; that to till the soil will not always be necessary; that human life in these bodies will have no end; and that an absent person can poison your health and happiness through malicious animal magnetism; or that a good person can give you absent treatment and cure your indigestion.

I agree with Mrs. Eddy as to the necessity of eliminating a medical fetish, but I disagree with her about religiously preserving a theological one. I have read " Science and Health with Key to the Scriptures " for twenty years, and I have also read the Scriptures for a much longer

348

period. Also, I have lived in the same house for many months with very intelligent Christian Scientists ⚬ And after mature consideration I regard both the Scriptures and " Science and Health " as largely made up of the errors of mortal mind. My intuitions are just as valuable to me as Mrs. Eddy's were to her.

My conscience is quite as sacred to me as hers was to her. And in being an agnostic I object to being classed as blind, stubborn, wilful, malicious and degenerate.
¶ We should honor our Creator by cleaving to the things that seem to us to be true, and not abandon the rudder of our minds to any man or any woman, be they living or dead. Let us not be dishonest with ourselves, even to rid us of our physical diseases. As for health, I have all of it that Christian Science ever gave or can give. I have no " testimony " of healing to relate, for I have never been sick an hour. And I think I know how I have kept well. I make no secret of it. It is all very simple—nothing miraculous.

My knowledge of how to keep well is not inspired knowledge, save as all men are inspired who study and know the Laws of Nature. Health, after all, is largely a matter of habit.

ACK of the reading-desks, in the " Mother Church," at Boston, are quotations from Paul and Mrs. Eddy, side by side. But the quotation from Paul, which is behind the desk of the woman reader, is not this: " Let women keep silence in the churches."

Mrs. Eddy believed the Scriptures are all true, word for word. Yet when she quoted Paul she picked the thing she wanted and avoided all that did not apply to her case. Personally, I like the plan. I do it myself. But I do not believe the Scriptures are inspired by an all-wise Deity. So far as I know, all books were written by men, and very often by faulty, human men at that. Mrs. Eddy's " Key " does not unlock anything; and she did not try to unlock any passages except the passages that seemingly had a bearing on her belief. That is, Mrs. Eddy believed things first, and then skirmished for proof. This is a very old plan. Says Shakespeare: " In religion what damned error but some somber brow will bless it and approve it with a text, hiding the grossness thereof with fair ornament." Let no one read " Science and Health " in the hope of finding in it simple and sensible statements concerning life and its duties. They are not there.

I append a few quotations, and in mentioning the page I refer to the pocket or " Oxford " edition of Nineteen Hundred Six. On page one hundred eighty-three of " Science and Health " I find, " The Scriptures inform us that sin, or error, first caused the condemnation of man to till the ground, and indicate that obedience to God will remove this necessity."

Mrs. Eddy evidently believed that work is a punishment, and that the day will come when God will remove the necessity of farming and making garden. Can a sane person reply to such lack of logic?

On page five hundred forty-seven is this: " If one of the statements in this book is true, every one must be true, for not one departs from its system and rule. You can prove for yourself, dear reader, the Science of healing, and so ascertain if the author has given you the correct interpretation of Scripture."

This is evidently inspired by Paul's quibble, " If the dead rise not from the grave, then is our religion vain." Lincoln once referred to this kind of reasoning by saying, " I object to the assumption that my ambition is to have my son marry a negress, simply because I am struggling for emancipation." Mrs. Eddy may heal you, but that does not prove that her interpretation of Scripture is true. Because this happens, that does not necessarily follow. Neither, because a thing precedes a thing or goes with a thing, is the thing the cause of the thing. On page five hundred fifty-three is this: " Adam was created before Eve. Herein it is seen that the maternal egg never brought forth Adam. Eve was formed from Adam's rib, not from a fetal ovum."

In reading things like this in " Science and Health,"
let us not be too severe on Mrs. Eddy, but just bear
in mind that such silly superstitions and barbaric
folklore are yet officially believed by all orthodox
clergymen and members of orthodox churches. You
can accept a belief in Adam's fall and the vicarious
atonement and still make money and have good health.
¶ Page one hundred two: " The mild forms of animal
magnetism are disappearing, and its aggressive features
are coming to the front. The looms of crime, hidden in
the dark recesses of mortal thought, are every hour
weaving webs more complicated and subtle. So secret
are its present methods that they ensnare the age into
indolence, and produce the very apathy on this subject
which the criminal desires."
This passage reveals the one actually dangerous thing
in Christian Science—the fallacy that one mind can
weave a web that will work the undoing of another.
This is the basis of a belief in witchcraft, and justifies
the hangings at Salem. On page one hundred three I
find this: " As used in Christian Science, animal magnetism or hypnotism is the specific term for error, or mortal
mind ⚹ ⚹
It is the false belief that mind is in matter, and both
evil and good; that evil is as real as goodness, and more
powerful. This belief has not one quality of truth or
good. It is either ignorant or malicious. The malicious
form of animal magnetism ultimates in moral idiocy.

The truths of immortal mind sustain man; and they annihilate the fables and mortal mind, whose flimsy and gaudy pretensions, like silly moths, singe their own wings and fall into dust. In reality there is no mortal mind, and consequently no transference of mortal thought and will-power." Page five hundred two: " Spiritually followed, the book of Genesis is the history of the untrue image of God, named a sinful mortal. This deflection of being, rightly viewed, serves the spiritual actuality of man, as given in the first chapter of Genesis. When the crude forms of human thought take on higher symbols and significations, the scientifically Christian views of the universe will appear, illuminating time with the glory of eternity."
¶ I append these two passages simply as samples of " inspired literature."

Any one who tries to understand such printed matter is headed for Bloomingdale. You must leave it alone absolutely or else accept it and read it with your mental eyes closed, mumbling it with your lips, and let your mind roam like a priest reading his breviary in the smoking-apartment of a Pullman car. The question then arises, " Was Mrs. Eddy sincere in putting forth such writings? "

And the answer is, she was most certainly sincere, and she was certainly sane. She was an honest woman. But she was not a clear or logical thinker, except on matters of finance and business, and consequently she did not

353

give forth a clear expression when she essayed philosophy. In order to write lucidly you must think lucidly. Mrs. Eddy had no sense of literary values. She was absolutely devoid of humor, and humor is only the ability to detect a little thing from a big one —to perceive a wrong adjustment from a right one ⚇ Style in literature is taste. But the lack of style, taste and humor is general in mankind. The world has produced only a few great thinkers, and one of them was Darwin, a name which Mrs. Eddy mentioned in " Science and Health " with reproach. Great writers are even more rare than great thinkers, because to write one must have the ability not only to think clearly, but the knack or technical skill to use the right word, the luminous word, and so arrange, paragraph and punctuate them that your meaning will be clear to average minds. To say that Mrs. Eddy was not a thinker nor a writer, is not an indictment of the woman, although it may be a reflection on the mental processes of the people who think she was.

To say that there are two million people reading Mrs. Eddy, also proves nothing, since numbers are no vindication. Over a hundred million people have kissed the big toe of Saint Peter in Rome.

And surely the Roman Catholic Church contains a vast number of highly educated people. The things you do not know, you do not know. And Mrs. Eddy, knowing nothing of literary style, knew nothing of

354

literary art. Her prose and her poetry are worse than ordinary. All inspirational poetry I ever read is rot, and all inspired paintings I ever saw are daubs. Mrs. Eddy should not be blamed for her limitations ⚘ ⚘ Many people who are great in certain lines labor under the hallucination that they are also great in others. Matthew Arnold was a great writer, and he also thought he was a great orator.

But when he spoke, his words simply fell over the footlights into the orchestra and died there. He could not reach the front row. Most comedians want to play Hamlet, and all of us have heard girls attempt to sing who thought they could sing, and who were encouraged in the hallucination by their immediate kinsfolk ⚘ Mrs. Eddy thought she could write, and unfortunately she was corroborated in her error by the applause of people who, not being able to read her book, kindly attributed the inability to their own limitations and not to hers, being prompted in this by the suggestion oft repeated by Mrs. Eddy, herself. The resemblance of Mrs. Eddy's thought to that of Jesus was never noticed until Mrs. Eddy first explained the matter. Mrs. Eddy was by no means insane. Swedenborg was a civil engineer and a mathematician. He wrote forty books that are nearly as opaque as "Science and Health." If you write stupidly enough, some one will surely throw up his cap and cry "Great!" And others will follow the example and take up the shout, because it is much easier, as Doctor Johnson affirmed, to praise a book than to read and understand it. The custom of reading to a congregation in a dead or foreign language, which the listeners do not understand, has never caused any general protest from the listeners. The scoffers are the only ones who have ever noticed the incongruity, and they do not count, since they probably would not attend, anyway.

Next to reading from a book written in the dead language, is to read from a book that is unintelligible. To listen to such makes no tax upon the intellect, and with the right accessories is soporific, restful, pleasing and to be commended. If it does not supply an idea, it at least imparts a feeling. Mrs. Eddy's success in literature arose from the extreme muddiness of her thinking and her opacity in expression.

If she had written fairly well, her mediocrity would have been apparent to every one; but writing absolutely without rhyme or reason, we bow before her supreme assurance. The strongest element in men is inertia—we agree rather than fight about it. We want health—and health is what Mrs. Eddy gives to us—therefore, " Science and Health with Key to the Scriptures " is the greatest book in the whole world. Sancta simplicitas! Why not, indeed!

MARY BAKER EDDY

EOPLE turn to Mrs. Eddy's book for relief just exactly as they formerly went to the doctor for the same reason. ¶ In addition to bodily health, Mrs. Eddy gives joy, hope, worldly success; and even superior minds, seeing these practical results of Christian Science, move in the line of least resistance and are quite willing to accept the book, not troubled at all about its medieval reasoning. In Ungania is a very great merchant who, not content with having the biggest store in the Kingdom, aspires to the biggest University. The fact that the higher criticism is to him only a trivial matter, and really unworthy of the serious attention of a busy man, simply reveals human limitation.

The specialist is created at a terrific cost, and that a person will be practical, shrewd, diplomatic and wise in managing the buying public and an army of employees, and yet know and love Walt Whitman, is too much to expect. This keen and successful merchant, an absolute tyrant in certain ways, has his soft side and many pleasant qualities. Why any one should ever question the literal truth of the Bible is beyond his comprehension

He is convinced that "Leaves of Grass" is an obscene book, never having read it; yet he knows nothing about the third, eleventh and thirteenth chapters of Second Samuel, having read the Book all his life. He has a pitying, patronizing smile for any one who suggests that David was a very faulty man, and that possibly

357

Solomon was not the wisest person that ever lived. "What difference does it make, anyway?" he testily asks. If you work for him you have to agree with him, or else be very silent as to what you actually believe. We often find an avowed and reiterated love for Jesus, the non-resistant, going hand in hand with a passion for war, a miser's greed, a lust for power and a thirst for revenge.

There may be a prating about righteousness while the hand of the man is feeling for his sword-hilt, and his eye is locating your jugular. The Ten Commandments are all rescinded in war time. The New York "Evening Post" noted the peculiar fact that nine out of ten of the delegates at The Hague International Peace Conference were theological heretics. As a rule, Orthodox Christians stand for war, and also for capital punishment. How do we explain these inconsistencies? ꙮ ꙮ We do not try to: they are simply facts in the partial development of the race. Why millionaires should patronize the memory of Jesus is something no one can understand, save that things work by antithesis. Mrs. Eddy was of the same shrewd, practical type as the merchant prince just mentioned. She was the greatest woman-general of her day and generation. She possessed all the qualities that go to make successful leadership. ¶ She was self-reliant, proud, arrogant, implacable in temper, rapid in decision, unbending, shrewd, diplomatic—and a good hater.

358

At times she dismissed her critics with simply a look. No man could dictate to her, and few dared make suggestions in her presence. To move her, the matter had to be brought to her attention in a way that led her to believe that she had discovered it herself. And of course all the credit went to her. In all Christian Science churches are various selections from her writings, and beneath every one is her name. " Thou shalt have no other gods before me!" is the one controlling edict breathed forth by her life and words. One of her orders was that whenever one of her hymns was announced, always and forever it must be stated that it was written by Mrs. Mary Baker Eddy. Always and forever, the " student " giving testimony refers, in terms of lavish praise and fulsome adulation, to " Our Blessed Teacher, Guide and Exemplar, Mary Baker Eddy." God Almighty and Jesus occupy secondary positions in all Christian Science meetings.

Mrs. Eddy is mentioned five times to where they are once. And I would not criticize this if Mrs. Eddy had but regarded Jesus as simply a great man in history and " God " as an abstract term referring to the Supreme Intelligence in Nature. But to her, God and Jesus were persons who dictated books, and very frequently she was careful to explain that her method of healing was exactly the same as that practised by Jesus. Side by side with His words are hers. Passages from the Bible are read alternately with passages from " Science and Health." If both were regarded as mere literature, this would be pardonable, but when we are told that both are " sacred " writ, and " damned be he who dares deny or doubt," we are simply lost in admiration for the supreme egotism of the lady. To get mad about it were vain—let us all smile. Surely the imagination that can trace points of resemblance between Mrs. Mary Baker Eddy and Jesus, the lowly peasant of Nazareth, is admirable. Jesus was a communist in principle, having nothing, giving everything. He carried neither scrip nor purse. He wrote nothing. His indifference to place, pelf and power is His distinguishing characteristic. Mrs. Eddy's love of power was the leading motive of her life; her ability to bargain was beautiful; her resorts to law and the subtleties of legal aid were all strictly modern; and the way she tied up the title to her writings by lead-pipe-cinched copyrights reveals the true instincts of Connecticut *

This jealousy of her rights and the safeguarding of her interests were among the emphatic features of her life, and set her apart as the antithesis of Jesus *
There is one character in history, however, to whom Mrs. Eddy bore a close resemblance—and that is Julius Cæsar, who was educated for the priesthood, became a priest, and was Pope of Rome before he ventured into fighting and politics as a business. Mrs. Eddy's faith in herself, her ability to decide, her quick intuitions,

the method and simplicity of her life, her passion for power, her pleasure in authorship—all these were the traits which exalted the name and fame of Cæsar ✄ The inventor of the calendar ordered that it should be known as the " Julian Calendar," and it is so called, even unto this day. Once Carlyle sat smoking with Milburn, the blind preacher. They had been discussing the historicity of Jesus. Then they sat smoking in silence. Finally, Tammas the Techy knocked the ashes out of his long clay t. d. and muttered, half to himself and half to Milburn, " Ah, a great mon, a great mon —but he had his limitations! " The same remark can truthfully be applied to Mrs. Eddy. And about the only point that Jesus and Mrs. Eddy have in common is this matter mentioned by Carlyle.

The superior shrewdness and the keen business instinct of Mrs. Eddy are seen in the use of the words " Christian " and " Science." The sub-title, " With Key to the Scriptures," is particularly alluring. And the use of the Oxford binding was the crowning stroke of commercial insight. Surely Mrs. Eddy must command our profound respect. She was undoubtedly a very great business genius, to say the very least.

HEN John Henry Newman became a Catholic, he gave as a reason for his decision that he had found no place in literature or art to rest his head. His reward for not finding a place in literature or art for his head was the red hat.

Let the followers of Mrs. Eddy take comfort in that their great teacher had plenty of high precedent for believing that Adam was created by fiat, and Eve was made from his rib, all the fiat being used; that Joshua commanded the sun to stand still and it obeyed, even when the order should have been given to the earth; that Lazarus was raised from the dead after his body had become putrid; that witchcraft is a fact in Nature; and that children can be born with the aid of one parent a little better than in the old-fashioned way—parthenogenesis, I think they call it.

These inconsistencies of absolute absurdity, existing side by side with great competence and sanity, are to be found everyhere in history.

Mrs. Eddy excited the envy of the medical world in her demonstration that good health and happiness are the sure results of getting rid of the doctor habit; but they got even with her when she said that virgin motherhood would yet become the rule, and tilling of the soil would cease to be a necessity.

Saint Augustine thought, as did most of the early Churchmen, that to do evil that good might follow was not only justifiable, but highly meritorious. So they

362

preached hagiology to scare people into the narrow path of rectitude.

Chapman, Alexander, Torrey, Billy Sunday and most other professional evangelists believe in and practise the same doctrine.

The literary conscience was a thing known in Greece, but only recently, say within two hundred years, has it been again manifest, and as yet it is rare. It consists in the scorn and absolute refusal to write a line except that which stands for truth.

The artistic conscience that refuses to paint for hire or model on order is the same. Wagner, Millet, Rembrandt, William Morris and Ruskin are examples of men who were incapable of anything but their highest and best creative work, and refused to truckle to the mercenary horde. Such men may be without conscience in a business way. And a person may be absolutely moral in all his acts of life, except in writing and talking, and here he may be slipshod and uncertain.

Mrs. Eddy was beautifully lacking in the literary conscience, just as much so as was Gladstone when he attempted to reply to Ingersoll in "The North American Review," and resorted to sophistry and evasion in lieu of logic. Absolute truth to Gladstone was a matter of indifference—expediency was his shibboleth. Truth to Mrs. Eddy was also a secondary matter; the only things that really mattered were Health and Success. Health and Success are undoubtedly great things and well

MARY BAKER EDDY

worthy of possession, but I wish to secure them only through the expression of truth. If you gag my tongue, chain my pen and cry, " Believe and you will have Health," I would say, " Give me liberty or give me death!" Christian Scientists ask you to buy Mrs. Eddy's book, " Science and Health."
When the volume is handed you, you are promised health and success if you believe its every word; and if you don't, you are threatened with " moral idiocy."
¶ It is the old promise of Paradise and the threat of Hell in a new guise. As for me, I decline the book.

TEPHEN GIRARD was a great merchant who had a great love of truth; but if he had been in a retail business, his zeal for truth might have been slightly modified.

As a rule, the world of humanity can be divided into two parts: the practical men and the searchers for truth. Usually the latter have nothing to lose but their head. Spinoza, Galileo, Bruno, Thomas Paine, Walt Whitman, Henry Thoreau, Bronson Alcott, are the pure type. Then come Theodore Parker and Ralph Waldo Emerson, crowded out of their pulpits, scorned by their Alma Mater, pitied by the public—yet holding true to their course

And lo! they grew rich; whereas, if they had stuck close to the shore and safety, they would have been drowned in the shallows of oblivion.

On the other hand, we find in, say, the directorate of the Standard Oil Company, many men who are zealous members of the orthodox churches, giving large sums in support of the " gospel," and taking an active interest in its promulgation. All of them say, with the late Mr. Morgan, " My mother's religion is good enough for me." So here we get practical shrewdness combined with minds that, so far as abstract truth is concerned, are simply prairie-dog towns.

These men belong to a type that will cling to error as long as it is soft, easy and popular. Most certainly these men are not fools—they are highly competent and useful

365

in their way. But as for superstition, they find it soothing; it saves the trouble of thinking, and all their
energies are needed in business.

Religion, to them, is a social diversion, with a chance
of salvation on the side. Inertia does not grip them
when it comes to commerce—but in religion it does.
Lincoln once said that there was just one thing, and
only one thing, that God Almighty could not understand: and that was the workings of the mind of an
intelligent American juror.

Herbert Spencer says that Sir Isaac Newton was one
of the six best educated men the world has seen. He
was the first man to resolve light into its constituent
elements. Voltaire says that when Newton discovered
the Law of Gravitation he excited the envy of the scientific world.

" But," adds Voltaire, " when he wrote a book on the
Bible prophecies, the men of science got even with him."
Sir Isaac Newton defended the literal inspiration of the
Scriptures and was a consistent member of the Church
of England. Doctor Johnson was unhappy all day if he
did n't touch every tenth picket of the fence with his
cane as he walked downtown.

Blackstone, the great legal commentator, believed in
witchcraft, and bolstered his belief by citing the Scrip-
tural text, " Thou shalt not suffer a witch to live "—
thus proving Moses a party to the superstition. Sir
Matthew Hale, Chief Justice of England, did the same.

366

Gladstone was a great statesman, and yet he believed in the Mosaic account of Creation, just as did Mary Baker Eddy.

John Adams was a rebel from political slavery, but lived and died a worthy Churchman, subsisting on canned theology—and canned in England, at that.

Franklin and Jefferson were rebels from both political and theological despotism, but looked leniently on leeches and apothecaries. Herbert Spencer had a free mind as regards religion, politics, economics and sociology; yet he was a bachelor, lived in the city, belonged to a club, played billiards and smoked cigars. Physical health was out of his reach, and with all his vast knowledge, he never knew why. All through history we find violence and gentleness, ignorance and wisdom, folly and shrewdness side by side in the same person.

The one common thing in humanity is inconsistency. To account for it were vain. We know only that it is.

HE very boldness of Mrs. Eddy's claims created an impetus that carried conviction. ¶ The woman certainly believed in herself, and she also believed in the Power, of which she was a necessary part, that works for righteousness. She repudiated the supernatural, not by denying " miracles," but by holding that the so-called miracles of the Bible really occurred and were perfectly natural— all according to Natural Law, which is the Divine Law. ¶ And the explanation of this Divine Law was her particular business. Thus did she win to her side those who were too timid in constitution to forsake forms and ceremonies and stand alone on the broad ground of Rationalism.

Christian Science is not a religion of fight, stress and struggle. Is n't it better to relax and rest and allow Divinity to flow through us, than to sit on a sharp rail and call the passer-by names in falsetto? May Irwin's motto, " Don't Argufy," is n't so bad as a working maxim, after all.

All Christian denominations are very much alike. Their differences are microscopic, and recognized only by those who are immersed in them. Martin Luther only softened the expression of the Roman Catholic Church —he did not change its essence.

Benjamin Franklin declared that he could not tell the difference between a Catholic and an Episcopalian. But Christian Science is a complete departure from all other denominations, and while professing to be Christian, is really something else, or if it is Christian, then orthodoxy is not.

Christian Science strikes right at the root of orthodoxy, since it divides the power of Jesus with Mary Baker Eddy and affirms that Jesus was not " The Savior," but A Savior.

This is the position of Thomas Paine, and all other good radicals. Christian Science places Mrs. Eddy's work right alongside of the Bible. No denomination has ever put out a volume stating that the book was required in order to make the Bible intelligible. No denomination has ever put forth a person as the equal of Jesus. This has only been done by unbelievers, atheists and freethinkers ॐ ॐ

Christianity is at last attacked in its own house and by its own household. It is thoroughly understood and admitted everywhere that there are two kinds of Christianity. One is the kind taught by the Nazarene; and the other is the institutional variety, made up of denominations which hold millions upon millions of dollars' worth of property without taxation, and parade their ritual with rich and costly millinery.

The one was lived by a Man who had not where to lay His head; and the other is an acquirement taken over from pagan Rome, and continued largely in its pagan form even unto this day. Christian Science is neither one nor the other, and the obvious pleasantry that it is neither Christian nor scientific is a jest in earnest. Christian Science is a modern adaptation of all that is best in the simplicity and asceticism of Jesus, the commonsense philosophy of Benjamin Franklin, the mysticism of Swedenborg, and the bold pronunciamento of Robert Ingersoll. It is a religion of affirmation with a denial-of-matter attachment.

It is a religion of this world. Jesus was a Man of Sorrows but Mary Baker Eddy was a Daughter of Joy ⚹ And as the universal good sense of mankind holds that the best preparation for a life to come, if there is one, is to make the best of this, Christian Science is meeting with a fast-growing popular acceptance.

The decline of the old orthodoxy is owing to its clinging to the fallacy that the world's work is base, and Nature is a trickster luring us to our doom. Mrs. Eddy reconciled the old idea with the new and made it mentally palatable. And this is the reason why Christian Science is going to sweep the earth and in twenty years will have but one competitor, the Roman Catholic faith.

Orthodoxy, blind, blundering, stubborn, senile, is tottering—the undertaker is at the door. Indeed, the old idea of our orthodox friends that they were preparing to die, was literally true.

The undertaker's name and business address attached to the front of many a city church is a sign too subtle to overlook. Not only was the undertaker a partner of the priest, but he is now foreclosing his claim. Christian

370

Science is not final. After it has lived its day, another religion will follow, and that is the Religion of Common-sense, the esoteric religion which Mrs. Eddy herself lived and practised.

As for her believers, she gave them the religion of a Book—two Books, the Bible and " Science and Health." They want form and ritual and temples.

She gave them these things, just as doctors give sweetened water to people who still demand medicine; and as if to supply the zealous converts, just out of orthodoxy, their fill of ecclesiastic husks, she built fine churches—churches rivaling the far-famed San Salute of Venice. Let them have their wish! Paganism is in their blood—they are even trying to worship her! ¶ Let them go on and eventually they will pray not in temples nor on this or that mountain, but in spirit and in truth, just as did Mrs. Eddy, one of the world's most successful women.

MARY BAKER EDDY

HRISTIAN SCIENCE is orthodox Christianity, minus medical fetish and the fear that a belief in sin, sickness, death and eternal punishment naturally lends, plus the joy of a natural, healthy, human life. The so-called rational Christian sects preserve their Devil in the form of a Doctor, and Hell in the shape of a Hospital.

My hope and expectation is that Christian Science will become a Rational Religion instead of a one-man institution, or a religion of authority, such as it now is. Its superstitious features have doubtless been strong factors in its rapid growth—serving as stays or stocks to aid in the launching.

But now, the sooner the ship floats free the better. Christian Scientists, being men and women, can not continue to grow if fettered with an Index Expurgatorius and mandatory edicts and encyclicals. That which binds and manacles must go—the good will remain ✠ Christian Science brings good news, and good news is always curative. Mrs. Eddy animated her patients with a new thought—the thought of harmony, the denial of disease, and the affirmation that God is good and life is beautiful. The animation thus produced is in itself the most powerful healing principle known to science. Life is born of love. Joy is a prophylactic. Christian Science comes to the " student " as a great flood of light. His circulation becomes normal, his muscles relax, the nerves rest, digestion acts, elimination takes

372

place—and the person is well. ¶ Fear has congested the organs—love, hope and faith place them in an attitude so Nature plays through them. The patient is healed. In it there is neither mystery nor miracle. It is all very simple ❧ ❧

Let us rid ourselves of a belief in the strange and occult! The Christian Science organization is an expediency. It is an intellectual crutch. The book is a necessity. It is a scaffolding. Yet he who mistakes the scaffolding for the edifice is a specialist in scaffolding.

Truth can never be caught and crystallized in a formula. Also this: truth can never be monopolized by an " ite " or an " ist." Eventually the label will be eliminated with the scaffolding, and the lumber of ritual and rite will have to go.

We will live truth instead of talking about it. Among Christian Scientists there are no drunkards, paupers or gamblers. Also, there are no sick people. To them sickness is a disgrace.

Orthodox Christians get sick and gratify their sense of approbation by receiving pastoral calls and visits from the doctor and neighbors. The biblical injunction to visit the sick was never followed by Mrs. Eddy—she always decided for herself just what injunctions should be waived and what followed.

Those which she did not like she interpreted spiritually or else glided over. The biblical statement that man's days are few and full of trouble, and also the assertion

373

that man is prone to wickedness as the sparks fly upwards, are both very conveniently glossed.

Christian Scientists know the rules of health, just as most people do; but what is more, they follow them, thus avoiding the disgrace of being pointed out. They have made sickness not only tabu, but invalidism ridiculous ❧ ❧

When things become absurd and preposterous, we abandon them. Unpopularity can do what logic is helpless to bring about. The reasoning of Christian Scientists is bad, but their intuitions are right.

While denying the existence of matter, no people on earth are as canny, save possibly the Quakers. A bank-balance to a Christian Scientist is no barren ideality. It is like falsehood to a Jesuit—a very present help in time of trouble. Sin, to them, consists in making too much fuss about life and talking about death. Do what you want and forget it. Quit talking about the weather, night air, miasma.

Knowingly or unknowingly Christian Scientists cultivate resiliency. They are proof against drafts and microbes. Eat what you like, but not too much of it. Be moderate. Christian Scientists get their joy out of their work. This is essentially hygienic. They breathe deeply, eat moderately, bathe plentifully, work industriously—and smile. This is all sternly scientific. It can never be argued down.

No school of medicine has ever offered a prophylactic

374

equal to work and good-cheer, and no system of religion has ever offered a working formula for health, happiness and success equal to that launched by Mrs. Eddy. The science of medicine is a science of palliation. ¶ Christian Scientists avoid the cause of sickness, and thus keep well ⚜ ⚜

There is no vitality in drugs. Nature cures—obey her. In this matter of bodily health just a few plain rules suffice. And these rules, fairly followed, soon grow into a pleasurable habit. Fortunately, we do not have to oversee our digestion, our circulation, the work of the millions of pores that form the skin, or the action of the nerves. Folks who get fussy about their digestion and assume personal charge of their nerves have " nerves " and are apt to have no digestion.

" I have a pain in my side," said the woman who had no money to the busy doctor. " Forget it," was the curt advice. Get the Health Habit, and forget it.

This is the quintessence of Christian Science. Your mental attitude controls your body. Happiness is your health. There is no devil but fear. As a man thinketh in his heart, so is he.

SO HERE ENDETH "LITTLE JOURNEYS TO THE HOMES OF GREAT TEACHERS," BEING VOLUME TEN OF THE SERIES, AS WRITTEN BY ELBERT HUBBARD. BORDERS AND INITIALS BY ROYCROFT ARTISTS, AND PRODUCED BY THE ROYCROFTERS, AT THEIR SHOPS, IN EAST AURORA, NEW YORK